And Promenade Home

To Alan Devoe

Contents

Illustrations appear between pages 116 and 117.

And
Promenade Home

And all should cry, Beware! Beware!
His flashing eyes, his floating hair!
Weave a circle round him thrice,
And close your eyes with holy dread,
For he on honey-dew hath fed,
And drunk the milk of Paradise.

SAMUEL TAYLOR COLERIDGE
(from *Kubla Khan*)

CHAPTER I *The Call*

I had one of those dates a bachelor girl manages to dig up for herself, not a really good date, but more entertaining than dining alone at Aunt Clemmy's. The young man with whom I made the date was a playwright and quite interesting, but he explained he had a dinner appointment with another young man; they had nothing against my joining them for coffee and a possible movie afterwards. This could not in any way be considered the invitation ardent, but it would serve. I was still to have dinner alone at Aunt Clemmy's. Aunt Clemmy's wasn't bad; it was handy, right under my studio; it was clean and freshly painted. Nice old ladies ate there who talked quietly. There was no Muzak and the price range just suited me: 35 to 60 cents without appetizer. I ate nearly all my lunches and dinners there while I read through the magazines I could not subscribe to.

Mother said to come eat with her. She always said this. Mother lived just down the street and she served much better dinners and there was no Muzak there either, but there were family affairs and the price of her hospitality was explaining what I had done all day and what I expected to do the next. It never seemed like much — not enough to talk about, anyway — and it was dismal to have to keep bringing in no good news. Everyone else in the house was succeeding. My sister Margaret had a fine job as assistant editor on *Mademoiselle*, earned a weekly salary, dressed marvelously, and although her husband was in the Army, was altogether in a better and more hopeful condition. Mother was divorced and sometimes very lonely, but she knew just what she believed in, which was the Single Tax (a faith she inherited from her father, Henry George), and she took great joy and comfort in doing good for other people. My niece, Margaret's daughter Judith, aged ten, led a terrific social and scholastic life; she was always very busy too, and had lots to tell at the dinner table.

So I didn't always go, although they loved me and the food was delicious. Anyway, it wasn't dinner alone I minded so much; it was coming back afterward in the early evening to the empty studio. But then, on the other hand, I hated to leave the phone. The great oak table beneath it had been all pricked out in floral designs where I had sat stabbing at the wood for quarter hours at a time waiting for a call. It might ring any moment. Any day or night it just might, and change everything.

There were several kinds of calls I had in mind: the one from the Theatre Guild notifying me that I had been selected dance director for their new musical and would I report at the office the following morning to discuss terms? It could happen just like that and I could then go pounding down the street and say, "Here, darlings, take back the check you gave me yesterday — and now lend me some fine clothes, for I must look tops tomorrow." Or, alternately, the call from Mr. Sol Hurok, impresario, stating he would like to tour me in concerts with my company and would I, etc.? Or the one from the Ballet Russe informing me that Mr. Leonide Massine felt indisposed and unable to function as head choreographer and would I oblige? Or the one from a rich relative who, believing in my ability, and touched by my years of struggle, had decided to put half a million dollars behind my career. None of these calls came; after twelve years, expectation had become a private hobby about which I did not speak.

Failure is a daily matter and one can get used to it. One can, if one does not watch out, begin to cherish it. My life was really quite cozy, and it certainly was private. There were only two unbearable hours between dinner and bed, but I'd learned a number of dodges for getting through these without facing up to my situation. This I was aware of dimly always, whether I wished to be or not, when sleeping or eating or joking with friends. The condition was close and never departing, like a head cold. I think the name of the state is despair, but I never dignified it by any such resounding title; I just went along grumbling.

That February Wednesday when I awoke, it was to hear the usual catastrophe of coal down the chute under my studio window. It was to hear the grinding of Ninth Street bus brakes and the honking of taxis. But mainly there was the sound of no hopeful morning bustle.

Mother kept saying to come down the street and live with her and there would be lots of sounds in the morning. People around Mother did things. And they started early, rising out of bed to Beethoven's Seventh on WQXR and disputing over every single subsequent action, such as whether to draw the coffee water from the hot or cold tap, or what constituted too much lipstick for the ten-year-old or too much eye shadow for her mother, or why my sister did not prefer to forgo a gala at Jascha Heifetz's in favor of a Taxation of Land Values meeting in our front parlor with hot chocolate and cookies. Every morning there was a whole new set of differences and by the time the kid had left for school, my sister for the office, and Mother had moved from the kitchen to her desk and world-wide correspondence, her size-one shoes resting firmly on the back of her red cocker spaniel, the whole family was emotionally used up. I believed in the Single Tax with all my heart, and I thought my sister the best and wittiest of company; but I had determined that the purpose of my life was to make up dances; I wanted them to be good dances. I thought it wise to stick it out where I was, alone, in quiet.

Mother's homes had been happier before her divorce, but they had never been peaceful. And this had tired my father as it had abashed me. However, we had had a wonderful childhood.

Father and his younger brother, Cecil de Mille, had been largely instrumental in building up the moving-picture industry in Hollywood. We had known considerable wealth then, lived in a tight family group and in what my mother chose to call a simple fashion, which meant that we children went to bed early, used almost no make-up, never went out unchaperoned, and neither smoked nor drank. But simplicity stopped right there. We had tennis and music, both on a professional level, writing and production conferences, amateur theatricals, lectures, legislative and economic reforms, civic projects, entertaining — adult, international or adolescent — dog-breeding and gardening. All these *divertissements* were lively. The house boiled with temperament. It wasn't easy living. Everyone was too preoccupied, too amusing, too passionate, and too successful. The members of my family succeeded brilliantly, aggressively and vocally, except possibly at marriage.

In the meantime we were happy and had everything we wished, except only the frequent presence of my beloved Pop and sufficient quiet for professional study.

I wanted a dancing career and this my parents were not prompt to permit. I found myself starting on a lonely path without plan or guiding example, and with scant understanding except from Mother.

It turned out to our bitter distress that I didn't succeed — not, certainly, on the family terms. Well, not satisfactorily on any. It wasn't for lack of trying.

In the course of the long effort, I had given self-sponsored concerts in five countries. I had danced for pay at society parties and without pay at osteopathic balls. I had appeared as soloist in Roxy's Moving Picture Theatre, New York, in nameless Southern movie houses and English music halls. I had performed in night clubs and restaurants, including Scandinavian beer gardens. I had staged numbers for Broadway and London musicals and an Irving Thalberg superspecial movie starring Norma Shearer. I had toured under every possible condition — alone, with my own troupe (Sybil Shearer, Joseph Anthony, Katherine Litz, Trude Rittmann) and as a member of a bona fide ballet company. I had played character bits in a dramatic stock company and a piano backstage. I had designed costumes and sewed them and I had helped to dress the stars. I had exiled myself for five years in London, where it was cheaper to study and perform. Whenever I could, I taught, and wherever I could, I collected girls and worked on choreography. I did anything and everything to get a stage under my feet and an audience seated and watching. Once there, the audience was usually moved, at least to laughter and occasionally to tears, and the press was often serious and flattering. But nothing ever led to anything else; nothing ever bore fruit.

"You're not pretty," said all the bosses in my trade; and even my folks agreed. They didn't think I was a bit pretty, and some of them went so far as to say I had no sex appeal besides. But I could hear people laugh where I danced. I could hear them roar at my comedy, so I must have been attractive in some way.

Very few concert dancers succeeded during the thirties. The opportunities simply did not exist. There were, for one thing, no ballet companies, and for another, the musical theater was closed to us. So I found myself with not even a checking account of my own — or, at best, one that, for obvious reasons, was turned on and off like a faucet. I tried to subsist on what I could earn teaching dancing classes, which was less than thirty dollars a week. Father, at this point, was struggling under bitter business reverses and so it was left to Mother, out of her savings, to make my dancing career possible. Mother had not much money, but she was sacrificially generous and was depriving herself of necessities. She was growing old. She had had a heart attack recently which was a warning to us all. I felt I had become a real burden to her.

I lived in a studio in Greenwich Village, unfurnished except for a bed, a chest of drawers, a piano and eight mirrors. It was not very tidy or even clean. Tidiness entailed time; time was for dancing. I naturally could not afford a char. Mother said my untidiness would one day cost me very dear. It would one day mean tragedy, she said. Loneliness destroyed the energy required for success; lack of success made me mad, and unattractive, and guaranteed loneliness. Round and round I chased my tail in the mare's nest on Ninth Street.

That Wednesday I lay in bed much too long, surveying a room neat only from emptiness and a situation bearable only from habit. And I hoped and prayed the phone would ring. By dint of concentration I made it ring. It was Mother. She wanted to know what my plans were. She always wanted to know this and she always asked it of me first thing in the morning before I had decided whether or not to go on living. I had no plans beyond practicing. Well, then, why not come to her for dinner?

Bed, by now, had more than served its purpose; it didn't ensure oblivion anyhow. I got up. The mailbox could not be expected to change my outlook and didn't. I bought a newspaper and proceeded to Romanoff's Pharmacy. They knew me there and started my breakfast as I appeared at the door, giving me the illusion of a household. I did not read the theatrical news. What use? But anything by John Martin, the *New York Times* dance critic, was a life and death bulletin. I turned to the dance column, which was on the society page, before looking at the war headlines. The war headlines — February 1942 — were dreadful. The dance criticism wasn't too hot either.

Then I wandered back to my studio, made the bed, took in the garbage pail and wastebasket, washed some cups, straightened out the bathroom and sat down in the chair in my big room.

The choice before me for the next two hours was wide: for instance, I could make up a dance; or I could not make it up. If I did, would I ever get to perform it? One partner, Sybil Shearer, had gone off to do her own concerts. The other, Joseph Anthony, had just been drafted into the Army. Indeed, we had only been permitted to finish out our tour because the contracts had been signed months before he was called up. So we ended our joint career with a series of paltry and ridiculous concerts in New England, where, in addition to the low fees and disenchanted audiences, we had to cope with stages that never should have housed a theater troupe. One stage, I remember, was backed by a cyclorama of gray velvet curtains without opening of any kind. "And just how am I to make entrances or exits?" I asked. "Oh," said Joe, "either by climbing over the top or creeping underneath, according to whether it's tragedy or comedy." (It is, among other things, this superb response to situation that has made Anthony today one of the finest directors in Broadway and Hollywood.) The very last performance was in Rhode Island, where the footlights resembled, as Joe remarked to cheer me up, "an ear of corn." And so we petered out ignominiously and rushed to catch our train home with a strange sense of relief and the desire not to be reminded in any way of our past endeavors. For all our tremendous efforts and our refusing for four years to be daunted by anything, dancing had become inadvertently a farce. At six o'clock the next morning Joe reported at Governors Island.

After a while I put on a record and began fiddling with a dance.

But I only got as far as a mood and a facial expression which I had to start with anyhow. I went on walking about to music, hoping an *enchaînement* of steps or a ravishing arrangement of arms would make itself known spontaneously as I crossed from bookcase to window and back to door and mirror.

It was at this point that in desperation, I called to invite myself to supper with the playwright. And having got through the morning I took the subway to Carnegie Hall for my ballet practice.

There is always courage in a classrooom, and the daily ballet class had been my salvation. The upper floors of Carnegie are a rabbit warren of heterogeneous, tattered and frenetic art. Here on a narrow corridor which is labeled sixth floor at one end and, without sufficient change of level, eighth floor at the other (visitors have been driven to exasperation hunting the seventh) one may hear pianos, betrayed and seduced voices, castanets, gramophones, heel taps, drums, toilets flushing. Indeed, the whole sixteen floors of the Carnegie studios are awash with cacophony, solfeggio and plumbing, when they are not clamorous with the young aggressive voices of drama students shouting in what purports to be their classroom jargon, but is a bid for attention, softened over and sanded down by the flatfooted shuffling of the ballet children who seldom speak at all. And here at an open door sometimes there is silence and the glimpse of a studio walled with signed photos of the great, a closed piano, and an old man sitting majestic and soundless in his armchair, sitting alone and waiting.

In these halls there is visible a kind of moldy coquetry, as the habitués dye, puff, enamel, pad and lift in an effort to appear otherwise than what they patently are. The truly talented work quietly beside the unrelaxing efforts of despair and deepening age. But we know they are there; they pass close by; and this gives us heart.

One could lose oneself here and draw sustenance from the bustle of poverty and from the absolutely unbeaten vegetable strength of the art impulse — pushing, pushing through all people, all barriers, all luck, all turns of fate.

Leonard Bernstein had a two-room apartment at the eighth-floor end of our hall and used to play for our dance classes at one dollar an hour until he was thrown out by an exasperated ballet master who screamed that he couldn't keep time. Bernstein is now conductor of the New York Philharmonic on another floor.

In the classes at Ballet Arts, sometimes teaching and sometimes practicing, were Vera Nemtchinova, whom I had seen as a star in Diaghileff's company dancing the leads in *Les Sylphides, Les Femmes de Bonne Humeur, Cimarosiana;* Edward Caton and Aubrey Hitchins, both of whom I had seen partnering Anna Pavlova; Sonia Wojcikowska, the daughter of Diaghileff's great character dancer; Iva Kitchell, the comedian; Theodora Roosevelt, who now under her married name, Theodora Keogh, writes strange and powerful novels; stars of current Broadway shows, night clubs and icecapades; transient soloists from the Ballet Russe; and the youngsters, perfectly neat and perfectly inexpressive except for intent. Among them were Bambi Linn, Diana Adams and Allyn Ann McLerie.

In ballet class, standing in an anonymous line, I was free from responsibility for one hour and a half, free to work through the gall of spirit, to feel once more the breath of revival and promise come into my heart, moving from the floor under my feet. Stretching about me was the beloved floor, the classic empty floor. It waited for the blow, for the caress, answering the striking as a musical instrument answers the player. I put my hot and readied foot on the wood, and felt the power up my leg and in my ready back. I felt with my toes and my strong instep and my heel that supported my spine and my lifted head — and from the heel I pushed. The floor pushed back and the instep held like a wing and

I suspended in the air and my arms were released; my throat and my back ached again with the good pain of supporting and my body was strong enough and held.

Does the sight of a white surface and colors laid out excite the painter as the bare and welcoming floor excites the dancer? Does wet clay send such a rush to the heart and yearning to the sculptor's hands? Or the open keyboard to a composer? Floor space is as irresistible to the dancer as cool waters to the thirsty. The sight alone is enough to make one hurry. The room, empty, the enclosing walls serenely bare, the mood of reservation protecting as a fortress; it is impossible therein to maintain rage or hate. Sounds cease and fall away. The dancer enters the arena of total lonely effort and works with spirit and flesh. Pattern is learned here and relationship and law, as communication is worked on the bare air. No dancer comes out of a good practice without exhilaration, and on leaving the room, the better self stays behind.

This is the area of "curious peace" that Martha Graham describes. The supporting feet are her root into life. Wherever a dancer stands ready, Graham says, that spot is Holy Ground.

I watched the children beside me. Bambi Linn or Diana Adams grinding and rotating through the merciless regimen with a controlled body line as ideal as a diagram drawn for instruction. The steadying blink of the eye in the hope of balance, the thrill of muscle at ankle and knee as the swinging weight is checked, the grip in the instep when the weight fights back, the nostril using life, the reflection of sweat under the soft throat and in the strong hollow of the neck, the mouth held like a guiding rope, the skin drawn taut, the heart thrust beating against emptiness — all these cleanse the performer like a prayer and render her universal. The long unbroken line fixed them in time and space as apart from common experience and lent them the immediacy of something fairy and immortal. Dancers in their yielding to physical involvements work stripped to the heart muscle. Truly, as Martha Graham says, they are God's athletes.

Bear in mind that when Bambi, Diana, and their contemporaries embarked on their course of study, as when I did, there were no guaranteed companies for our services. And yet, with a vision no one can explain, the youngsters began and pledged their whole youth and their parents' savings and when they were trained and ready, there were, in fact, two repertory ballet companies waiting and available for employment. And the doors of the American theater had been opened. But without that blind faith on the part of the dancers, the companies could not have been formed, nor any other timely opportunity exploited.

After class I could speak without snarling, even smile at my comrades — and I went for my postpractice coffee in a benign mood. And then, still happy, I subwayed home.

And when I put my key in the door, the phone was in fact ringing. I lifted the instrument just as the bell thrilled off. It was Martha Graham.

"Don't you ever get depressed?" I had asked her once.

"All the time," she answered, "but I never tell."

Her path has never at any time been easy, for she is the greatest pioneer in our theater and she has had to buy her way dearly.

Whenever Martha speaks, no matter how trivially, when she says, "You're looking well," or "Let's go eat," or "I need a new hat," there is excitement and the vitality of relationship. The folks who work with her are dazzled by this. She brings quickening to all who hear, colors deepen, sounds reverberate, little experiences fall into the lovely patterns of continuing life. This has nothing to do with glamour; it is rather an act of consciousness, an awareness of reality. But although she lives in an aura of immortality, her manner is never didactic or pontifical. She remains as eager in discovery as the person to whom she talks.

She was my friend and I counted myself blessed. I leaned on her whenever I could arrange to. I had become an expert, I began to realize, at leaning.

It was not often Martha called me; usually I called her. Tonight, however, she was asking me to a party.

"I've been trying to reach you all day. Can you possibly come with me to the Ralph Kirkpatrick recital tonight? Wear your prettiest dress. Walter Prude is coming."

"Oh, thank you, Martha, I'd love to." I felt frisky. "I'll gladly break the date I had. I don't wish to seem rude, but who the hell is Walter Prude?"

"Ah, you'll see. Pick me up after dinner."

My prettiest dress had been purchased with tumultuous effort in a mass of quarreling women at Klein's on Union Square for $11.59. It was slinky and black and made me look as though I'd been pulled from a lake. I pinned my costume hair on and blackened my eyelashes and covered all with a veil. Through half-closed lids I thought I looked pretty good. (En route to Martha I did remember to cross Washington Square and wish the young men a pleasant good evening.)

One steps down to the boxes in Town Hall. When Prude stood at the top entrance he seemed taller and slimmer than he was — and he was six feet tall and weighed 140 pounds. The black and white of evening dress has never showed up any straight back to disadvantage. His face and skull were long, like an Englishman's, his cheekbones high, his nose straight. His eyes were deep gray and brilliant. His mouth was full, even sensual, the lips set quizzically. His hands were as large and strong as a pianist's. It struck me at first glance, although reason told me I was crazy, and although I took care to give no evidence of my opinion, that he was a nice combination of Gary Cooper and George VI of England. In addition, he seemed to know a great deal about music.

At concert's end we adjourned to a German *Hofbrau* called the Blue Ribbon. It devolved he was a member of a concert agency called WGN, Martha's management, which had recently slammed its doors in my face. He had never heard of me and appeared to be as unimpressed by my achievements as by the false hair and the veil which I kept vibrating eagerly. He turned his attention assiduously to Martha, and they had many amusing experiences to remind each other of, for he had recently shepherded her tour of the South and the Caribbean. When neglected, I tend to get raucous, and between bites of my triple-decker Swiss cheese, cole slaw and ham, I snapped out my views of the concert situation.

"Saucy little thing," he said, and went on talking to Martha.

Every so often, even at first meeting, his face seemed to be shadowed by a sudden stillness, an absolute breaking off of all communication, and one could not guess whether he was disturbed, or bored. The eyes went opaque, the mouth still. There followed a pause, while I fluttered in panic with no direction or bearings and all interchange suspended. Suddenly, as the twinkle reappeared, the eyes saw again and with a caustic and altogether unexpected quip he expunged the lapse and pushed conversation back again into gear. Some people found this rude; I considered it tantalizing. I was damned if I couldn't hold his attention. He saw me home and came to tea the next afternoon.

As he stepped into my bare and untidy studio, he drew back affronted. "Ah, a housekeeper," he murmured, and taking off his coat, set about putting things in order while I made the tea.

He later told me he found me exhausting, for I never stopped chattering, and as his business involved talk all day, often with disgruntled and clamorous women, I did not furnish a refreshing contrast. In spite of this, however, he kept coming back. As I recall it, we didn't talk much about dancing or theater. Mainly we discussed sex and the war and communism and other social amenities.

He was chary of information about himself, but under insistent prodding I discovered the following: he had grown up in Dallas with a lot of cousins — very tall ones, he said — and he knew the cattle ranches of West Texas; his grandmother had lost nine brothers and a husband in the Civil War; he had entered the university at fifteen; he had heard his first serious music at seventeen, Brahms' Fourth, and decided not to study medicine, as his father wished, but somehow to dedicate his life to music; with this in mind, he served as an able seaman, which brought him to New York and Olga Samaroff Stokowski, whose secretary he became. He liked Buxtehude, Dvořák, Brahms and, most surprisingly, Tchaikovsky. He had never seen any dancing except Martha Graham and Harald Kreutzberg and he didn't think he'd care for ballet dancing. He had walked from Stockholm to Zagreb and enjoyed the scenery. He spoke without accent and he seemed to have none of the expected Southern prejudices. He didn't ask me about my life and habits, but I told him anyway. In full. He always left looking exhausted. He always came back.

And I always waited for him. He made me laugh. Laced through his polite manner, as brandy through milk, was a savage wit. He seemed often like a wild animal, gentle enough, but never wholly within reach, and he could not be made to temper his conduct. He recognized me right off as a fighter and spared me nothing. But this I was used to, having been brought up just so by my father, who, if anything, was tougher. "Who is crucifying you now, dear?" Pop once asked after an absence. "Or am I talking shop?"

But the predominating impression Walter made was one of gentleness, an instant and careful divining of hidden hurts and terrors. He recognized the mechanisms of behavior as a doctor does, or a novelist. And this is, I think, why he got on so well with artists and animals.

Then one evening I found him waiting with a new look on his

face. The exhaustion and teasing had disappeared. He'd received Greetings from the President. "That makes things clear, doesn't it?" he said. "I report for duty next week." So we stopped talking nonsense.

The next day he flew to Texas to say good-by to his father, leaving with me all his writings, his lyric verse, his opera, his stories and his journal, not to be considered ever again, he said — never to be finished. He didn't seem morbid or regretful, just convinced; he expected to be killed. I said of course he wouldn't, but then, on the other hand, someone was going to be.

When I put him on the BMT subway for Governors Island at Eighth Street and Broadway, we kissed good-by. He didn't like kissing in public places like BMT stations, but I seemed to take it for granted, so he indulged me. "Write me often. Whether or not I answer, keep writing. This is important," he said. Then he was gone away to the war. We'd known each other two and a half weeks.

I kept writing. And I ate at the tearoom downstairs alone as before. But now it was different. I didn't mind any more walking up in the silent and empty flat. Even the coal falling across my sleeping face was a good indication of life and vigor — a sign from the great hustling city.

I took care of my clothes, washed my stockings and brushed my hair and tried to be tidy, and I know I was more polite. I went happily down the street to Mother's for dinner and was kind and attentive — and I paid some heed to my sister and to Judith. People I met no longer seemed like animals trapped in the same cage.

While I was practicing an adage I was not going over the list of everyone who had been mean to me. I kept my mind on the adage; it improved. And when I thought about dance patterns, I kept my mind on them. Miraculously I decided to stop failing because, briefly, I no longer had the taste for failure. It had always previously taken me forty to fifty minutes to work myself up to the point of composing anything, twenty-five minutes devoted to being mad at things as they were, fifteen minutes to evoking things as I'd like them to be, four minutes of direct transference. Forty-six minutes after entering the rehearsal hall I was ready to start work. Now I could start without emotional preambles. I couldn't wait to start. All hesitations and doubts were absorbed into daily activity — and no residues of stagnant emotion fouled and clogged my mind. I could hardly recognize my mind. It was like a shiny new machine.

I began to write letters; all the lovely feeling of knowing who I was at last budded and flowered in the letters. I wrote him everything, although I realized he knew little of dancing and cared less. He'd never seen a class or any rehearsal outside of Martha's group. Nevertheless, I wrote him of ballet exercises and what the girls had said in the dressing room. I told him when I decided quite simply to quit dancing because of economic reasons. All right — he was in Biloxi at that point peeling potatoes. I wrote that I had had an interview with Lee Shubert, who didn't remember who I was although I had once choreographed a whole show for him. That was a funny letter. He read it as he came back from tarring a road in Shreveport, Louisiana, in July. I wrote that I had asked for a job at the Metropolitan Opera and been curtly refused. He now hoped to be a weather observer or maybe learn to operate a glider. I wrote him in panic not to. I wired him in God's name not to. I drew him pictures of the new dresses I had bought at Klein's. I illuminated one letter in color and gold with a wreath of all my dancing roles. He had decided to go home to Dallas for the week end and had forged his own pass, found the official stamp, stamped it and dismissed himself. He came back vastly refreshed and formally readmitted himself.

When he failed to answer at equal length, I read his poems over and the journal he had left with me. I wrote him I had unexpectedly been given a job with the Ballet Russe to do a Western piece. He wired congratulations. It was about a cowgirl and I told him the story. He didn't like it and suggested in its place a girl and a tribe of Indians who were to be indicated merely by a cloud of feathers blowing around the stage. This would save costumes and rehearsal time, he promised, and be in the best modern stylized tradition.

He wrote about Army life — and how he didn't want to get into special services. He had taken care to keep the authorities from learning that he was a concert manager or that he knew anything about music. He wished to get the war finished and he didn't believe arranging violin recitals could expedite matters. He decided to try for artillery. He was, among other things, a pretty good shot — but, of course, this didn't count with a cannon. He went through every menial and exhausting service a foot soldier, no grade, can be put to. He grumbled continuously, but he got on with the jobs. In time, he was private, first class, and permitted to supervise the peeling of potatoes.

I wrote him that I was about to entrain for California with the Ballet Russe. My concert money was long since exhausted. I traveled in coaches to save fare and I carried everything I owned in baskets to save tips.

And how far was Shreveport from Hollywood? I wrote to ask. Too far, he said. He was not dazzled by the Ballet Russe but hoped I would have a nice success. "Come back with your shield or under it," he said.

He was now a corporal and in Tennessee. He had missed weather forecasting because of faulty calculus, but he had been accepted in weather observing. From time to time there were requests for books. I sent him *Totem and Taboo* by Freud and *The Sexual Life of Savages* by Malinowski. These were not what he expected and threw the barracks into an uproar. He asked for a chromonica. I bought one; it cost me my phone for two weeks.

The epistolary courtship was getting on his nerves. He wanted to see me, he had something important to discuss. Well, I said, I would stop off on the way from Seattle and call on him — and where was he exactly? Smyrna, Tennessee, he'd told me — and the calls were all routed through Atlanta, Georgia. O.K. By exchanging my Ballet Russe Pullman ticket for second-class fare and going coach, I could afford the extra trip. I phoned him once more, Seattle — Atlanta — Smyrna, that I could manage forty-eight hours on the way east. He was delighted.

Mother was, of course, dreadfully shocked. This was not her idea of the winning of a fine woman. In her day it was the men who crossed continents and oceans. There had been no bunches of violets, no boxes of chocolates, no pressed leaves in letters, no constant attendance, no pining for me. It was all somehow "not quite fine," she thought. But, I asked, how could she tell? He was being kept on the double at very odd occupations far away. I knew that he was terribly mistrusting of marriage under these circumstances. I always had distrusted marriage too, and had driven away every likely young man, believing I could not have dancing and true love at the same time. Oddly enough, under the present curious circumstances, I was no longer afraid.

CHAPTER II *Smyrna*

I set out from Seattle. I had been rehearsing and traveling all up and down the West Coast and I was tired. I slept right across the continent, unnoticing and unhearing. I slept as though I'd been hit on the head, rousing myself days later to change trains in Chicago and in Cincinnati and then start due south for Atlanta.

The train was like all the coaches at this time, crowded, restless and permeated with smells that seemed to be more emotions than odors; the air into which we were sealed was turgid with body atmosphere, coffee, peanuts, chocolate and dust. At first I could find no seat and settled with two women and three children in the washroom. We were extremely indignant when a sailor with remarkably bad manners came in and, after looking around bleakly, brushed his teeth and washed his neck. He then even had the effrontery to enter the little toilet. The women clucked like a hencoop and hid their little girls' faces. One of them rang for the porter. "Outrageous indecency. The war's no excuse!" said the ladies. The porter grinned. The boy combed his hair doggedly and left. "Excuse me, ladies," said the porter, "I don't believe you know. You're in the men's room."

Several cities later, I found a seat out in the coach and we all settled for the night on our reclining chairs, I with *War and Peace*, a carton of coffee tasting strongly of cardboard, and one of those flat, opaque sandwiches, of the consistency of damp tissue, sold regularly in such places.

My first seat companion was a rabbi traveling South to a religious conference. He completely disregarded the noise around and talked to me in a low, accented voice. This was his first trip away from his wife and he sent her a postcard at every stop. He was a Hungarian and had been hurled from a third-story window in Budapest during an anti-Semitic student riot. Several of his friends had their necks broken that night. He said he could never feel the same about the university again and had emigrated to America. He shared his box lunch with me and he patted me on the shoulder when the conductor found him a quieter seat where he could study. "Godspeed," he said, smiling with incredible kindness.

A rear gunner now replaced the rabbi, with a blonde who informed him she was on her way to join her husband. The blonde was accompanied by a child to whom she paid no mind at all. So the child ran loose through two cars all night, protesting. Finally a mother, not his own, gathered him in and he fell asleep in her arms. The gunner and his responsive friend passed from group to group being companionable and sometimes, in moments of mounting intimacy, invisible, but how, I could not guess, since every available spot was occupied either with drowsy people or luggage. Whenever they vacated the seat beside me, a marine who had been standing the entire way quietly slipped in and fell asleep with his head on my shoulder. I found this rather comforting except that he groaned and ground his teeth. Once, when we both jolted awake, he opened the shoe box he held on his knees and offered to share the lunch his mother had put up for him. The box was filled with neatly wrapped homemade sandwiches, apple pie, an orange and a banana.

A landscape, more luxurious with every mile, changed softly to gray. Lights budded on the hillside and the dark was threaded with fireflies. The great trees of Tennessee, festooned and weighted with wild grape, bowed toward the tracks. The woods stood under the moon in blankets of flowering vine. Inside our car, where the light was turned low for sleeping, people jostled and nodded. We clung together, weaving a kind of relationship that would be sustaining for an hour or so until stations cut the vague safety and threw us out toward decision.

At 1:10 we went through Nashville, Tennessee. I looked out. It was dark, lights winked. The marine moaned and shifted. Nashville seemed to be quite a large place. At 8:45 we were in Atlanta. I rose creakily and collected my various belongings. The sailor instantly slipped into my seat. He waved to me out the window.

I got a very slow porter and said, "The Hotel Jackson at Smyrna."

"Ma'am," he said with extreme leisureliness, "there ain't no Hotel Jackson at Smyrna — not that I heared of."

"There certainly is," I said with objectionable Yankee dispatch. "Now you just find me a taxi while I phone."

"Yassum. Not that I heared of," he muttered ominously, lifting my bags very carefully onto his little truck and proceeding with caution across the nearly empty station. It was a clear, hot, brilliant morning that promised prostration. I ran for the telephone and gave the name and service number. "Smyrna, Georgia, or Smyrna, Tennessee?" asked the operator.

I was in the wrong Smyrna.

I laid the receiver down and flew out to the ticket office. "Where is Smyrna, Tennessee?" I gasped.

" 'Bout three hundred miles back north. You passed through it at two thirty-five A.M. There's a big weather base there. A train goes out in four minutes."

Ten minutes later I was settled in another coach, and the lush green scenery started to slide back the other way.

We were to have had forty-eight hours together. One whole day was lost.

I sat biting my lips and winking back tears, as the chasms, rocks and gorges, the green irrepressible growth of the strong South slid by unheeded. The same sort of social rumpus was going on and as we approached the air base, seemed to increase in volume. A colonel, gray-haired and decorous, sat beside me.

"Excuse me, sir," I said, "do you know anything about Smyrna, Tennessee?"

"Yes. I am stationed there."

"Then you can tell me about the Jackson Hotel."

"There is no hotel at Smyrna."

"Oh, yes, there is. I'm going there." I looked at him steadily. "Isn't there? Really? Isn't there?"

He shook his head. "There's a Hotel Andrew Jackson in Nashville. That's fifteen miles beyond; Smyrna is a flag stop and the town consists of a platform and two or three stores. There is absolutely no hotel."

My eyes filled.

"Tell me about it," he said.

So I told him what I could. My speech was halting and I felt, due to shyness, quite uncommunicative. It was difficult to indicate to this strange gentleman that I thought my life's happiness depended on there being a Hotel Andrew Jackson in Smyrna and on my getting there within twelve hours. He listened discreetly.

"Well," he said, putting out his cigarette, "we're getting in. I'm going on to the Hotel Jackson in Nashville, where my wife awaits me. I think your corporal meant to have you stay there. Did he say explicitly Smyrna?"

Then I dimly realized that perhaps he had mentioned one of the better-known Southern cities.

"The train slows up at Smyrna," said the colonel, "but it does not stop. We will look over the station. If he's there waiting, I will have the train halted. But I will not let you off this train alone if he's not waiting for you in plain sight. Not at Smyrna. That's out of the question. It would be . . . well . . . inadvisable."

When we approached the station, he braced himself squarely in a doorway and clasped both arms around my waist. I swayed forward at right angles and swung back and forth searching the platform as we eased past. Soldiers were dropping off all down the long train and swinging their duffle bags to the ground. My bags were stacked right behind me in case they had to be thrown out abruptly and the porter stood by ready, one hand on the emergency cord. I looked and looked. A few men in khaki lounged on benches, three jeeps waited, an Army car was coming down the road. In my anxiety, every single G.I. soldier looked exactly like Walter and my heart stuttered as I gazed past each face and wondered if I could possibly fail to make a mistake and recognize him just as the train gathered speed. "No . . . no . . . yes? Oh, no, indeed . . ." The train was picking up.

"I was afraid so," said the colonel, pulling me inside. "Here, you'd better wipe your face." He offered me a spotless handkerchief.

He drove me to the Jackson Hotel. I sat, speechless.

"My wife and I would be pleased to have you for cocktails," he said, "as soon as we've freshened up."

I asked for my room, but the clerk stared at me in concentration. "You didn't come," he explained. "It was booked for last night and we had to give it up. The town is crowded. You can have that divan over there in the lounge. We're not supposed to let you, but I will." At the moment there were three soldiers on it. "I'll get them off," he reassured me.

"Oh, please find something!"

He looked hard, said 614 and handed over the key.

The colonel's wife phoned me minutes later, but I sat rigid and unbudging with my hat on. "Forgive me, no cocktails. Thank you." I kept staring at the telephone, now and then trying to get a call through to that mysterious green settlement up along the line through which I had passed twice in the last sixteen hours, and which seemed to close itself away from my searching like a place in a dream. It was dusk now — exactly the hour I had boarded the train the day before in Cincinnati. Finally he rang me.

"Good God, honey, what were you doing in Georgia? I have night duty tonight."

I have no recollection what I did that evening or where I ate or if I ate. I fancy I read a lot more of *War and Peace*.

He arrived at nine-thirty next morning, white for sleep. I was overstrung and tired. "What I need at the moment," he said, "is black coffee." So we ate breakfast in the coffee shop. It seemed odd that people were slamming waffles and biscuits about and calling coffee orders while these enormous moments were gathering carefully between us. He yawned a lot. It made explaining about the ballet hard. I did not particularly want to explain about the ballet or any other work, for that matter, but he said almost nothing. I danced some of it for him. I showed him the illustrated Ballet Russe program book. "This is Freddie Franklin, who has been so kind to me," I said. "And this is Youskevitch, who is probably the greatest male dancer in the world."

"They all look alike," said Walter. I hastened to re-examine them. This was a novel point of view, but on consideration, it did seem that one man in armpit tights looked very like another, and their faces were all photographed from below to heighten their jumping prowess and virility, or in shadow because of the intensity of their emotions.

"Tell me what you do all day," I begged.

"Oh, honey, it's boring and it's tiring and I do it all day and many nights and I hate to talk about it."

"Do you think a little walk in the fresh air would make you feel better?" I asked.

"It might." He gave himself a glum look in the mirror. "My God, I didn't even stop to shave."

We walked around the main square several times, and we talked about the war headlines and where he would be sent next. He had no idea, nor when, so that discussion was short and quite gloomy. We walked behind the World War I Memorial and then we went in it. There was not so much inside: some flags and guns brought home by Nashville veterans, some medals and photographs of out-of-style trenches. The men and situations looked very old-fashioned except that there is no style in death and the cadavers seemed up-to-date. We got the most out of that display and went back on the streets again. The shops were attractive, but neither of us had any money to speak of; our examination was therefore academic.

"That is the store where the wool was purchased for my new pullover. I was taken in yesterday to be measured," said Walter.

"By whom were you taken in?"

"By the knitter, of course."

"Walter, are you interested in a girl here?" My voice probably shrilled.

"I'm interested in her father. He's a wonderful cook. He did me the best dish of curried prawns last night I ever ate."

"That's where you were last night! Did you know where I was?"

"Yes. Going as fast as you could to Smyrna, Georgia." He pinched my cheek.

We went for a walk in a sort of park. It was mangy and bare underfoot and the dusty trees hung like mops in the heat. All the grass had been worn away. He told me limericks he'd made up — some of them were very funny. I did not particularly want to hear limericks. I thought I'd better laugh, though. I told him a limerick or two back, and by that time we'd walked right through the bare park. He kept yawning. I suggested we sit down.

"Why don't you describe your dance to me?" His head drooped. "I'd better keep walking," he said. "I haven't been in bed for thirty-eight hours."

"What about a nap?"

"If I lie down I'm gone for good. I'm due for eleven hours straight. Besides, you didn't sit up three nights to see me sleep."

Then he thought of something interesting to do. We boarded a bus and went out to Andrew Jackson's home, The Hermitage, now a museum.

"I really haven't any idea what you do all day," I said, while joggling along.

"Can't hear," he yelled. "Wrong ear. Deaf in the left ear, you know."

"Didn't know. Change places."

"Nearly there. Keep the window."

The Hermitage was beautiful, I guess.

We ate dinner at The Two Keys. A young corporal brought his steak over and joined us. I minded, but he was Walter's friend.

"Could we go somewhere for a quiet talk?" I whispered.

"There's a ball game on tonight," said the friendly corporal.

"Wanta go?" said Walter.

That, as the English say, tore it. It also conditioned my feeling about baseball for the rest of my life. When I boarded the train for New York some hours later it was with the intention of never seeing him again.

The next week of silence was dreadful. But I had to finish up *Rodeo* and I worked six hours a day in full company rehearsal at the jolly finale. Occasionally I just stopped. The tears stood in my eyes and I forgot the counts. The Russians took no notice; they were used to people crying. It was part of normal rehearsal atmosphere. They just figured I was mad at them. I went to Freddie Franklin on the unbearable fifth afternoon. "Freddie, I feel sick." I didn't feel sick a bit. I was sound as a nut, but I looked pretty awful. "Duckie, here are the keys to my room. Lie down for an hour. I'll clean up this bit until you get back." So I went to his hotel room and sobbed in the luxury of perfect quiet, washed my face, and came back to the Hoe-Down.

Walter phoned on the eighth day. "Do you think you could pretend none of this happened? I'll be here for at least two weeks. Can you possibly come back?"

"I can't. Oh, darling, I really can't. Now the ballet is going up to Montreal for their season there and I have to go with them. It's my only chance to keep rehearsing. We open soon."

"Oh, hell, honey, I must see you."

"But we open cold at the Met in two weeks. Where will you be on October sixteenth?"

"I don't know. Possibly on my way to Aberdeen Officers' School. I think they're at last paying attention to my petitions."

"Could you possibly be at my *première?*"

"Maybe."

"We'll hope for that."

But it was to Aberdeen I phoned at midnight on October 16, where he was becoming, with unprecedented complaints and misgivings, an officer. "It's a hit. *Rodeo's* a smash hit. We got twenty-one curtain calls."

"I'm not surprised. I expected you to. Now, when can I see you?"

"Can you come here?"

"Good God, no. I can't budge. You come here."

But in Candidates' School he could have visitors only when his conduct was unblemished, which, naturally, it never was. Oh, those demerits, those "Gigs" that turned me back despairing in Philadelphia and Wilmington — back to New York without ever having seen him, bearing all my little presents and food packages, chocolate cakes and muffins, back to eat in solitary nonmartial gloom! I told him I had been hired by the Theatre Guild to stage the dances for their new musical based on *Green Grow the Lilacs* and that Richard Rodgers was enthusiastic about my work. Good girl, said Prude. But he began to be impatient and wanted to see me urgently, and he seemed apprehensive.

By the time he got his bars and his seven days' furlough, which he had to spend in Texas because of his father's illness, I was in New Haven, sunk beyond all personal plans in dress-rehearsal chaos. After the New Haven opening, I phoned him, stationed now in Omaha. I phoned from the lobby of the Shubert Theatre. Dick Rodgers was walking up and down the lobby, smoking.

"It looks like a hit," I said. Rodgers nodded at me and grinned.

"Yes, it does," he said.

"Never mind all that," said Prude. "When are you coming out here?"

"In about three weeks with luck."

"Why so long? Whatever are you going to do for three weeks? It's opened in New Haven, hasn't it? And it's bound to open in New York?"

"We think it is."

"Well, what's there for you to do now? Get here quick!"

After three weeks of the hardest work I'd ever experienced, we did open in New York. The show was now called *Oklahoma!* I telephoned Omaha again. "It really does look like a hit."

"O.K. O.K. When are you coming?"

"Aren't you glad I'm a smash? I'm told I've pulled off something rather special."

"Sure I'm glad. When can you be here?"

"In five days."

"Hurry."

I should have stood by my new hit for some weeks to tidy up and consolidate matters. But once the understudies had been seen to, I fled. My leading dancers saw me off. Joan Mc-Cracken handed me an old-fashioned bouquet, complete with lace frill and ribbons. And Katharine Sergava brought me a magnum of Pommery. These items were not handy on an overcrowded train; they also did not pass without remark. This time I had a berth and this time there was a nice hotel room waiting for me.

"With Katya's love," I said, handing the champagne to the lieutenant just in from a 700-mile motor-convoy trip.

"Very sound," he answered, hefting it.

"Can we have some now?"

"No, not yet. This is not the right moment."

We spent our time aimlessly, amiably and serenely.

I danced for him the whole of *Oklahoma!* and he was amazed that I knew one foot from another and had thought out all those funny little gestures by myself.

"Just what do you think I've spent my life learning to do?" I demanded in astonishment.

"God knows," he answered, *"not* keeping your clothes in order or your studio."

And every day there were long-distance calls from New York and from Hollywood. I, who had spent hours and days in outer offices, was now hunted down and searched out so that I could not have three uninterrupted hours with my guy. The phone rang in the morning and in the evening when he was sitting with me having drinks.

Suddenly, one twilight, he stated quietly, looking over his glass, and with no preamble of any kind, that he thought it was time we got married. I burst into tears.

"In God's name," he said, "what's the matter? Surely this is not the first time anyone has asked you!"

"No," I blubbered into my cocktail napkin, "but it's the first time I've said yes."

Katya's champagne, he informed me as he wiped away my hysteria, was cooling at the best restaurant in town.

The next day we discussed the practical side of our situation. I was agreeing to marry a young man I barely knew, who stood in immediate likelihood of being shipped overseas. He knew better what he was getting, or believed he did: a frowsty woman, no longer really young, who made him laugh and who appealed to him for certain reasons — among others, the losing, game fight she had put up in her chosen profession.

"It's nice you've had this success, dear," he said. "This will buck you up. And now you can get another job. One more and you can get the business out of your system altogether."

I nodded. Two years before, a young man had proposed marriage with the unfortunate provision that I quit dancing. That fixed his wagon, but this peculiar misapprehension of the lieutenant's fixed no one's. I believed him, or I hoped I did. One or two more shows and then anything he wanted, even idleness. So I nodded — but everything was not settled yet.

"There is something you don't know about me," I said.

The lieutenant turned pale. "Good God, is there more that you haven't told me?"

"You haven't seen any of my work."

"But I'm marrying you. I'm not marrying your work."

"Aren't you? But you may not like it."

"Possibly not."

"That would be dreadful."

"Oh, you'd get used to it."

"I should find that very hard."

"Is it so important?" I nodded. He put an arm around me quietly. "I know what you want to do. That's the really important point. Whether or not you succeed matters less."

On my return to New York, I told Mother about my engagement.

"I'm not surprised," was her laconic remark.

My niece, Judith, was enchanted. She thought Walter was handsome and very romantic. My sister Mag was glad to see me settling at last.

I called up Martha with the joyful news. "What do you think?" I said. "We're going to be married."

"Yes," she said, "he told me a month ago."

"But he only asked me last week. Do you mean he discussed this with you before me?"

"He was worried about a war marriage and about his own qualifications."

"He took a lot for granted, I must say. I wish I'd refused him."

"Oh, yes, I know," said Martha. "Have you set a date?"

CHAPTER III *Success*

I wanted to spend all my time on a trousseau, but professional concerns engulfed me. During my few days' sojourn in Omaha a lot seemed to have happened. A reporter from the *Times* remarked suddenly during an interview, "Miss de Mille, I don't believe you realize what kind of a success *Oklahoma!* is."

"What kind is it?" Never having had any commercial success at all, I didn't realize this was unusual in degree.

He struggled to find words. "I think it's the biggest success that's ever occurred in the theater — ever — but certainly the greatest in this century." Well, this was nice, if inopportune.

The week after the play opened, financial wizards of my acquaintance began advising me how to invest the money they were sure I was earning. My *Oklahoma!* contract stipulated a moderate lump sum and no royalties at all, but after the out-of-town triumph, the Guild had generously granted me fifty dollars a week. I was carrying ten years of debts owed to Mother and friends and I was intending to marry a second lieutenant with, as far as I knew, no resources beyond his Army pay. It would be nice, I thought, if I could afford to stay with him, if I wasn't forced to take another job immediately.

But no entreaties could persuade the management to better my weekly royalty from fifty dollars to seventy-five dollars. I was, for this sum, expected to rehearse replacements in the dancing cast, and refresh and coach the veterans from time to time. The bargain was hard; but this is the essence of our theater — the hardest and the sharpest bargain possible under any given circumstances. The treatment accorded me was by no means discriminatory. Managements attempt to maintain this line universally, and dancers, on their part, retaliate whenever they can, which is not quite so often.

There were immediate and visible evidences of success all around, many of them helpful to me. The box-office line on forty-fourth Street, which did not diminish for thirteen months, ran right down the block past the boardings where men on ladders were busy painting the management's name in larger letters. When I entered Sardi's, I was recognized and ushered to a front table. I was recognized also by the box office. They were courteous although they never had any seats for me, either free or for sale; I stood for every performance of *Oklahoma!* I saw in line of duty — all but one; they did, however, say, "Good day." The bank managers and clerks who had been so concerned about my overdrafts stopped me as I deposited my new weekly fifty-dollar checks and begged for help in getting tickets. My sister Margaret called up to say it would be an enormous business boon to her to give certain wholesale manufacturers the privilege of buying a pair.

I kept remembering how, only a year before, my mother had been forced to bully and nag her friends to enlist any kind of audience for my concerts and how humiliated we had always been, on the afternoon of a performance, when it had become certain that the box office would be disastrous. Now I was invited out by people I had never heard of, just in the hope of cajoling tickets at any prices named. John Martin reported that the current year was becoming known on the street as the "de Millennium." The *New Yorker* planned a profile. *Collier's* wanted colored photos — pages of them. When a photographer, famous for his fashion pictures, came to my studio, I tried to hide the fact that there was no furniture by filling the corners with pots of laurel leaves and flowers.

Dress designers on Seventh Avenue began making full-skirted ginghams and rayons like the *Oklahoma!* dance costumes (as full as cloth rationing permitted) and I was photographed with my girls for *Vogue*. The high topknot and the pony-tail, Bambi Linn's hairdos, began to appear, first on dancers, then on every teen-ager, then on mothers and aunts. Capezio devised a ballet shoe for street wear and every woman with or without an instep went flat-heeled. Sally Victor put out a line of straw hats with feathers and flowers like the hats on Laurie's friends and they were widely imitated. Helena Rubinstein considered a new cosmetic called "The Ballet Look" and I was taken to lunch at the Russian Tea Room and asked to describe "The Real Ballet Look." "Exhaustion," I replied, and the idea was abandoned.

The boys and girls with the true ballet look, the erect, brisk and quiet figures carrying their boxes and baskets of practice clothes, began to scuttle hatless through the 40's of Times Square during that April. They were to become a familiar figure in the next decade. Frequently, their long black woolen tights could be glimpsed under their coats as they rushed from audition to audition.

The chorus girl and the chorus boy of the past, corrupt, sly, ruthless and professionally inept, gradually disappeared. And in their place came singers and dancers, trained and self-respecting. Rehearsal halls began to lose their overtones of boudoir bargaining.

One heard "Beautiful Morning" in every restaurant, on the air at midnight, in cars as they passed on the highway. Every taxi driver whistled it.

And every night at the theater the crowds jostled and pushed and laughed and went out singing. And always at the back of the house was a double row of uniforms standing and gazing with misted eyes at the final joyous statement of what they were leaving behind. These were the songs the men and women went away whistling and taught to others under heartbreaking circumstances. This was the show the soldiers kept asking about. New York meant not only the gateway to home, but this show. *Oklahoma!* became almost as important to them as Rita Hayworth, but there was a good bit of sweetheart and kid sister involved in *Oklahoma!*

It meant much to my mother to hear friends talk, to see my name mentioned in all the columns, to be pestered by managers and agents for my whereabouts; she who had humiliated herself for so many years, begging these very people to take notice of me. She used very frequently to go see *Oklahoma!* because she loved it and because I think the sound of audiences cheering my dances mended her poor damaged heart. There were no seats available and she used to sit on the stairs at the back of the auditorium and peer through the rail. Sometimes she stood in the wings. She often did this when I was away from home. It made her feel less lonely. A member of the cast said later, "When we noticed her there the performance became more important." Those performances had cost my mother a very great deal, twenty years' work in fact, and all her savings. She was being repaid now, and somehow the cast sensed this.

When I was away my dancers used to telephone her and ask advice; Bambi Linn, for instance, who called herself my "First Daughter." Mother tried to think what I would say and counseled accordingly. She had remarkable practical sense — better than mine. She endeavored to spare me all she could — and there was need to do this.

I changed my telephone number. Having been a failure for so long, my name was still hopefully in the directory. Now there was no retreat from attention. Managers, agents and dancers phoned by day and night and once I found a dancer, poor desperate creature, lying across my stairs when I came home in the evening. I was suddenly very, very wonderful and important and there had not been five minutes' preparation for it. But the constant interruption of my privacy made me nervous, and my temper snapped. Naturally everyone thought my head had been turned. I was like a deep-sea fish brought suddenly to the surface: I exploded.

My agent, Dick LaMarr, urged me to get a secretary and a tax expert, but I did not understand how to delegate responsibility. I had not been in the black for eight years and I'd never in my life had a secretary. He begged me to try taxis instead of buses and to get a mink coat. But I was, I kept reminding him, still living on fifty dollars a week and there were ten years of debt to pay off; I had the leopard skin that Clara, my stepmother, gave me, relined.

Dick also kept urging remunerative long-term contracts, but I resisted with every instinct I had and my lawyer stuck by me. Dick grew frantic.

"I can get her fifty thousand dollars a year," he said. "Easily fifty thousand dollars."

"You can do nothing of the sort," said the lawyer. "With taxes she can't keep it — and what good is it to her if she loses her self-respect?"

"What's so disrespectful about fifty thousand dollars?" cried Dick. He broke out in a sweat and threw open a window, walked up and down and rubbed his hands over and over in a handkerchief. "I never heard such talk. You're keeping her from getting her just returns. She's been poor. Do you understand? Poor."

"Dick," I said, "let's have a drink. I'll try to explain."

"This will take some explaining," he said, wiping his hands and his forehead again. "Some explaining!"

"You see," I said over my sherry, "either you believe I can only do it once . . ."

"There's a time to strike — a time to cash in —"

". . . or you believe I have real talent, and given a good chance, can repeat the success and maybe even do better. But I must be free to choose — and there will always be risk."

He had a triple Scotch.

Dick had been born William Merlin Hanrihan in Boston but decided for exotic reasons to change his name to Richard LaMarr when he entered the theater as a baritone. In the customary process of elimination, he became well known as an actor's representative and his almost unnaturally handsome Irish face grew familiar at Sardi's and the night spots as he browsed for helpful and likely rumors. He worked in a mysterious way, mostly at midnight and seldom in his office, but he got things done. He was quick-eyed and nervous with restless fingers and a flicking cigarette, his Irish charm marching before greetings and negotiations like a gay and hopeful banner in the changeable breezes of our climate. He minced words. He smacked his lips on them until they faded and were useless. Over and over, with the prayerful monotony of an Ave, he denounced our betrayers or our rivals. He reported business progress something in this wise: "You should have heard what he said to our proposal. But I remember. Only too well do I remember. It's as though he were speaking now. Goddammit, it's as clear as though he were right here. He said to me, he had the audacity to say — and Goddammit, I couldn't wait to tell you. I want you to know everything exactly. Oh, but he was sure of himself! Believe you me, he was sure, until I surprised him. He said — but wait till I tell you — we were walking down Shubert Alley and I can see the rain on the poster with your name. I called his attention to it. 'Do you think a girl with her name up there will listen to anything like that?' That's just what I said. 'Do you think a girl —' But then I thought of something he didn't know — and, Goddammit, you should have seen his expression change. Brother, did his expression — right then when I — and he tried to make a comeback. Oh — oh — oh. But I wrote that book. He couldn't tell me anything! Imagine his gall in suggesting a thing like that!"

Under these remarkable and mysterious arabesques was a hard core of business accomplishments. But how it maintained itself, I could never follow.

Dick always wound up as he began with personal solicitude. "How's your guy, how's the bridegroom? God love him! Oh, this war is terrible! If it wasn't for my bad leg! And your mother? There's a little lady I love. But anyhow, let's drink to Walter. Have another, it won't hurt you! Good for you. God love you! I'll settle the deal tomorrow."

He squired me everywhere, met trains, escorted me to interviews, arranged all mundane details, waited in offices, waited outside rehearsal halls, treated me like the heir apparent, the Promise, Joan of Arc. For the first time in my life I had a courtier, a devoted attending cavalier. He was my permanent equerry and I found this a very attractive comfort. He had been grounded in the Broadway theater in its dirtiest, most merciless period, and he tried to understand a point of view accumulated elsewhere — namely, that I liked as much money as I could get with no compromise, but I liked other things more. No compromise is the most expensive luxury in the world. Dick tried to understand this. He tried so hard he succeeded. He placed his trust in my hunches, which, in the beginning, must have been horribly awkward for him, going against an agent's instincts, seemingly those of a bulldog's for a beefsteak, but, heaven knows why, he controlled himself. On every subsequent show I knew I would have to hazard my whole career, the rule in show business being that you are as good as your last job — not the one before, but the last. Nevertheless, he stood by. He was stalwart about Hollywood offers, even shaking his cigarette and roaring at the representative for M-G-M who was trying to bully me into a long-term deal.

And no matter where I went or what I did, there he was with a taxi and magazines, and the latest rumors. This was an act of faith, because he was drawing no percentage on *Oklahoma!*, as penance for the contract. And there were always other people who earned more and were not so difficult or full of vagaries and hampering ideals. But God love him! He caught on; he began to believe in what I wanted to do.

During this chaos I attempted to buy a trousseau and wedding linens. I attempted to clarify my life so that I could terminate all business plans and stay with my husband or, in case he was shipped, resume business plans and stay alone.

LaMarr eventually contracted me for a new comedy, *One Touch of Venus*. He procured handsome terms; for the first time in my life, I was well paid. Walter was apprehensive and somewhat disappointed. He was not sure this was a good enough show to follow up *Oklahoma!* But Dick was firm and very pleased.

"Goddammit," said Dick, "you've been exploited all your life. Right here it stops. A fair price is fair. I'm not going to have you swindled in the name of fine art any longer. Don't worry about the book. Don't worry about anything. It will all be fixed. The people involved aren't exactly punks." And this could not be denied. The staff included Kurt Weill, Ogden Nash, S. J. Perelman, Elia Kazan and Cheryl Crawford. I had to admit that the prospects as they stood were, in fact, better than hopeful. They were splendid.

Rehearsal dates were set for early August. The wedding date was determined by the U. S. Army. Walter's furlough came due in June.

"Leave everything to me," said LaMarr. "God love you both! Go out and have a wonderful wedding."

CHAPTER IV *Marriage and Hobbs*

SO, with my advance royalty for *One Touch of Venus*, I went out to buy my trousseau — new dresses all my own. Now, for the first time, I was able to go into the expensive shops, not the bargain counters. Since this was a war wedding, I thought a gown and veil inappropriate and chose instead a little brown gabardine suit to match the lieutenant's summer khakis. Mag gave me a hand-embroidered blouse, and Mother, an heirloom diamond brooch. Katharine Sergava gave me Victorian gold-tasseled earrings. Out of sheer habit, I got a cheap brown straw bonnet and then decided that for the first time in my life I would spend as much as for a costume, and selected a creation by a name milliner. It was no more becoming than the inexpensive one, which was not very, but I felt better for the gesture.

We received a few gifts, but most friends said they would wait until the war was over, with just what precaution in mind they never made clear to me.

Walter had told his father, who said not to be a fool, there was a war on. He told a Texan uncle, who gave him a very large and sharp hunting knife, whether for marriage or the South Pacific he did not stipulate.

We planned to meet with our acquisitions in Hollywood and I preceded him West by two days, which gave me time to make all the preparations. I found a pretty Episcopal chapel in Beverly

Hills called All Souls. It was small and charming and since we had never been divorced, the minister was willing. No music, I said; we both wanted the ceremony to be simple.

Then I shopped for my bouquet. Wild lupine, the Texan bluebonnet, was what I asked, but they were out of season, so I settled for some garden flowers.

Then I invited the guests. Not more than nine, and all very dear to me — "Because," as I told Father, "Walter is alone. There is no one on his side."

"I'm on his side," said Pop. "I'll double in brass."

Then I arranged for a matron of honor — my dance assistant and soloist, Mary Myer Green, who had helped me in many difficult situations before. Dennis and Mary Green were among the very few of my friends whom Walter knew. Actually, I'd introduced him to her when she was in the hospital. They got on well and I knew he would want them with us.

Then I arranged for a U-Drive car.

Walter had ordered the ring from our friends, the John Gershgorns, and designs had been submitted through the mail to Hobbs, New Mexico.

Then I had my hair and nails done.

Then I met Walter at the station. He had been having a bachelor dinner at Las Vegas with brother officers and he came toward me with a strangely distracted air. He kept looking over my head as though he expected me to have grown an inch or two taller.

We had nothing to say to one another.

Then doubts assailed me and then doubts assailed him, I learned subsequently.

Then we went to get our license and there was such a traffic in divorce documents we could hardly attract the clerk's attention.

Then we had a chocolate soda.

"You're nearly caught," said Walter with a taut face. "Three more hours and you can't pull out."

I laughed heartily and gave myself up to wondering.

He asked about the arrangements. The church seemed all right. Music? No music. What? I'd bungled the wedding. He grabbed the telephone. There followed a brisk twenty-minute conversation with the church organist while a tasteful program of Bach and Handel was arranged with a very old Swedish wedding march to lead off. I'd forgot he was a concert manager.

"I guess that's all now," he said.

So we got ready. He didn't like my hat and he didn't like the way my hair was done, but he didn't say so. Only I knew. I'd had doubts myself.

As the whole family sat assembled in Father's living room waiting to go to church, the phone rang. It was Sam Goldwyn. He wanted to speak to me. Goldwyn hadn't called Father in fifteen years and he'd never called me at all, but he chose this moment. Nobody ever has succeeded in saying no to Goldwyn, but Father tried.

"She's getting married, Sam, in ten minutes."

"I won't keep her longer than ten minutes."

"No, Sam."

Walter looked odd and Clara, my stepmother, shook her head.

Walter and I left early. We fetched the ring, but it was too small and had to be stretched and there was no time. How does one stretch a gold ring? All right, so they stretched it and we ran to the florist. Too stiff, too awkward. I began to bite my nails. Walter paced up and down, grabbing a tousled but more natural bouquet from the hands of the bewildered professional. We drove to the church. The organist went over the program with Walter. It seemed in order. The minister gravely instructed us. Walter, round-eyed, studied with solemn dawning comprehension the extremely binding and inclusive commitments he was about to make. Like all brides, I gave my attention to wondering whether or not my hat was or was not really unbecoming.

"Where are Mary's flowers?" suddenly asked Walter.

"I didn't order any — a simple wedding, you remember."

"Well, I must say!" he snapped, again grabbing the phone. "You didn't forget yours." He rang a florist. "Can you make up a handsome matron-of-honor bouquet in five minutes? Thank you. Really, Agnes!"

"It is considered wise by some," murmured the Reverend Smith, "to keep the bride and groom apart before the ceremony."

Walter met Mary and Dennis on the curb. "Here, Dennis, here's money. Hurry and get Mary's bouquet."

"I can see you're both in the traditional state," said Mary.

Father arrived. The nine guests were assembling. David Hertz leaned over to Michael, his wife, and audibly said, "I think, on the whole, I prefer funerals, don't you?"

Dennis came back. Mary's bouquet and mine didn't match in any way except that they were both alive.

"Oh, my God!" said Walter, white to the lips. "I can't go in there alone!"

"I'm with you, old man," said Dennis. "I'm right with you. I'll stay right there. Here, let me hold that." He talked as though it were a Bren gun he was relieving Walter of, but it was the wedding ring. Dennis was a six-foot-four-inch Englishman of military bearing and he looked reassuring. The two men marched purposefully away toward the door which led to the altar.

Pop took my arm and we proceeded to the vestibule.

It was five o'clock in Beverly Hills and the sun came long and golden through the avenues of date palms and the green gardens. There was a sound of traffic and children which seemed strangely irrelevant.

Suddenly the march started, a high peal of chirping antique sound. An entrance is an entrance and I braced instinctively and attacked. Mary insists that I gave her the tempo and the starting signal, as I'd done so often before camera or curtain, by snapping my fingers smartly. "And!" I said as an upbeat and stepped out. One does not loiter on an entrance or the audience leaves. At that pace in eight bars of music I would have been past the altar. I was two yards beyond Pop when he grappled me back. Sedately, properly and decently we entered, Father's arm like a vise clamping me quiet, and proceeded with propriety between my standing beloved friends toward where the minister and the two men waited, one in uniform.

Then we were married.

At the conclusion, I turned toward Father, who was in the first pew, standing with Clara, his wife, and threw myself on his breast.

"Oh, someone embrace me too," said Walter. "Oh, come here, my Mary," and she dropped the two bouquets she was carrying and threw her arms about him. At this point the ceremony broke to pieces. The organist was playing Mendelssohn doggedly fortissimo, and there should have been an orderly exit. But there wasn't.

"Why doesn't everyone go on the lawn?" murmured the Reverend Smith. "There's more room," and in an undertone, "and it will probably be quieter."

There came the time for signing the register, and as Walter took the pen, he looked across at Mary Green. "Why, Mary," he exclaimed gaily, "this is the first time I've seen you out of bed! You're taller than I thought!"

"No, really?" cooed Mary.

The Reverend Smith straightened suddenly and shot them a peculiarly searching look.

"It's all right, old boy — I mean, Reverend. My wife's been ill," said Dennis hastily. "They met in her hospital room . . ." But the Reverend wandered weakly off.

Outside in the afternoon, Mary and Dennis faced us. "Now, it's just beginning for you. It will all be quite different — oh, entirely different — you'll see. And better."

Walter was stationed at Hobbs, New Mexico, seven hours by bus from the nearest railroad train. We found ourselves on a flat, flat plain higher than the rest of America, with no chance of getting back and no promise of going forward, and there we waited out our cruel, lost, lovely honeymoon. We waited among strange companions, some of us surely doomed, all hopeful. The bugles blew at sunup and sundown. The great planes revved up their motors and took off and returned all day and all night. All day and all night the sky over our heads vibrated with a sound that meant no danger yet, a sound that was only practicing with death. And without surcease, like a sign on the horizon, streamed banners of flame from the natural-gas towers. They were flower-pale in the sunlight and ghastly at night — and they blew out and out and out.

There is a timelessness and impersonality about very high places which frightens away habit and frees the spirit from daily responsibilities. This is everlasting life visible upon earth; it is beyond calendars, like deep emotion. And bodily functions, speech and duty fall back as one endures with rocks and high waters. One can be homesick for this for the rest of one's life even if one has known it briefly. In this way Hobbs, on the lofty prairies, seemed cut off from all other life experience and the people as isolated as though they were survivors on a lost continent. We were totally out of communication with the rest of the world, however much we prepared for the melee. We lived each day separately as though it were our last.

The wind never ceased. The grasses moved to it and the flowers bent. There were no trees. It fanned with furnace heat our cheeks in the noon streets and it ruffled our hair and carried a reminder of sage and prairie weed. But it did not alter the heat. In the daytime the lid was off the sky and we were up there bare, so that the very asphalt moved under our shoes. The little flowers one picked were hot as though cooked, and little frying crickets sang like a sizzling in a pan. The sun beat down on the back of our necks, black and heavy. Everything appeared in double, one image dark. At high noon the air was alive with dazzle, the sky moving up in a maelstrom of spangles. But the wind never stopped. Overhead the planes carried on.

I found it unwise to walk abroad until the sun turned — but it was hard to know what to do. I spent a great deal of time in the hotel coffee shop. It had a cement floor which was unattractive but comfortable and it had a cooling system of sorts. I could kill a half hour or so over iced coffee, reading or watching the stray wives around me trying to amuse their straggling heat-ridden kids or entertain themselves, who had never before met and had so little to say. Quite a few were pregnant and feeling depressed and poorly. When I went upstairs to our very hot bedroom, I tried to study the *Venus* script and invent dances between the bureau and the bed — but there were disturbances. Outside in the inferno of our yard four dogs were tied up. They didn't like the heat or being tied up. They didn't like it from five-thirty in the morning until six-thirty at night. In the hall the four children of a major shot each other down in Jap planes for two or three hours at a stretch; all doors were open in order to catch what air there might be. The young wives played cards or sewed and called out remarks to each other until midafternoon when news began to come in.

This young man or that couldn't get off the base for dinner. The doors began shutting. The girls tried not to be sick with disappointment. There was the hush of fear about and it was very contagious. Did detention at the base mean something? Were they going to be moved out? Babies wailed. Whatever happened, the babies kept wetting and wailing.

Walter always got back. He was not a pilot and his hours were long but regular. We had dinner in the morgue light of our cement and oilcloth dining room and then walked out on the prairies.

The evenings were superb, the west a carnage of color. "Byronic," Walter called them. Out there beyond blue ether Lucifer and his hosts fought in glories of terror and space, while in the east a faint false dawn appeared where the night was coming, pale green and clear blue, and in the darkening heights a few brilliant enormous stars hung burning. I hunted for tiny microscopic flowers in the dusky grass, trying to find one of each, my "scorched earth" policy reproved by Walter, who liked things to remain living. Wherever we walked, animals came to the fence to see him — donkeys, dogs, chickens. Walter had an extraordinary power over them. He would speak softly from the road, and then, as they pressed against the wire, walk over and have a satisfactory, quiet conversation. I can see him still, a straight dusky figure just lighter than the surrounding twilight in his khakis, bent over the head of some animal, a goat or a dog, softly fondling the ears, talking low and understandably. They always seemed gratified and quietened by the exchange. Across our path loped great long-eared Mexican rabbits. Sometimes they sat on their enormous haunches, whiskers and ears twitching against the striped sky. And always the wind blew and the flag of fire burned over the town with its pale ominous flame.

On Sundays we went to the only trees in town, which were around the electric plant, trespassing under the barbed wire, to sit in shade while I coached him in German verbs, just in case, or he read Sid Perelman or George Moore aloud to me, the scenery revitalizing and dimming as the great New Mexican clouds passed over.

For variety, there were movies.

We saw *One of Our Aircraft Is Missing,* and I nearly jumped our of my seat to recognize Robert Helpmann, a ballet colleague and friend, not dancing but acting this time, and in very good Dutch. "You see how smart dancers are?" I said proudly. "I've had other reasons to think so," Walter murmured.

There was a meal or two at the officers' club. The young men with wives sat not talking to them. They looked depressed, but Walter and I looked beaming and we chattered like squirrels. There were officers' cocktail parties where, for the first time, I became less ashamed of dancers' gossip. The old familiar ballet grapevine for once seemed innocent in comparison to the venality of those desperate and ambitious men.

Well, there was all this that was new and stimulating and also there was a rain of frogs. One night the heavens opened, water gushed, a ball of fire fell straight down the sky ("suitable to bring any primitive man to his knees," Walter said, picking me off mine) and the next morning the parched land was a world of puddles and frogs, whose croaking rose and fell in banks of sound like gigantic machinery. Where did they come from? I asked. No pool or stream or lake for miles around — and then in three hours, hatched from the clay, a plague was upon us. And this visitation gave rise to village fun. Young rowdies speeded through the puddles with their shrieking girl friends, wetting and muddying every officer in town.

There was an evening — I remember it well — bright with color and wind. I was hurrying to meet Walter at the officers' club. I had on my new black cotton frock and it whipped annoyingly high over my knees. I ran to meet him and the wind tore my breath out and heightened my heartbeat. I had to run with both hands to my hat, a saucy straw with geraniums. I saw him running too, lean and quick, and the long brown legs of his khakis winking, his slim cap in his hand. And as we met and started to kiss, the notes of Retreat sounded and I was not aware of what was happening, but he said, "Excuse me a moment, dear," and put on his cap and stood at salute. We were quite alone on a great field and no one would have noticed, I thought, if he hadn't. But he did. And this very close person, my intimate and gentle friend, became suddenly a stranger, obeying laws and plans I had nothing to do with. All over the grounds wherever one could see were silent unmoving figures, fixed in amber light and the bugle tones, still as though forever. Continuance stopped, or rather, the moment endured past the normal instant and so saved itself from the regular disappearing and losing. Nothing in all those acres moved but the wind and the planes, which had become an element of nature and beyond politeness. And, of course, the flag dropping. We all watched it together; all the unassorted people watched it and were strangers to each other and then were not, because of the watching.

Once Walter had written to me to get a book, *Hail and Farewell* by George Moore, for "our library" and I stared at the page in a new and startled perception. This was the first time that the word "our" had meant anything in my life. I who had been living and working alone in rebellion against family restraint, had never before grasped any such concept. "We" and "our" now stood on their rights. I had a stake in life beside my own wits and, more important, beside my own wants.

So all this was new, all was important and zestful. Even the frogs were new to me — not the multitudes — but each frog separately and each flower and every spoken word. I was traveling in an unknown country with senses quickened and infinite anticipation and relish. This is part of what it is to be a bride.

The time went by. It wasn't any more. I had used it up.

I must leave for New York. After fourteen years of waiting, victory of sorts had come. The tide was with my career. I dared not tempt fate by delaying. But how do you tell a bridegroom this?

It is seven hours by bus to El Paso, nine hours by car. Walter drove me down and we chatted gaily. It was a strange unending trip and I thought, as hour after hour passed, that if Hitler could see all this, some of his confidence must dissipate. Surely no European could imagine such amounts of space; for in the two hundred and thirty-four miles between Hobbs and El Paso there are no towns of any kind, one settlement at the Carlsbad caves and four gas stations. An invading army could get thirsty on such a trek.

We talked. Why had he no prejudices about colored people, for instance? (He just shut his lips and shook his head. "I saw it. I didn't like it, any part of it.") Were there other young Southerners so liberal? (Yes, many.) It turned out he was in fact a good deal more liberal than I.

"You know," I said after serious consideration, "I think I'm liberal mainly because it gives me such a dandy chance for hating conservatives. You're not so rude as I am. I get mad all the time."

"Oh, nobody's as rude as you — and nobody's ever as mad."

We had our last evening across the border in Juárez. I wore a large brown straw hat and my wedding suit, and everywhere we went, he pulled me back with gentle tact. "Not in there, that's private. Don't stare so. They're not animals." But I, quite oblivious, was trying to fix all in mind and, like the eye of God, sought to stamp forever each color and odor and gesture so that I could duplicate it later. I could not tell then how often during the next years I would try to recapture that lovely evening and the spicy delicious food and wine and the faces in the first lantern light, the deep hard regard of the dark-faced people as they lifted their eyes to ours!

We stood on the banks of the Rio Grande and watched naked brown boys dive for silver in the muddy milky water. On the one side of the great gully was an ordinary American town, and on the other were the naked boys emitting cries like water birds, and shivering and glistening silver. We passed across a bridge and through a wire mesh gate and there we were in Baghdad, Port Said, strange speech, strange walking, faces not ours, and the steady glowing quiet of a Mexican sunset on the mud walls. Inside the great vegetable markets the tropics spread their unfamiliar fruit, not one piece of which was ever sold or ever seen on the other side of the wire gate, and women in *rebozos* lifted the magic vegetables in black-rimmed hands and brushed off the halo of flies and called and beckoned, and I pressed tight to my soldier and begged to stand and watch while the animal odor mounted about us like a tide and the red of the fruit rinds glowed in the last day, and underfoot everything was soft and rotten and musky and rich.

"Don't stare so," he kept whispering. "Darling, they're human beings. You can't stare at them this way. You'll hurt their feelings."

"They stare right back."

"Not the same way. You stare like a child. You'll have to learn manners."

"I might forget — I might forget some little thing."

Behind the lattices, eyes moved and hands rustled. Now and then our happy aimless path was blocked and we looked straight into the face of a cutthroat. G.I.'s sauntered and lounged. Tourists plodded and bargained. But always the stream of silent people moved past, fourteen-year-old madonnas, fat and prolific mothers, the old and the spent, diffident, stepping aside with closed faces until their eyes lifted and they saw straight in. Little, pretty, dark, vicious girls darted from doorways, brushed past Walter and called in their polysyllabic quick tongue. He took my hand and smiled and we continued along, floating on the iridescence of mutual apprehension and serene soft excitement.

We ate a strange and wonderful meal that scorched our mouths in a candle-lit restaurant, but we had tequila to make us not notice the burning and Walter showed me how to take it with salt licked delicately from the wrist, and in a spirit of camaraderie we presented a bottle to two lonely G.I.'s and they stood by our table and toasted us.

"This should be champagne," we said, "considering the circumstances."

"We've never had champagne," the soldiers said. "This does fine."

"There's a really beautiful woman," said Walter of a white-haired lady who sat with her daughter across the room, and the courtly creature let her enormous dark eyes rest on us and just didn't smile and then saw we were holding hands, and did.

We carried our tiny purchases home in a bright green fiber basket trimmed with pink passion flowers — a tea set, a kitchen apron for me with JUAREZ cross-stitched on it, some baked dishes. These were very nearly the first household purchases I'd ever made in my life, my mother having always previously furnished me with what I needed.

I suppose the hotel we stayed in was ugly. I can't recall. The town itself was small, commercial and hot, accented only by jeeps. There was a pool in front full of dejected alligators and a ring of frazzled palms that crackled and clattered in the night air. The building was of stucco and furnished hideously, like any small-town American hotel. It stands in my memory, with its cheap swing doors shut dark against the mysterious and beckoning light, as a place apart, as magic and strange as the *Arabian Nights*.

CHAPTER V *Trude*

THE train he put me on came from the Coast and was crowded. We waited for it in the last Western sunset. We waited in the cinders between tracks, sitting on my luggage, and as the great transcontinental monster huffed to a halt, Walter shouldered his extra foot locker (full of my trousseau) and the brand new suitcase with my new initials, which was his father's gift to me, onto a platform. I had a coach seat as always, but he pushed me into an empty bedroom and summoned a conductor. The conductor was white-haired and gentle. (Most conductors are elderly, but during the war they seemed more than usually seasoned. They were a whole lot frailer when it was over.)

"My wife must leave me to go to terribly exacting work," said Walter. "She must sleep. Can you get her something?"

"There's nothing available," said the old man wearily.

"I know I can count on you to do what you can. I know you will help. She must not arrive in New York exhausted." Walter began pulling loose bills and coins out of his pocket. "Here, take it all — get her something — anything."

"There's nothing available. I would if I could. There really is nothing."

"Oh, look!" said Walter, and found another ten-dollar bill folded up in a buttoned pocket. "Please try."

The kind old man winked at me. "Somebody's taking good care of you!"

I hadn't been able to speak for the past hour — so I smiled palely and looked out the window. Walter's arms were about me. "He'll get something. I've got to get off the train. Keep in touch."

And now the train was gathering speed and there was his face straining up in the dusk, and the other young men beside him, all watching us go away. The tracks clicked underneath; I leaned my face on the hot glass and couldn't see. I knew so well the road he would take to the hotel, and the room in which he would pack his bag alone, and the nine hours' way back to Hobbs, and the barracks, and the dreadful wooden office where he spent his days, and the officers' club, where the men read comics. There were two and a half months of this ahead of him — unless, of course, he were suddenly sent away. I was on my way back to New York to the first well-paid job, with power, control, opportunity and the promise of brilliant collaboration — everything, in short, that I had wept and prayed to have for so many years. Walter and I had discussed the whole matter and had decided to be realistic and practical. I had learned that opportunities do not wait; even he had recognized my need for "one more."

I was going to be extremely occupied and strained and disconcerted, but what in God's name was he going to do? I kept seeing his face as I tossed in my bunk, his white face, as he smiled and said, "Don't change," and the train slid past him to the eastern darkness and the lights of El Paso winked away in a chain against bald mountains. It had been such a short time since our train had rounded the valley and I had first seen at the foot of that abrupt precipice the little Spanish town lost in the earth ramparts and desert shadows. I had watched for it with quickening senses as the lovely adventure just begun gathered force about me. Now it was over — this part was over — not fading gently to tranquility but ruptured, cut off. This could be a very dangerous trip for me! What hell-hold, what compulsion dragged me back and away? Like a sailor forced again and again to sea — but I was not a sailor; I was a woman.

It was in this frame of mind that I was preparing to consolidate the *Oklahoma!* success.

The heat that August in New York was oppressive. Indeed, it has been every August and I have spent most of them right there and similarly employed. It is hard on the dancers, for, although they move more easily in warm weather, they have to eat salt tablets to fend off prostration. Their clothes soak through in an hour and they must devote every evening to enormous laundries. Hands drip and slip, making lifts dangerous as the girls slide like fish through the boys' insecure clutch. Feet blister. But the dancers work without complaining. At least they work for pay, however small. At this point in my story, rehearsal pay was twenty dollars per week, and after decades of no work and no pay, they were delighted to slip and blister in their beloved vocation, and when I sent out the call for auditions, they came flocking in the hundreds. After preliminary script study, a Broadway musical begins for the choreographer with dance auditions. All auditions are held on an empty stage lit by the one overhead third-degree light permitted by the electricians' union, a 500-watt bulb which makes the actor or dancer look like something in a badly kept morgue. It matters little. The management is in any case half blinded by the bulb.*

This light persists for the duration of rehearsals and may not be altered. Sometimes the house curtain is lowered below the light to protect the eyes of those in the auditorium. To lower the curtain,

---

* Not until 1957 did Actors' Equity finally force the theaters, through their contract, to install a strip light of three bulbs.

the house carpenter must be called for a four-hour minimum at $5.20 per hour. He charges as much to raise the curtain later. If any additional light is used, the house electrician must be called on the same terms, that is, $41.60 to put the lights on and off for rehearsal, allowing a four-hour interim for work. It is understood, on pain of union blackball, that the carpenter will not touch a button nor the electrician set his hand to a rope. The actors generally, therefore, arrange to make do with the single 500-watt bulb. Most directors and actors, who pass their entire working hours for the five or six weeks of rehearsal time under these conditions, attempt to protect their eyes with shades and dark glasses. Six weeks in this glaring tomb without any sunlight at all has a noticeably debilitating effect.

Whenever I call the dance auditions, every single member of the staff is on hand, invited or not. In particular, all the men are present. The dancing girls, like the singing girls, are required to run a gantlet that is nothing short of formidable; they must be under twenty-five; they must be pretty, fresh-looking and bright. So far all would agree, but beyond this there is a margin for differing personal taste. The choreographer has requirements of his own; but these are considered academic by the rest of the staff. There exists, for instance, a widespread belief in the Broadway theater that I don't know a pretty girl from a three-legged stool, so the boss men gather to instruct me. They fear that I will lean in the direction of ability as against charm, nor believe, as I do, that lack of ability cannot be pleasing no matter how presented. Apparently they do think I know the difference between a good-looking boy and a three-legged stool, because they leave the theater in a body when I start to audition the men; among these I am allowed to pick and choose as I like. This is not always happy or easy. During the war, for instance, the choice was paltry; the U. S. Army and I saw eye to eye and they got first pick. But I am not ashamed of my record with either young women or young men. Diana Adams, Virginia Bosler, Nelle Fisher, Lidija Franklin, Pearl Lang, Gemze de Lappe, Bambi Linn, Betty Low, Annabelle Lyon, Joan McCracken, Allyn McLerie, Raimonda Orselli, Sono Osato, Katharine Sergava, Emy St. Just, Evelyn Taylor, Jenny Workman all entered the Broadway theater in my shows. Also, Peter Birch, John Butler, Ray Harrison, James Jamieson, Kasimir Kokic, Scott Merrill, James Mitchell, Marc Platt.

Whatever ideals the staff has in mind, there are certain physical characteristics peculiar and constant to dancers. Dancers are nearly all smaller and more tautly knit than other people. They appear always so much smaller than the singers or the actors on any stage, the difference in height is so marked as to make them seem like another species. Their chief and most appealing characteristics are their slenderness and their posture, a soldierly spine and a sense of supple readiness that no other people acquire, not even great athletes. They are as relaxed as cats, alert for any demands even while resting. Their walk can be recognized by any professional, but it is not particularly attractive. Ballet dancers walk splayed out and flatfooted, very nearly a shuffle. The moderns stride with what amounts to a spring or lope. They all walk from the hips like Indians. They put the heel down hard because the ground is their ally; they trust their feet. The dancer's face is intelligent, quiet — unlike the actor, who feels called upon to practice his faculties of response every minute in every conversation. Dancers who are comedians are more alert in expression than lyric dancers. The dancer waits and watches, trained to keep the countenance clean of grimace, to express only what must be expressed with an effort of total will.

At all auditions a brisk horse trading goes on in the front row where the staff sits, a high jump for a redhead, the promise of passion in a face for a model's thighs. We agree upon a balanced group at last while the poor wretches stand half naked in line in front of us, swaying with embarrassment, hope, despair, fatigue and anger. The union permits us three chances in which to weed out twelve or fourteen from, roughly, four hundred applicants. We make mistakes. It will become clear in rehearsal later, and only in rehearsal, who can act, who can follow direction, who can play comedy, who can phrase music, and which beauties can do none of these things. Every replacement costs delay and confusion — several hours of wasted effort. At the time of our new show, *One Touch of Venus,* choreographers were permitted by Chorus Equity to hire extra recruits and given three days in which to make a final choice. This practice, although prolonging the suspense for the doubtful few, made the final decision fairer and saved the choreographer and group the terrifying waste of work thrown away on a casualty. For it must be remembered that there is no dance script, and accordingly, every individual body that leaves the rehearsal hall takes away in head and muscles part of the actual texture of the composition. In deference to the performer's feelings, the rules have been altered; we may start work now only with the exact number we require, or fewer. We may not, for any reason, diminish the number once rehearsals start. But since no studies of any kind are permitted before rehearsals, since every step must be demonstrated by the choreographer and learned by rote in rehearsal, the situation becomes almost insurmountable.

And as all steps are developed on live bodies, hired by the hour, and as each dancer's body is a unique instrument with individual modifications, the composition must be achieved in rehearsal; any departure from formalized class technique necessitates experimentation. The choreographer, for reasons of sex, strength, or virtuosity, cannot always work out problems beforehand on his own body. That is why even the most skilled and experienced craftsmen plan, before rehearsal, little beyond sketches and are usually unaware of the exact types or even the exact numbers of people needed. No musician would be required to hire orchestra players before his piece had been composed and scored. But composing, scoring and rehearsing occur simultaneously in dance composition.

I had projected the *Venus* dances in a light lyric mood full of what I hoped would be irony. I immediately got to work with favorites sweating through hours in the studio all day. Such preparation is now forbidden by union ruling — but in those days a choreographer was permitted to find out what he wanted to do before getting into full rehearsal. At night I plotted steps and patterns on paper close to the telephone. A call from Hobbs might come through at any time.

Few Broadway composers are responsible for any of their own orchestrations. Most of them furnish only the song melodies, while the overtures, the incidental action accompaniments, the transition pieces, the ballet and vocal variations, the musical reinforcement and "glue" of the show will be arranged by someone else. There are, for this purpose, a handful of experts who function as musical amplifiers and arrangers. The most notable of these and the most helpful to me over the years has been my former concert accompanist, Trude Rittmann.

Trude sat knitting and whistling between her teeth while I pushed people around the room. When an amount was blocked out she would go to the keyboard.

"Jean," she would say, picking the most musical girl in the room, and Trude always knew within minutes who was musical, "count for me in eights at this rhythm."

Then she improvised melodic variations on the song tunes as we went along, playing full out, changing keys, modulating, developing a musical climax where the choreographic climax was shaping.

"How would it be if we were to have two fives right here? And if I play three-four against your four-four? Don't change a count. You keep going. We come out together, you see. It gives a brilliance, a shimmer, no?"

"Gee whiz," said the dancers, "that's wonderful."

"It is not," said Trude. "I work it over tonight." And that's what she would do, taking her glyphics and scrawls home — she worked — how late? — how early? — in her impeccable little German flat with the window corner full of potted green plants. And in the morning she would return with a new arrangement — but every count exactly as rehearsed. We proved it with excitement and joy. The blueprints of this musical arithmetic were to be handed to the composer, Kurt Weill, to translate into his own style.

"Now I'm tired," said Trude, stretching out full length on the floor of the studio, her music case under her head, her glasses off at her side, her slender ankles crossed. "You go on."

The dancers mopped up on their towels, changed shirts and started in again. After a time, we would be aware that our musician was sitting up on the floor. Her glasses were back on.

"Now just where is all that going?"

"I thought at the beginning."

"And just what am I supposed to play for that?"

"I thought the verse —"

"Impossible! Impos — maybe not! Wait a minute." And on she tried, changing, inverting, shifting keys and rhythms. "What's happened?"

"Nelle's fainted. It's her hay fever again."

"Ah, poor child!" And Trude was back on the floor, Nelle's head in her lap. "Give her air. Don't crowd. Lift up her feet. There, dear, lie quiet. Keep fanning. Some water — not too cold — wouldn't hurt — at the back of her neck. I think I'll faint myself. Lie quiet, Nelle. There's no rush. What a life!"

It was always Trude who raised the dead, comforted the sick, counseled the forlorn, and who found out and informed me of what I should know in order to help. She was big sister, mother, schoolmistress and scoutmaster.

Oh, the tears she had wiped away on our long transcontinental concert trips! "*Liebchen,* dear heart, sisterle, don't. It's not worth it. Pull yourself together. Your work is getting clearer now. Be grateful for that."

"Oh, Trude," I said at the end of these long hot August afternoons as we picked up the mess in the emptying studio. Trude policed a studio like any sergeant — she couldn't bear mess. "Oh, Trude — what you have watched me through! — to have waited so long in such confusion and loneliness." I looked to the west where was the sunset and, farther along, Hobbs, New Mexico. "And now to abandon him and come back to the rat race in this hot stinking city."

"Dear heart," said Trude, "you have to do your work. Later you can stop."

"Later! Will there be a later?"

"*Ach, ya!*" said Trude. "One hopes." Trude had had precious small reason for hoping. Trude at the beginning, at the first flush of her success, had had to abandon everything and come out of Germany, leaving so much she loved behind.

"If I could choose," I continued, pacing up and down, "if I could live one way or another, cut my pattern clean — be like other women, simply a wife or mother, or like great artists, sure and undivided. But all parts of me are set against each other."

"Do not question how you are, Agschen. This mixture may be a strength. Use it. You may have something to say for women that the others will not know. But in any case, that's how it is. We live with ourselves. And you have decided this way for now. Has he written?"

"Oh, yes — and phoned. But it's hardly the same."

"I should think not." Trude laughed. "However, the time will pass — it always does."

"You think so, Trude?"

"Absolutely — but, Agnes, watch the new girl, Lizzie. There's trouble there. I think she will not last rehearsals. Maybe if you could praise her a little — just once — no matter how it goes on your nerves. I know you think she's disgusting, but one word would do miracles."

"Lizzie is dreadful and stupid and off beat."

"Agnes, have some pity!"

"No."

"Well, then, have some tea with me. We talk about Walter. It will settle you. You say he likes music?"

Trude is a small brown-haired woman with a dry piercing laugh and thick glasses. Her body is that of an adolescent European schoolgirl, neat and plain and very young in appearance, but as she lives slumped over the keyboard, one hardly notices this charming fact. Her hands are small, with the square spatulate fingers of the professional pianist. She was, when I first knew her, victimized by constant migraines that nearly knocked her flat and her Empirin bottle was a fixture beside the erasers and five-lined paper.

Before every concert performance, she used to go on the stage, complain about the piano, arbitrarily readjust the lighting Joseph Anthony had spent four hours setting, and while her headache mounted, start in on forty minutes of five-finger exercises that had obviously been arranged by the Gestapo. She played the performance excellently, although her nerves were tense. We quarreled afterwards about tempi; this is traditional with all dancers after every performance.

I grew very fond of her. She never gave way, but she developed in compassion, understanding and tolerance and I like to hope I did also, but I rather doubt it.

At the time of our *Venus* rehearsals, Trude had not only head-
aches but backaches. This condition in no way improved when a
few years later Mary Martin, while rehearsing *South Pacific,* cart-
wheeled exuberantly right off the stage and into the orchestra pit
where Trude sat playing. Martin, who was appalled, was picked
up shaken but intact. It was Oscar Hammerstein who noticed minutes later that Trude was lying on the keys and had not moved at
all. She was out cold.

Trude always arrives for rehearsal promptly, neat as a dressmaker and full of solicitude, inquires about family news, bodily ail-
ments, or any musical revolution that may have occurred since the
night before. The dancers stand around ready in practice clothes.
They have been warming up for fifteen minutes. Trude carefully
folds her coat, polishes her glasses, deplores the state of the piano
and, sitting back and taking a deep breath, sounds the opening
theme of the rehearsal — *andante sostenuto.*

"You know how I admire you, my dear. You know what a
sympathy I have for your work. Yet in all sincerity I must say I
don't see where we're going. It is my impression we are smack
bang up against a blank wall."

The dancers quietly, without one further word, sit down and
open coffee cartons. Some light cigarettes.

I lean over the piano. I am too rehearsed in this to be dismayed.

"Why do you think so?"

"Last night," says Trude, shaking her head dolefully, "I worked
for four hours. Four hours is quite a time. One can try much. I
tried everything. It simply won't go. It is not unwillingness. You
know I work myself to the bone for you. I tried everything."

"Some of it may be good." This is the contra-, or second, voice,
usually taken by me, but occasionally by one of the soloists.

"It was not good. I threw it away."

"Oh, you didn't!" *Doloroso.* Someone brings me some coffee. Coffee is slipped between Trude's square worn fingers.

Repeat *da capo* — second ending.

"Perhaps you can remember some of what you didn't like."

Sotto voce, cantabile, poco a poco accelerando. "Please, Trude, please."

"No, what's the use? It was no good." She walks to the window and stares down at the city in ruins. "Perhaps another arranger . . ."

"Trude, I implore you. Let me despise your music too."

Trude emits an unwilling yelp. Dancers *tutti chorale,* "Oh, Trude, what were you working on?"

"Oh, well, that's all very well and good — no —" She plays sixteen bars grimly.

"I think it's lovely."

"*Ach!*" Trude makes the sound a good *Hausfrau* utters when she finds rats in the larder.

"Play it again, Trude. The rhythm in the base. Please, I implore you. Look."

Trude looks. "Why do you put the accent on the third count? Here, do it again for me. Wait, let me mark that."

Her pencil is on the music paper. She whistles between her teeth. I rush about the room. The dancers have risen and are following. Coffee is kicked into corners. *Allegro con brio al fine.*

These are Trude's warming-up barre exercises and she must go through them full out at least once every three days. This opera can be varied — as, for instance, *lento,* when Trude looks through me and says morbidly, "Do you believe in what you're doing? Can you honestly say you do? From the heart? We know, we have to make compromises in this field, but there is a level beneath which —" Or it can be the scherzo attack, *giocoso.*

"I have something quite nice. It's a surprise. Hold on to your heads — same counts —"

The cast yells. The leading male dancer kisses her. I kiss her.

"Now you think of something good for a change," she says, very smug, picking up the morning paper and reading as though she were on a train going far away, into the mountains.

"What a girl!" the dancers sigh.

This gift for arranging and developing popular songs into dances and for underscoring scenes, dialogue and business is unique. Her unparalleled help in infusing variety and dramatic effectiveness into shows as well as into accompaniments is common knowledge on Broadway. She has worked with me on seven shows since *Venus* — *Bloomer Girl, Carousel, Brigadoon, Allegro, Paint Your Wagon, Gentlemen Prefer Blondes, Girl in Pink Tights* — every one I have done, in fact, after *Oklahoma!* She has worked on others I have had nothing to do with: *Finian's Rainbow, South Pacific, The King and I, Fanny, Wish You Were Here, Look, Ma, I'm Dancing, Billion Dollar Baby,* the two *Peter Pans* — Jean Arthur's and Mary Martin's — and *My Fair Lady.* She has composed on her own original melodies the ballets in *Look, Ma, I'm Dancing, The Girl in Pink Tights,* and the Uncle Tom ballet in *The King and I.* She is more than an arranger. I rely on her taste as on no one else's and in all departments of my work. I herewith make her my deepest reverence, and there are other choreographers, and the very best, bowing beside me. Several thousand dancers and all orchestrators and conductors rise to testify to the taste, good sense, musicality and creative force Trude Rittmann brings to every show she touches, and the cheer and decorum she maintains in rehearsal.

"She is indispensable," say Alan Lerner and Frederick Loewe.

If in the tart and rather lugubrious exchanges which I have quoted I have given any indication that Trude was depressing, this is not accurate. She was stern and demanding, but the hope and solace and patience that woman could summon when everyone else had stamped out disappointed was why some of us were able to weather the jobs. I cannot number the times she has cleared the hall, brought me tea, or taken me to dinner and then returned to work quietly all night, if need be. The sane musicianly counsel she supplies, the expert eye, the humor and the large background experience which reaches into the best Europe could teach and embraces all forms and styles — these are at the disposal of every colleague who will listen — as well as her courage. And let no one underestimate what courage it takes to make an innovation in the commercial theater. But Trude, like all good artists, proceeds by instinct and not by rule.

Trude says quietly, "I had tonight in the theater a feeling about this work —"

And Trude's feelings are like the needle on a ship's compass.

CHAPTER VI *Show Biz*

A good part of the success of a musical comedy depends, I should say, on three elements: first, a strong skeletal plot line; second, good songs and dialogue; and third, someone who can coordinate all the disparate ingredients — dialogue, singing, dancing, acting, clowning and spectacle. This will not necessarily be a great director, but a man of experience with the ear and eye to maintain style, to balance and to edit. He must know what is possible in his medium and, most important, he must know how to organize the various lines of work, all of which have to proceed simultaneously. He is, in effect, a kind of train master. No one element can succeed without the other two.

A musical comedy begins when composer, lyricist and book writer agree on an idea, or rather, more often, an adaptation of someone else's idea. They compose a series of songs which presumably include two or three smash hits, several funny pieces and, in the case of the most sophisticated authors, a couple of numbers so special that they pertain only to the play on hand. These last are luxury items because, although they undoubtedly heighten the dramatic effect, they cannot be performed indiscriminately on other occasions, and it is in repeated performance on records, television and radio that the big money lies.

By the time three quarters of the songs are written, a producer and a star have been approached and the plot and dialogue will be more or less complete. It is unlikely, however, that the book or play which goes into rehearsal will closely resemble the book that opens in New York. The songs will undergo smaller alterations; metrical verse and music are harder come by and require substantial time in the composing — also, any alterations that involve an orchestra are expensive — just how enormously expensive, I will shortly make clear.

When the show, or at least a hopeful blueprint, is on paper, scene and costume designers, a director, a choreographer and orchestrator are summoned.

Cheryl Crawford, our producer, had assembled what her press agent, Jean Dalrymple, termed "The Brain Trust," top people in each field, Ogden Nash, the best-known light-verse writer in America, S. J. Perelman, a leading humorist, Elia Kazan, the coming director (he had long had a name as an actor with the Group Theatre, and had now directed his first hit, Thornton Wilder's *Skin of Our Teeth*), Mainbocher, the *couturier*, Howard Bay, the scene designer, Kurt Weill, internationally known opera composer and author of two smash Broadway successes, and me. "How can you go wrong?" demanded Crawford complacently, "with these people? Just reading over the list of names makes one begin to chuckle and rub one's hands in anticipation."

But this was the first creative venture in the musical theater for Nash, Kazan, Mainbocher and, with the exception of a revival of *Porgy and Bess,* for Crawford.

Perelman has since described himself as "button-cute, rapier-keen, wafer-thin and pauper-poor." All these epithets were exact except the last. He was charming, brilliant and slender; a slouch made him look thicker. He seemed inadvertent, both hopeful and startled either by what he couldn't believe he was hearing or by what he couldn't believe he was about to say. And his expression alternated between professorial dignity and raffishness.

He spoke in a sententious monotone, and there was always a raising of the eyebrows behind the round glasses, an intake of breath
and a clearing of the throat as though in preparation for public
address or a Noel Coward song. His most casual observation was
delivered in rounded periods of incisive misquotation. Through
every deliberation his staccato laugh cut like the signal given by
deer when alarmed, like the ejaculation of a fencer before the
thrust to the heart. "Ha!" he would warn us, roll off a couple of
balanced and slightly soiled Addisonian phrases and then lie in am-
bush behind his glasses. He never failed any occasion. There was
always an appropriate cliché which could be rubbed up and have
its neck screwed around. Technical discussions and the dialogue of
the play were decorated with these wry and disheartening observations. "They broke the mold before they made Perelman," he
said.

Ogden Nash appeared quieter and younger (although he was
not), like a bashful and nicely reared college boy. He brought in
superb lyrics from day to day and seemed happy and surprised if
we liked them. The two went around together through our rehearsals like visitors on a vacation, bubbling with curiosity and an
enthusiasm which lasted a good three weeks. Unfortunately, first-
class light verse and racy irony do not always make effective dialogue nor does all verse sing well. The lyrics of songs are a special
art. There is the disturbing fact that no amount of humorous detail strengthens plot.

There are the peculiarities of musical comedy construction, of
a piece that must play without pause, with only one interval
between the two long acts. For this reason, scenes requiring large
sets must alternate with scenes playing at the front of the stage
before a curtain or in "One." When the script of *Venus* was
handed to designer Howard Bay, the novice playwrights had made
no provision for the changing of any sets, no dialogue or songs be-

fore the curtain in "One." In perplexity about the practical mechanics of scene changing, Bay suggested a series of arches with
curtains that could be rolled up and down (by motor) at any
depth on stage. The staff agreed with alacrity.

The plot of the show is hard to remember. It had to do with the
coming to life in modern suburbia of an antique statue of Venus.
There was a gang of thieves who turned out not altogether reliably
to be comedians, and there were several leading men who responded to the Goddess of Love in the expected ways.

In support of the star, Mary Martin, I had engaged two splendid dancers, Sono Osato, of Ballet Russe and Ballet Theatre, and,
from the Carnegie Ballet Arts Studio, Diana Adams.

Osato was the happy result of a Japanese father and an Irish
mother. With great good fortune, she had been born with a tall
slender body and not, as might have been expected, with the low-
waisted torso characteristic of the Japanese. She was slim as a
houri, and like a houri she danced, although her strong sinews
had been trained by Russian ballet masters. Blessed with the figure
of a Petty calendar and the manner of a minor deity, she danced
secretly with no apparent effort, ivory bones and sleek flesh functioning smooth as an animal's. Her spell lay in her delicate but
proud posture, in the sense of antique refinement and the discre-
tion of mouth, in the ceremony of hand and wrist, in the display
of torso which seemed to be — how shall I say? — ready. It lay also
in the black lightning of mischief and perception that escaped
from time to time from her opaque pupils.

Thanks to her fastidiousness, she was able to perform comedy
no lesser actress would dare attempt, managing most wonderfully
to be irresistible and outrageous, sensual and funny at the same
time.

Wolcott Gibbs was to write in his review in the *New Yorker*:
"Sono Osato is a marvelously limber girl of cryptic nationality,

who led the dancers and alarmed and fascinated me almost un-
bearably."

Sono was plain-spoken in six languages and she talked in a flat
Omaha voice and took no nonsense from anyone. She was brave
and sweet, but she was not stupid. She trusted where she could
trust, which, in the theater, is very seldom. This combination
of mystery, courage, sportsmanship and magic drove people, I
mean men, stark mad. She had just married a handsome young
Moroccan, given up touring, and in an attempt at compromise, decided on a Broadway career to help the family budget. Because
she was a bride herself, and because she was a dancer, she was
able to understand my plight. We had long girl-talks over sodas
and sandwiches.

"Oh, Lord, Sono," I said. "I suppose it's important I make a
success of this."

"It is," she said, "for all of us."

"But nothing I do seems to have any meaning now except in
relation to him. I only see and feel in order to tell him about it
later. He's right beside me in the rehearsal hall, and that's funny
because he's never seen a rehearsal. I don't see how I can possibly
stick it out for two and a half months."

"It's lousy," she answered gently. "I'm lucky that my Pash was
rejected. But it's imperative for both of you that you clinch this
success. Top *Oklahoma!* and you're fixed for life."

The days weren't too bad. They went along. There were problems right from the first to take my mind off personal matters.

The other soloist, my pupil and protégée, the sixteen-year-old
Diana Adams, was working as an Equity chorus girl in *Oklahoma!*
at forty-five dollars per week. I asked for her release, offering a
solo role, double the salary and real opportunity. I was promptly
informed by the management that taking a performer from one of
my shows for the benefit of another would be regarded as a form

of "incest." My rivals could pick and choose among my discoveries and, quite naturally, they did, recognizing a good thing when they saw one. But I was forbidden to. I must think of the Good of the Show. When professionals talk about the Good of the Show they mean the Good of their end of the Show and it is generally not the dancers who do the talking.

Managements, I noticed, made quite free to transfer their employees from one of their shows to another when it suited them and there was never any inconsequential babbling about incest. At the time, Diana, who was a girl of high conscience and delicacy, was treated as though she had broken with all fine feeling. After three weeks of censor and chivying, her nerves began to give way.

I suggested that if the child was so valuable, a higher salary was in order, maybe even fifty-five dollars per week, and a run-of-the-play contract. But this seemed to be out of the question.

Diana was desperate for opportunity. She and her folks were by no means sure of her gifts. Several times her father took me to tea and begged me with deprecations for advice on the matter, believing there was no point in her continuing unless she had a chance at real success.

She thought she was ugly and this made her shy. As a result, she tended to be overlooked in spite of her height. She was very tall, five feet eight, and when on *pointe* topped most partners by two or three inches. This can be a disaster and is always a disadvantage, but so impeccable was the child's deportment that there was never a hint of aggression. Her height appeared a yearning up and out rather than a dominating and she seemed strangely most to yield when stating the full expanse of her gesture. She had a waiting face and a cloud of dusky hair that tumbled from her dollar-fifty beret. She looked, as Oscar Hammerstein said, like everyone's younger sister.

But when she took the stage, when the lights were on, behold,

there was the huntress, chaste and cruelly strong, every gesture
absolute as though there were no possible other gesture. Like a
great sea bird, wild and mysterious, she balanced on the exact compass points of definition. Her whole life's effort and hope were
hazarded on her skill.

We began rehearsals in the great studio rooms of the American
Ballet School, now officially closed for the summer. The heat was
overpowering. Sono showed up for rehearsal in the white cotton
wrap-around pants and shirt which is the native garment of the
Mexican peon, neat, cool and, on her lovely legs, startlingly attractive. Her waist-long, thistle-silk hair was braided Mexican style
with colored yarns and her waxen skin glowed amber under the
ink-black plaits. The staff, on hand to wish me luck, surveyed her
outfit and drew me hastily aside. "You're planning to use this girl
quite a lot, aren't you?" they inquired.

"That was my intention."

There were other beauties — Pearl Lang, Nelle Fisher, Allyn
McLerie — all young and appealing in their black woolen tights,
worn even in August for the practicalities of warm muscles, light
sweat and no floor burns. (Diana got free at last after weeks of
negotiation — none of us wanted hard feelings — and I composed
her a number about adolescent love whose essence was bewilderment, which she performed most touchingly. Her father came to a
rehearsal and laid his fears to rest forever.) And, of course, there
were some men, good ones — Peter Birch and Robert Pagent —
but no one except me paid any attention to them. The staff had
eyes only for the white peon pants.

"Maybe we'll have to revise our ideas about ballet dancers,"
they murmured as I pushed them reluctantly out of the room. They
marched off to watch Elia Kazan, who didn't mind the attention.
Cheryl Crawford, our lady producer, swung her great leather
pouch pocketbook over her shoulder, adjusted her summer seer-

sucker suit, winked at me and stamped out in her sensible shoes. "We've got a winner there, kid," she said in her low even voice. The door closed on what they foresaw would be magic communion with delicious creatures. This was a misapprehension. No dance rehearsal is delicious; not, certainly, in its preliminary stages. I rolled up my sleeves, Sono rolled up her pants, and we got at it.

I was working in a studio instead of on stage because I need privacy and because I prefer sunlight and air to union light excruciation and migraine. Furthermore, there is no advantage to rehearsing on stage. We may not use sets or any exact props of any kind. If we rehearse with any equipment whatever, even hand props necessary to the dance that will eventually be used in actual production, we have to call not only the house heads of departments — head electrician, property man and carpenter — but our own special head stagehands, and these latter, once hired, must be retained for the duration of rehearsals. We work, therefore, with token props, never anything of the exact weight, shape, size, or material.

We began, accordingly, in a studio, more or less in privacy, without props and with only space approximations marked out on the floor. The respacing of dancers to the actual sets and props would be one of the grueling jobs waiting for us in the out-of-town dress rehearsal. If we were lucky, we would be allotted before curtain two hours of uninterrupted stage time in which to make all necessary choreographic adjustments.

Kurt Weill, the composer, sat at the piano, bright eyes gleaming behind thick glasses. Maurice Abravanel, the conductor, sat beside him. Weill had composed a stunning six-minute bacchanal which they now played for the cast four-handed. It was a grand encouragement and it is the only show music of any development or length that has ever been handed me at rehearsal's start; we usually have to put our feet forward to nothing but the bare melody. This piece was, in Weill's opinion, the finest orchestral composition he had turned out since he had come to America from Germany, on a par with his great early work, *The Three-Penny Opera, Mahagonny*.

I always thought this gentle-voiced little German suggested a gnome from a Grimm fairy tale. He was short, with a head unnaturally large in proportion to his body, and his balding skull and glittering eyes behind thick double lenses gave him a slightly underwater appearance. His smile was sudden. He seemed to peer through decorum and lean against every idea as though he were pressing his mind to the windowpane of thought. But his intelligence was so apt, his knowledge so wide, that one was flattered if a trifle abashed. He had a wry sense of humor and viewed all matters, even his own music, with sardonic appraisal. Weill was one of the very few who did his own orchestrations and he used to score in the rehearsal room and later in the theater through the chaos of shouting, counting, orchestral reading and rows. He never faltered; his concentration was absolute. He composed on the back of the Steinway, standing up, or sitting in an empty box, inking in freehand the nineteen staves of the conductor's sheets. He composed and orchestrated in ink because he made no mistakes. What's more, he was always aware of everything going on in rehearsal around him, whether musical, scenic, vocal, choreographic, or emotional.

Weill insisted on being part of the active workshop. At first, as a matter of course, I begged him to leave, according to my morbid custom, but he was so sympathetic, so wise and experienced, that I soon got over my terror and became grateful for his help. He stood quietly at the piano, his back to the mirror, eyes gleaming behind his thick glasses, and when he spoke, it was with the authority of a doctor. Trude had the keyboard now and kept it for the duration. Weill came and went, for he had also to supervise the rest of the score and all the songs in another theater.

We blocked through two ballets in a week and then our star, Mary Martin, was ushered in to be placed and taught her role. She was just back from Hollywood and looked like the Sugarplum Fairy, a pretty, rather unimposing Southwestern girl with a straight body and a flat Texan voice as carrying as someone calling cows, almost unsexed like a choir boy's, of trumpet clarity. Whenever she spoke or sang, there was a sense of distance, and that is why, I think, she could later sing beside opera voices like Ezio Pinza's and hold her own.

Hollywood had just finished glamouring her up. The Western experts had curled and fluffed her hair, covered her with ruffles and ribbons, hidden her long neck under froufrou, persuaded her to wear enormous heels for height and sexiness, taught her to dip her knees and slouch for grace, and to purse her lips and to pout for humor.

When she came to rehearse, she was extremely nervous and shy. It is no easy thing, whatever one's reputation, to walk into a room full of professional dancers, many of them soloists with the great companies. Miss Martin was accompanied by her husband, Richard Halliday, and she wore a special little rehearsal suit, a sort of romper that showed off her lovely unmuscled legs. She had taken off her spike heels and now paddled across the floor childishly in flat ballet slippers. She was irresistibly charming. She was sweet and eager and dear and pretty and she was a very real problem. She couldn't walk. She walked like Miss Atlantic City 1927. She couldn't stand. She couldn't raise an arm simply or directly. She could do all these things to please and catch the eye of Daddy but not, I felt, of Jupiter Omnipotens.

The next day she literally couldn't walk because she could not put her heels to the floor; having worn high heels for so long, her

Achilles' tendon had shrunk. She limped for a week, but she was hell-bent on continuing. It was her husband who forbade further practice except in heels. He didn't want her opening in a wheel chair.

Our black-wooled athletes regarded her with interest and speculation. She had to take her place in front of them, dominate and lead them. None of us were fools — least of all our star.

"I'm not very good at this," said Miss Martin to me simply as she put on her beautiful costly hat before leaving that first day. "I'm going to need lots of help."

Sono and I looked at each other over a soda at the end of the rehearsal. I was disheartened.

Sono spoke crisply. "I've made a decision. I'm going to be a gentleman. I could dance, I could move so that Miss Martin would look very poorly. Why, my God, we've spent our lives learning just how to walk across a stage! But what good would that do? I'm going to fix it so that she looks better than all of us. I'm not going to be an ass, of course, and dance down, but I'm going to help her if she'll let me. Do you think she'd mind if I coached her a little?"

Over my chocolate malted, I gazed at Osato with something close to awe. Sono had spent her teens with the Ballet Russe de Monte Carlo. "Sonotchka," as her colleagues called her, had learned theater entirely with the Russian dancers, whose second technique is chicanery. They expect nothing else and they give nothing else. From the outright criminal compassing of planned accidents (broken glass and slashed slipper ribbons) to constant ungrounded suspicion, they never, under any circumstances, practice anything but deviousness. Trust and mutual help occur only in emergencies. They do occur then, I must admit, and as these are chronic, the companies often present to the casual eye the aspect of hearty camaraderie, but this impression is inadvertent and against intention. Sono, however, was gallant and, as she said, a gentleman.

So she approached Mary Martin and the coaching began very gently and unobtrusively.

"Why do you stand like that," said Sono, so honestly and decently that Mary, who was equally honest, could not fail to accept the question as a disinterested challenge, "with your knees all slack and your chest caved in?"

"They told me to in Hollywood," said our star meekly.

"Never mind Hollywood. This is Olympus. My goodness," Sono said, "you've got a fine body. Be proud of it. Throw out your chest — and here, tuck your tail in. Stand on your feet. Put your heels down and stand hard. Be proud."

"I can see you're right," said Mary, gazing in surprise in the mirror. "I wish I could move the way you do."

"You're going to move like yourself," said Osato, "and it will be dandy. But you've got to have confidence."

And thereafter every day I could see, from the corner of my eye, Sono take her quietly aside to work out their problems. Mary straightened, Mary walked and stood like a deity, and it didn't take her very long to learn. Beside her were five veterans of the Ballet Russe, two future leading ladies and one future prima ballerina, standing and walking right beside her, and she did, as Sono had promised, dandy. Mary has never scorned coaching since. Today she dances creditably and moves with real authority, freedom and expression.

Great theater figures of various categories differ widely, but they all have this in common: they do not tire, they do not flinch, they never give up, and they never become discouraged, or if they do, like Martha Graham, they never tell.

Some stars acquire what they know by instinct, some by paying attention. The latter, I believe, was Mary Martin's method. She might be called the Great Learner. No one ever said anything useful to her twice. She was pretty always; she took advice: she invented a style. She found the man to dress her and now is one of the world's fashion leaders. If she crops her hair close, as in *South Pacific* (and at the time this was without precedent except in cases of typhoid), a whole generation of women do likewise.

Mary epitomizes the average American girl, her gusto and unlimited force being her only startling characteristic — and her enormous skill (but this is hidden and not apparent). She seems like anybody's sweetheart, just usual folks. And as there is a legend that any mother's boy can become President, so Mary seems to prove that any man's sister or cousin can become an International Star, and everyone's bosom swells with vicarious pride. She appeals straight to good sense and liking. She is neither mysterious, nor unfathomable, nor dangerous, nor maddening. She is effective, and whatever she plans to do she succeeds at with bull's-eye proficiency. Behind this knack is intellectual and emotional machinery as intricate as a Packard motor — and a life of dedication and of undeviating service shared by her husband, Richard Halliday, and now lately, to some extent, by her daughter Heller. Together, they plan every move; together, they try to sense whether it is right for Mary or not; together, they succeed.

As she studies a new role, absolutely no nerve is spared, and the whole family bends its efforts to the cause. The whole family usually triumphs. It is a composite effort, but Mary carries the flag and her arm never falters.

When Mary knew her part in the dance we showed it to the company and she proudly displayed the considerable amount she had learned in one week. We then repaired to her hotel suite, where Lotte Lenya, the great *chanteuse* (Mrs. Kurt Weill), discussed singing techniques. Mary listened to all carefully. Mary continued to profit. Mainbocher discussed costumes. He had just finished dressing the female members of our Navy, the WAVES, to look as though history and not he had designed the cut of their coats, and he had been chosen by our producers for the dissimilar but equally tricky task of making a Hollywood star look like a divinity whom men still do not wholly disbelieve in. He attacked the problem drastically. He peeled everything off little Miss Martin — curls, bows, ginghams, flowers. He cut classic gowns in classic materials. He bared the wonderful long throat and, contrary to Hollywood's doubts, advertised it by lifting her hair away neat and high and by tying a small ribbon about it. The fine little skull balanced on the wand of her neck with nobility. He gave her a back which is strong as a boy's and flawless, and he gave her lovely free arms, the trim waist, the hips and the fine legs, the sprightly and elegant figure we know now as Mary.

Mary's five Mainbocher costumes cost ten thousand dollars, and there were additional charges for suggestions and corrections for other clothes in the show. But they were worth every penny, and although the backers may have opened their eyes at this item on the statement, what they bought for the sum was a new star, Mary Martin, and an over-all style. This show could well have been tacky; it had, as it turned out, great chic.

After two weeks came the first run-through — always an evening of horror. Here were the numbers unshelled, out of the protection of the studio and the studio atmosphere and placed as they must be in the middle of dialogue and songs and jokes — all their values altered, before a jury with special powers of life and death. It is invariable on these occasions that the authors discover that they have furnished too much material and that, consequently, the dances must be cut. This is axiomatic and the dancers and choreographers expect it.

To this run-through came as expert witness Moss Hart, who had, with Kurt Weill, created the prodigiously successful *Lady in the Dark*. He didn't think Diana's pretty dance had anything to do with the plot and he was, unfortunately, quite right. Kazan had thought so too, and besides, he had never understood it. He could not see why adolescent love should be in any way bewildered. Sex, he said, was gay and confident. (It is since this conversation about gay and confident sex that he has devoted his strength with such distinguished effect to *Streetcar Named Desire, Cat on a Hot Tin Roof, Camino Real, Flight into Egypt* and *Baby Doll.*) So five minutes after it had been seen for the first time on stage, the dance was out of the show.

"How shall I tell Diana?" I asked.

"Oh, she's strong," said Kazan. "Don't pity her. She's got real talent. Don't underestimate her strength. Treat her like an artist."

She learned the news, of course, immediately somehow, and before I could find her, disappeared. I went all over the empty theater hunting and crying her name. Finally, sticking out from under a low wooden platform on the darkened stage, I saw the sole of a foot. I pulled on the ankle. She was crying silently. I hauled her out by the legs, and she lay, dust-covered, sweaty and weeping, in my arms. I remember men were loading in cables and electric equipment past us. I sat on the floor and tried to tell her it was not important, that Kazan was right, that she was young and very gifted. She wept without answering. Behind her disappointment lay eight years of daily practicing, no games after school, and history and English learned under hanging practice clothes in a dressing room that smelled of sweat and old malted milks, and a young back, weary every night when it went to bed with a weariness like old age. Behind it lay the fear that if she didn't justify herself quickly, the family could not continue the expenses of her career. Behind it lay the fear that if she didn't hurry, she'd never make the grade: a ballerina must be well on her way by twenty.

I got her to wash her face and took her out to tea. She rehearsed her chorus bits the next day like a veteran and the matter of her solo was never mentioned again between us. Although she lost her dance, I had the consolation of knowing she was doing her chorus work at double the salary she had earned in *Oklahoma!*

Diana Adams is now one of the ranking ballerinas with the New York City Center Ballet, an internationally known figure — but only after years of penury and effort. Diana made good. I can name you three with equal talents who have not.

After that run-through Kazan took me aside. "You don't appreciate Sono."

"I don't what?" I gasped in blank incredulity.

"You're not using her enough. The authors want more of her. They've made a place for a solo dance and another bit."

They had, it seemed. They had asked for more dancing, a demand unique in my theater experience.

Our producer, Cheryl Crawford, was sorry about Diana and glad about Sono but unwilling to go against the men in anything and worried about money, an attitude characteristic of her trade. A producer's occupation is one of unrelenting stress, the rewards uncertain, and the creative satisfaction intermittent. Smash hits pay off handsomely; failures net absolutely nothing in return for considerable outlay of time and worry. And always one does business inside a cage where it is unwise to turn one's back on any of the performers. The terrible wear and tear would seem to unfit the job for a woman except that two of the requirements are tact and patience and these women are apt to have. Crawford added another of her own, humor. She also proved, as rehearsals progressed, steadfast and kind, but she seemed determined to persuade all business associates that she was nothing of the sort, apparently wishing to be thought a woman of iron with decisions as irrevocable and fearsome as edicts from the Supreme Court. From her manner, one would suppose that she lived in a house with solid brick furniture. She wore square-cut suits of durable tweed, or, in summer, unmodified seersucker. Her hair went straight back and no nonsense. Glasses unsuccessfully screened off her piercing eyes. Her voice was a controlled soft baritone, her speech laconic.

Actually she proved, on acquaintance, to be everything she strove so hard to belie. She was vague, girlish, giggly and changeable, and because she must have been aware of all this and considered it weakness, at least in her field of operations, she usually entrenched herself behind a business manager of formidable habits and vague scruples. These remarkable associates were given their head until stopped by Cheryl's conscience.

Mary's clothes were, thank God, Mainbocher's concern. The rest of the costumes were designed by two men, Paul and Kermit. Paul did the bulk of the show, but for the ballet costumes I demanded Kermit, having a great admiration for the *Rodeo* costumes which he had designed for me the previous year.

He was a long slender creature of indeterminate age, sandy hair cut *à la brosse,* a moon countenance with a long chin, a small precise mouth, thick nose, and expectant bright eyes browless and behind glasses. His voice stayed high with constant excitement and seemed to wail even when expressing pleasure or enthusiasm. His manner was amiable and mollifying. He had an amusing gift for mimicry, always, however, an octave in alt, and nothing about him could be predicted but uncertainty. He was gone like the morning dews when needed. He appeared regularly and conscientiously at all appointments not his own. His promises were heartwarming, his views of his capacities unlimited, likewise his willingness to undertake everything mentioned, his tendency to disappear thereafter reliable.

He had a diffuse and watery charm, a character transparent in the sense that it was invisible. There was an iridescent sheen of manner but no discernible form. You knew something was there because of the reflection of humor, but you were damned if you knew what; uncertainty or absence had filmed over the impression. The Dusty Wraith the scene executant called him. During the *Rodeo* preparations I had learned that patience with him paid off, for in the end, his costumes turned out to be works of art.

The other designer's work I was not familiar with.

"But then you realize, my dear," said Kermit with the liveliest enthusiasm, "he's copying everything out of *Harper's Bazaar!* Everything, my dear!"

"Oh — surely not."

"Yes, I swear. He hasn't done one dress himself — except — but they're hideous!" His voice reached treble with sensuous excitement in this tribute to his colleague. "And let me tell you about the direction —" He proceeded to outline what he thought were Kazan's morning mistakes. He worried about the casting and the musical arrangements. He worried a lot about me. He was always present, interested, noticing, advising and fretting.

"Kermit," I said, beginning to be rather worried myself, "how is your work coming along? Who is supervising the execution of your costumes?"

"Being done. Being done!" he sang. "No cause for alarm. And, my dear, they're lovely. But when I see what Paul is up to and when I realize how his things are going to hurt your wonderful work, my heart breaks."

The authors and director were also getting a little nervous about his constant prowling. "Dammit," said Kazan, "has the man nothing to do? If I throw him out again, it will be out of the show." And, indeed, Kermit's behavior was unusual. Costume designers barely get a production ready in their allocated span, working sixteen hours a day.

I finally insisted on seeing with my own eyes. So I was reluctantly summoned to Eaves' costume house. Kermit chose to model the satyr's outfit himself. He stood on a podium under a spotlight surrounded by mirrors and his glasses winked joyously. He was a very pleased exhibitor.

"Not many people have seen my legs. They're good, aren't they?"

It wasn't the legs that held my attention.

"Kermit," I said, "I'm shocked."

"Oh, my dear, no! Not really! Do you mean it?" He became as gravely solicitous and respectful as a drugstore clerk selling an unmentionable. "You see, I've emphasized all the virile parts of the male body with dark plush to simulate hair. I think it's very strong."

"It does give an unusual piebald effect, but I think it's also pornographic."

"Oh, my dear, I do so hope not."

"Possibly I'm naïve. Let's ask Sono. She's cosmopolitan."

Sono stopped as though struck. "Oh, no, Kermit, certainly not. Take it off. Those things! Those things! Have you lost your mind?"

"Are you girls quite sure?" said Kermit, turning wistfully in front of the glass. "I thought we really had something here. And it was difficult to sew!"

"Kermit," I said as kindly as I could, "don't strain so hard. The less a dancer wears, the better. Just let's have plain bare arms and legs and the trunk as bare as the law permits. Let's not try to reinforce them sexually. They do very nicely let alone."

"Oh, dear!" said Kermit. His glasses had misted opaque and he ran a tender hand over the strong plush.

"There, there now! I'll go see Sono in the dress Paul has fixed for her."

"You won't like that, I can tell you," said Kermit, his spirits rising immediately.

Alas, he was right. Paul had turned Hebe into a fat frump.

And our Sonotchka looked at us ruefully over a mass of wrinkled velvet, every line in her beautiful body cut and obscured.

"You know, Sono," I said musingly, "there won't be a costume ready for opening night in Boston?"

"Here's a nymph," said Kermit, thrusting Ann into our curtained enclosure. "Now, isn't she lovely? You see, she doesn't look like anything at all you've seen before. Quite unworldly. Where you'd expect a breast, there is just sea foam. Extraordinary! You didn't like Sono's dress, did you?" he whispered in a piercing parenthesis sibilant with satisfaction. "I wanted to warn you about that. But I thought it would be better to let you all see for yourselves."

"About the nymph, Kermit. There seem to be breasts under her arms and on her back too."

"That's the mysterious part. But as she dances, you won't know where they are. The spangles will make just a film of light, sea spume, or cloud iridescence. You wouldn't want ordinary anatomy on nymphs, surely!"

"What I want —" my voice rose a fraction — "what I want is to see the dances for what they are. I don't want you to put spangles where the boys have to place their hands for lifts or you'll cut the flesh off their fingers."

Kermit put down the scissors and gazed fixedly out the window. "I simply will not be banal. Nobody can make me be." He threw down the scissors and retired in dignified misery behind a screen.

Paul's costumes were all finished in time, but they presented difficulties. Part of the dramatic point as well as the rhythmic accompaniment of "40 Minutes for Lunch" was nervous finger snapping. He put the entire cast in gloves, long gray velvet ones on the girls at forty dollars a pair, thereby rendering all finger work inaudible, snapping or clapping. The boys were in Madison Avenue suits of green and rust red and lavender.

Kermit always tried to do what was inventive and original, experiments that required a great deal of time and effort, and the successful costumes were fine, but so many of them seemed to remain unfinished. The good ones, we kept reminding ourselves, were the reason we'd hired him. Everyone worried a lot. Oh, we did a peck of worrying.

Throughout all this, a never-failing source of strength was Elia Kazan, who, notwithstanding his inexperience in musicals, brought humor, zest and insight to every situation, and a sense of command which made these ridiculous disturbances bearable. I fought him off my work, as I did everyone, at the start. He later told me that when he entered the theater or rehearsal hall, he could see from across the auditorium all the muscles of my shoulders and neck tighten as I withdrew inside my core. But he teased me out; he treated my work with tenderness and respect. He was not so polite about the book, which was his special province. The authors complained, with some reason, that he distorted their intention.

"Their plot!" he moaned with his head on my shoulder. "Their plot! They have asked me to study their character development! Oh, my God!" and he leaned, rocking with laughter, against the walls of the outer lobby and wiped tears from his eyes.

This was not quite fair. The plot was, as Ogden Nash said, as substantial as *Puss in Boots*. They wanted style and fantasy. Style is a very tricky business, and the realistic method of the Actor's Studio, in which Kazan had trained, proved no help. Our particular brand of nonsense needed a technique as developed and ritualistic as Noh dancing. The authors, nonetheless, behaved like gentlemen, and were friendly throughout. Kazan had said at the start that he saw no reason for confusion; there was none in the nonmusical theater. He kept repeating the opinion for quite some days. Confusion and terror, however, mounted steadily throughout the rehearsal period according to tradition.

It must be remembered that musical comedy is not an art form but a compendium of many art forms, collected and smashed into pattern during rehearsal.* The work is largely improvisation on the spot. There are no known recipes for success and when those that have proved most useful are copied, the resulting form seems stale. Work proceeds, therefore, freely, in anguish, doubt, foreboding and conflict, with lighter moments of true creative inspiration and recurrent bouts of hope.

One Wednesday at 2 P.M. the cast met at Grand Central at Gate 51 and entrained for Boston and the tryout period. They left gay and hopeful — in spite of history, they were hopeful. The staff was, as was fitting, riddled with apprehension.

Cheryl Crawford and Kazan, who had preceded us by two days, were finishing their early dinner in the Ritz dining room when I found them.

"Well, rest easy on one score," said Cheryl. "We've seen the sets and they're fine. In good taste, beautifully built. They're very successful."

Kazan nodded agreement.

"Thank God," I breathed, and sinking down before my roast beef, I ate with a quiet stomach for the first time in ten days.

Most of the scenery in any show is designed for purposes quite outside dancing and the ballets are fitted into limited floor space, broken levels, furniture and props which may aid book scenes and songs but provide real hurdles to movement. The same applies to the costumes. The difficulties cannot always be corrected. Very few professionals and no layman can diagnose the precise reason a number fails to make effect. It may lie in the size of the floor,

---

* A real synthesis of the ingredients has since been attempted with only partial success in Rodgers and Hammerstein's *Allegro*, with more notable results in the Robbins-Bernstein-Laurents *West Side Story*.

in the lighting,* in the cut of the coats, in their color, in the color of the background, in the placement of the dance within the act, in its length or shortness, in the orchestration, even in the rhythmic sequence and duration of the final chords, in tempo (every conductor holds the dancers' and choreographer's fate in his right hand). It may also very well be that the choreography is poor. Even directors do not always know where the trouble lies. But the dance stands or falls on its audience effect and the choreographer must diagnose and correct immediately or his work will be scrapped no matter what the reason.

So the news about the sets was to me good news. Kazan and Crawford went off for a dialogue rehearsal. Trude and I repaired hopefully to the Shubert, where we were to open forty-eight hours later. We entered together at the back of the auditorium and walked down the aisle and there we stopped stock-still. In the single naked watch light there was revealed the permanent masking frame of the play behind which the painted drop would be slipped. This frame was composed of a series of gray velvet arches, extending back like a dark subway tunnel, from which hung cobwebs and frills of velvet looped in a kind of mortuary-parlor elegance. These curtains were run by motors and could be dropped at any depth on stage. They were Bay's solution to the authors' failure to invent any cover for scene changes. Whatever the backdrop, these would never be removed. I thought of my nymphs lifted against the stars and peering up into those drab and dirty-looking skirts. I thought of the hurrying crowds in "40 Minutes for Lunch" rushing about under shawls instead of blue New York weather.

---

* The ballets are always lit last because the singers and actors have to go home to rest. It has happened, not once but several times, that when all else was done and the turn allotted to the ballet finally arrived, time was up and the electricians walked off the controls and went to bed themselves. Many dance numbers have been *premièred* without a light cue of any kind.

"We are lost," I said.

Trude set her lips and marched down to the piano. She slipped into the pit and tried to adjust a light for herself.

"Try to work, Aggie. We face the other problem later."

"I can't work. This is defeat. What is the use of all we've tried to do? This is pompous and permanent. We cannot for one minute get the impression of fresh air and sky."

"Have a try at Sono's dance. Plainly they must fix the set. That is obvious. Now, how would it be if we started like this? The piano is not precisely in tune either. And the orchestra coming in at nine tomorrow morning! What are they thinking of? Stop looking at the stage. It will do you no good. Do you like this rhythm? Or not? I don't like it myself, come to think of it. I dish something better." She tore up the paper. I dove to retrieve the pieces and we were off!

They found me rehearsing steps between the seats and up and down the aisle when they came in at midnight to resume lighting. Trude was asleep, sitting at the keyboard with her head on her folded arms. Her glasses and the new piece rested at her side.

They came in force, the entire staff, and sat down in a group. The designer switched on his talk-back box and the crew climbed into position, on ladders, catwalks and in the balcony.

The lighting rehearsal resumed. As each scene was revealed, the staff sank lower in its chairs. There was no sound of applause or comment. After a bit, Nash and Perelman and their wives moved to the other side of the house. Kurt Weill and his wife, Lotte Lenya, joined them shortly, then I. Kermit roved the background, wringing his hands and moaning and rolling his eyes to heaven behind his glasses. Halfway between the camps sat Mainbocher, silent in his smart gray raincoat, looking with a sort of benign incredulity at the spectacle before him.

These sets were exactly what had been approved in sketch.

The designer had made no alterations. But few people in the theater have the gift of visualization. Naturally Bay was surprised and hurt that we were surprised. There had been no secrets. In the face of our cold disappointment he struggled to bring order from backstage chaos and get the lighting charted. It is a tedious and slow process and therefore our hopes did not crush; they slid downwards ponderously for three hours.

Then we came to the ballet. I put my head in my hands. Here I knew I was partly to blame, for, although I had not liked his original sketch and had said so, I had not been able to give him specific suggestions. Not knowing what else to do, he had gone ahead and executed it. Perelman jumped up and spoke for me.

"Look here. Do you think this has anything to do with the choreographer's intentions? Do you think this helps her work?"

Kurt Weill was on his feet also. "None of this will do. This is disaster. Plainly and simply disaster."

Nash rose. "I'm a mild agreeable sort of fellow usually, but I think we might as well not open."

Then Kazan, who remained seated, spoke firmly, forcefully and with the voice of complete authority. "We open. We open tomorrow night and with this scenery because that is all we have. We know that it is not all in order. Corrections will be made later. Now, I suggest you all leave and let us get on with our work."

We left in a body. Kazan, Crawford, designer Howard Bay and the crew maintained the death watch. We walked, muttering and exclaiming, along Boston Common (it was now two o'clock) to Childs' and had coffee.

"You do realize, don't you," said Weill, "that this is just plainly catastrophe — two years' work thrown away?"

We all nodded. We realized. We walked on to the Ritz and got into the elevator. Kurt raised his hand.

"Look, friends, we're deserting. Back to the theater."

We returned. This time in taxis, posthaste. Nobody's head turned as we entered. We continued to sit in a small clump on one side of the house, quiet now with despair. At eight o'clock in the morning (a lovely September day) we went home. The musicians came in at nine.

Later that day we had dress rehearsal. The rehearsals for the past few days had been mounting steadily in nerve tension, hubbub and confusion. The last two weeks of any musical are a hell of conflicting disturbances — book rehearsals are undermined by music consultations and music rehearsals by costume conferences. Everyone stamps in and out of dance rehearsals talking — mainly about possible cuts. But hardly anyone seems to think silence might be a help.

Singers, for instance, always arrive for work in full cry and their approach can be heard corridors away as they enter any situation full of head resonance, breakfast and gossip. So firmly have they come to identify sound with working effort that they cannot bring themselves to believe that thinking is sometimes done quietly. When attention is diverted from them for one second, they hum, chew, stroll, chatter and munch.

Dancers are quiet partly because they have little breath to squander, but mainly because all their training has been in group work and by imitation and rote; and under these conditions, silence is rewarding. Unique among theater people, they respect other artists' working efforts, an appreciation they have learned from having to stand by during actual creative spasm.

When to the usual rehearsal distraction is added the cacophony and uproar of instruments and their owners, nerves really stand still. Notwithstanding, this must be the moment of our major effort. Once the pitmen are with us, any change in the show is preluded by full orchestral cooperation. Of all the theater workers, the musicians are the noisiest, and I don't mean by virtue of their

art. Twenty minutes before any rehearsal they have to build the
pit and furnish it, moving chairs and pianos, and even comman-
deering the boxes when necessary. Also, they have to test every
instrument to see if it still works, and they sort out an entire music
library. This is necessary. But due to various union restrictions,
we are forced to overlap our rehearsals and compose and invent
through chaos, until the baton is raised. The musicians' time is
bought in blocks of an hour, and a ten-minute delay is prohib-
itively expensive. A prolongation or stretch for anything under
an hour (or one hundred and sixteen dollars) is not allowable.

The last half hour of our final preparation for any orchestra
rehearsal will therefore be in pandemonium. Sometimes the fire
curtain is lowered to help us. But an English horn makes itself
known even through asbestos; besides, the carpenters and electricians, with the sounds appropriate to their trades, are walled up
on our side.

All dress rehearsals begin alike. The theater is dark and it is,
for a blessed wonder, at last quiet. The pit is full of silently
attentive musicians. In the front three rows sit arrangers and
usually orchestrators. Unseen before this moment and usually unseen again they live holed up in some hotel suite working around
the clock and ghosting for one another in a tacitly admitted anonymity. Only one man's name will be on the score; but the work
may represent a compendium of the best talent in the country.
During the *Venus* rehearsal Weill himself is in a stage box scoring
the finale and in the front row are the music copiers and their
piles of new sheets ink-wet. Midway in the orchestra, seated at
a desk with telephone and two-way talking box, works Bay in
direct constant communication with the stage manager, the spotlight
booth and the backstage switchboard, where four or five electricians are manning the 268 levers and where the head electrician
reads from his notes and briefs the men on the catwalks and up

in the flies. They are all wired for sound. Close beside Bay sits
Kazan and Crawford. Weill finishes and goes to the back of the
auditorium where he can hear a balanced sound from the orchestra
and voices. This will not be exact because a full audience will
change all the acoustics, but he knows how to correct for the
difference. He will instruct the stage manager which of the singers
to amplify on the over-all sound system. He will edit on the spot
orchestration for audibility of speech and vocal balance. The authors and their wives sit quietly in a cluster midway. I am seated
on the tops of the seat backs, my legs stretched out before me.
This gives me a good vantage point and makes it easy for me to
run in any direction quickly. Beside me is the dance captain with
a notebook and a flashlight. Trude is in the front row, hanging
over the pit rail, conferring with conductor, copier and musicians.
She runs up and down the front row, jumping over piles of music
to check mistakes at each desk.

Kermit and Paul and the Eaves costume executants sit near an
exit where relays of seamstresses and tailors can shuttle conven-
iently between them and the backstage army of dressers. The cast,
as they are ready, take places in costume and make-up in the
empty seats. And this is the last time that any member of the
cast will be permitted to see the show from the front.

A new unknown group of men, scene shifters and grips, now
take over, the crew in whose hands the entire well-being of the
production rests. They have not seen the play, and the actors have
never seen them. The stage manager captains all. He knows who
they are — we don't. He gives them orders — we don't. Not even
author or producer or director or theater owner can speak on the
other side of the proscenium arch. The stage manager takes and
transmits orders from the staff in front; backstage his power is
absolute.

Everyone, front and back, holds a stop watch. There will be

no halting for anything except technical production matters. We, the show people, are supposed to be perfect. This rehearsal is for the mechanics and technicians.

The lights go down. The house curtain goes up, revealing the specially designed show curtain. The boys and girls, sitting with their arms around one another and their feet up over the backs of the seats ahead, applaud and snuggle excitedly, that is, they usually do. The *Venus* group is unhappily not very responsive. The orchestra starts on the temporary overture; there will be another and presumably better one written before the New York opening when it is discovered just which songs must be dropped and which are likely to be hits. Everyone looks at his stop watch and makes a note. Bay's voice is heard droning monotonously over the telephone. "Bring up the blue balcony rail to five. Take down your pinks. Take them out. Take the first pipe freneles to two. What's the matter with the frenele on the first boom? It's winking. Peter, get a ladder and fix that. I said the blue balcony rail down to five."

The assistant stage manager appears at the entrance behind the boxes and signals. "Company on stage for the opening."

Abravanel lifts his baton.

This is the moment of transfiguration. This, only theater can give. Close to fifteen hundred people have been working all over New York City in separate workshops, without checking or comparing or testing, never knowing their collaborators or understanding the plan or even the purpose of their work, and within this hour the groups come together, the purpose becomes distinct and effective. A show emerges.

The real professional knows nothing better. It is our wine and bread and comfort. It is our time of power.

We had better savor it, for within hours this theater will become an arena wherein will assemble fellow prefessionals who have gone to the most remarkable trouble to judge their colleague's work in an unfinished state. They will come with no thought of mercy.

CHAPTER VII

One Touch of Venus

I thought about Walter as I bathed and dressed for the opening that evening. He would have liked to be beside me through this, but there was not even a wire from him. He'd lost track of the days. This Saturday night in Hobbs, New Mexico, was no different from any other Saturday night. And I had not written in the last week, as I'd wished to. I'd been up all night for three nights running.

Dick (God Love You) LaMarr took me to dinner and said, as he raised his glass, "Here we go." (We were to have seven subsequent dinners with similar toasts — "Here we go again, dear.") He stood beside me in the theater. I watched in a sick panic at the back of the house, mortified that each number looked so confused and feeble in comparison to the effect on a bare unlighted stage. I stood because I always stand, not being able, through sheer nervous tension, to sit still. Everyone knows that the opening performance will not be the final version, but I knew from bitter black experience that if the ballets did not succeed on the initial showing, they would be drastically cut or even deleted. So when we got to the major ballet, I gripped the rail and prayed.

The scenery revolved, the lights came on and the dance started, but the central figure, the star, Mary Martin, was absent from her place. The chair on which she was supposed to be seated remained empty while the dancers pivoted around, gestured and grimaced toward nothing whatever. I wanted to shout to the orchestra to stop, to the electricians to black out. What was going on before us was meaningless and the thread of the story could never now be clarified. After the first eight bars, the ballet was a lost cause. And still she did not appear, and still the orchestra continued to play. The dancers revolved again and gestured toward the unresponsive chair. The press representative who had never seen the dance before was unluckily standing beside me.

"This is not clear. I don't understand the plot at all," she said in a loud whisper. "It needs cutting."

"Well, here's ten minutes they can save," said an unknown voice on the other side.

"Shut up," I gasped, striking out sideways in both directions. Very few people care to stand near me during an opening. I dance each number nearly full out, conduct the orchestra and pull up the curtains. I learned later I had caught the press lady square across the mouth.

"My God, where is Mary?" I moaned.

Mary walked across stage, sat down quietly just in time for the climactic scene with Sono, which they played exactly as though everyone understood and loved what they were doing, which was not the case. The cause for the delay, it later devolved, was an eager and insufficiently rehearsed grip who, rushing in the black-out between scenes, had shifted to the wrong side of the stage a flat on which were hanging all of Miss Martin's changes of costume. The star, stripped nearly naked, found she had nothing in which to clothe herself. Naturally, she suggested somebody fetch something. But the men were all too impressed to go near her. The ballet by then being on in full illumination, Miss Martin had to run the whole way round the set and slip into her dress before she made her entrance. I think neither Mary nor I will forget this heroic interlude — nor Sono either, for that matter.

The ballet played on to its end, rolled through its finale to flat and discomforting applause. If the beginning had been incomprehensible, through no fault of mine, the end was inconclusive, and for that I was to blame. I had planned the choreography carefully and I thought it looked fine in rehearsal and run-through. It was good as dance design but not very, it turned out, as drama, two elements difficult to fuse. It should have wowed the audience; somehow it did nothing of the sort.

There was a wretched kind of party after the show, but we all left early; a good many other things beside the dancing had fallen apart and we had a lot on our minds.

The court-martial began the next morning, Sunday, at ten-thirty and was held in Cheryl Crawford's Ritz room, one of those large corner suites that make such an imposing item on the out-of-town expense list. When I joined the meeting, the entire staff was seated in a semicircle heckling Bay, who stood with his back to the fireplace. He answered back with considerable spirit and reminded his judges intermittently that he had to catch the one o'clock to New York, there to hold conference with Oscar Hammerstein.

"You know," said Kazan to me later, "when that man stood up there in front of us for three hours, he hadn't been in bed for two nights. He is designing four shows simultaneously."

Bay was proving a convenient scapegoat. He had built, with the exception of my ballet, only what he had been encouraged to build. But the staff which admits the misapplication of money and time as their own fault has not yet assembled. His next job, *Carmen Jones,* brought him renown, and his record of successes since makes it permissible for me to tell this story.

"I think we need a gayer house curtain," said Nash.

"We certainly do," said Perelman. "This one looks like the entrance to Ramses' tomb at Thebes. Who would ever suspect we were playing a comedy?"

"Who would suspect it when the curtain was up?" murmured Bay.

"Possibly," suggested Mainbocher suavely, "something lighter and more delicate in coloring. Doves are suitable to Venus — a delicate design in grays and flesh pink."

"Like this?" said Bay, doodling a dove with patient scorn.

"Good God, man, that doesn't look like a dove."

"I'm not up on dove research."

"Look out the window." Mainbocher waved an arm toward the opposite church tower, whose every ledge was being methodically dirtied by a fluttering mob of grunting and cooing birds.

"I want something quite simple for the ballet," I interjected. "Lots of sky, please, and a low horizon like Manhattan seen from Brooklyn Heights. Very lyric and aerial. And, above all, simple."

"Yes, yes, yes," said Bay. (Two nights later he presented me with a sketch, a very interesting one with a remarkable perspective. It looked like the slum areas outside of Pittsburgh and would have been suitable for one of the more bitter Arthur Miller plays. In the end, Cheryl and the stage carpenter painted three little houses on a plain drop. They were exactly like outhouses and they certainly set no trend, but they served. Cheryl herself took scissors and step ladder and punched holes in the top of the drop for the stars to appear. I've never understood how the union men permitted her to do this.)

Nash found something else not to his liking. "That statue of Venus! An abomination! What was that fancy-pants sculptor thinking of? It in no way suggests Venus. And it is certainly unlike Mary Martin, who, as far as I can tell, is a handsome woman. This thing is a monster."

"Well, you know," said Cheryl evenly, "the sculptor took her measurements meticulously. He even measured her bosoms with calipers."

"Lacking a ten-foot pole," murmured Perelman.

Bay saw his chance to escape, bowed, and left without further ado.

"And now," said Kurt Weill, "how about our second comedian? There's a disappointment. Did you hear the audience not laughing throughout the play? That was a startling sound. We must change him, obviously."

"That's pretty drastic," said Crawford. "He has a run-of-the-play contract."

"Not a laugh," repeated Weill after a moment's thought. "Get someone good."

"Hear, hear," said Nash.

"Gentlemen, gentlemen." Crawford once again tried to keep hysteria low. "I must remind you that for five weeks you sat watching this same guy, nearly falling off your chairs laughing."

Kazan, the director, explained this curious phenomenon. "There were no costumes, no sets then to fight him, no lights, none of the nerve strain of performance, no audience —"

"Something we certainly never counted on," said Perelman.

At this point I found it expedient to walk up and down the hotel hall. Mainbocher joined me. We did not say much, but there are certain kinds of understanding that bring quick intimacy. When we had quieted down, we went back in.

The conference lasted fourteen hours. Sandwiches and coffee were served at intervals. There was no plan of agenda and no rules of order, but in our haphazard way we covered very nearly every point. It was decided to commission twenty-five thousand dollars' worth of fresh scenery* and three new sets of costumes (Mainbocher was put in charge with no budget for this particular Witches' Sabbath). I was asked to add a new finale to Act I, and

* In order to raise this sum, there is an apocryphal rumor that Cheryl sold 125 per cent of the stock of the play.

end the ballet altogether differently. They didn't specify exactly
how, but something that would get a thundering hand instead of
a puzzled silence.

"We know you can do it," they said with that grim cheeriness
one always suspects under the surgeon's mask.

It would have been convenient to withdraw the work and consider at leisure, but every night the dancers had to continue on
in something and wait panting at the end for the pitiful response,
a demoralizing experience that was repeated eight times a week.
They worked all afternoon long with me on alterations, hoping
my wits wouldn't fail us a second time. Sono kept begging me to
fix the ballet before anything else.

"Don't bother about my solo. You and I can throw something
together in the aisle or in the train washroom on the way home.
Fix the ballet first. Your reputation is at stake."

I was frightened. When one is this wrong unexpectedly, one
gets frightened.

Mainbocher, with no budget as specified, was handling the costume problems brilliantly. He kept unchanged the costumes he
liked. Kermit's stunning first-act-finale dresses he would not touch,
nor any other successful ones. But he reorganized the other scenes
dress by dress, seeing the soloist first in action under the lights before he ordered a second costume.

Dress designing, like cooking, depends for success on immediate
reception. Clothes do not properly exist until they are worn well
and they cannot be successfully worn unless related to the particular body they cover and the occasions and stresses in which they
must function. They reflect, therefore, not only the designer's point
of view, but the wearer's; they should be a second integument.
Mainbocher knew always what was needed and, equally important, what was possible to obtain. How grateful I was for this
creator's perception that the clothes should heighten the dance and

not the dance serve as a parade for the dresses. Mainbocher, watching me rehearse, also studied what I wore. It wasn't smart and it wasn't always pretty, but it was me as much as my steps. Under the dark rehearsal dresses I wore fluffy petticoats, starched and embroidered and lacy, from my mother's trousseau. They were my one frivolity and I doted on them. So Mainbocher duplicated the petticoats on my girls. At the time women wore straight slips. The vogue of the crinoline petticoats, I believe, stems from these dances.

Sono's mussy velvet was thrown away and the long gray velvet gloves in which she had found it difficult to snap her fingers. Sono was redressed in an American Beauty cashmere sweater and a velvet skirt the same shade. Her wonderful hands were bared. She glowed on the stage like the heart of a burning coal and all her beauty — waxen skin, dark hair, Greek breasts, delicious modeling of arm and leg — suddenly showed again. From her, Mainbocher keyed in tone all the other girls — and one by one they emerged for the lovely supple creatures they were. He stood over the Boston needlewomen himself. Suit by suit, he got the green and lavender coats off the young men and bought them regular, believable clothes. But at this highhandedness, Paul was outraged. "I've stood enough of this dressmaker's meddling," he screamed in the theater. "Where's my green suit? Where is it? That green was chosen specially for the boy's hair — on purpose. Now see what he looks like!"

"He looks like a nice young man — possibly a gentleman," said Mainbocher quietly.

"I won't stand for it," shouted Paul. "I'll go to the unions. I'm the designer of this show."

"With me — don't forget," came a treble voice from the dark where Kermit sat eating a Tootsie Roll. There were two of the possible young gentlemen sitting with him.

"We'll both go to the union."

"Look here," said Mainbocher, advancing to the orchestra rail. His gray head bent forward; he seemed like a high-echelon diplomat. "Look here." No one ever interrupted Mainbocher. "I'm trying to keep you from making fools of yourselves. I'm trying to help. I'm Mainbocher himself." He tapped his blue custom-made double-breasted suit with a manicured forefinger. "Himself. And by the way, Kermit, where are the new nymph costumes? We haven't even seen designs yet."

"I can't draw here. You know that. I can't think here. I've told you so repeatedly. Let me go home."

"To New York?" we cried, aghast. "There's no time. The seamstresses have all been engaged for tomorrow."

"I must go to New York. I'll be back with the designs. There's a seamstress there, a little old Russian, who lives in the Bronx, who can do miracles — and I can have quiet and peace and be let alone."

What could we do? He went to New York — I suppose it was New York — and he came back forty-eight hours later with a brown paper parcel. We selected the prettiest girl as model. She stood in a white leotard on a table in the dancers' dressing room. Kermit pulled a most unusual piece of pleated and pinned muslin from his package and laid it against her right thigh.

"There," he said happily.

"What is that?" Sono and I asked.

"When that is finished, she will look like an Ionic column, all flutings and ribbings."

Mainbocher cut through. "Man, you're out of your mind. Pleating like that would take two weeks and all the resources of Fortuny. Do you think these little plain needlewomen up here could handle that? I've never seen such pleating on this side of the Atlantic. Here, put this nonsense away."

He picked up a bath towel, took up a handful of pins from a dressing table, and fixed the towel to the girl's brassière.

"Give her breasts, give her thighs, give her a waist."

She stood in classic robes, free-moving and superb.

Five of the watching girls applauded. Kermit spat. "I think it looks like a bathing suit."

"So?" said Mainbocher. "It looks like a girl. Now get on with it."

We lost track of time. We lost track of days. I rose at eight, half drugged with sleeplessness and heavy with bewildered fear, and started composing around my breakfast tray. When I went to the theater at nine-thirty I found Trude hard at work at the upright piano in the ladies' room, where she had been for two hours.

Through corridors, halls and foyers coiled the great tubes of vacuum cleaners which roared and sucked all morning. The charwomen mopped and dusted around us and roared and shouted their conversations. A favorite exchange was between the old lady with the mop in the top balcony and her confidante with the rag polishing the orchestra rail. They always seemed irritated by our presence as interlopers. On stage the electricians banged and scraped and hammered in their welter of cables. They shouted only about business, but they strolled and dragged and banged and dropped and they also resented us. I have yet to see one deviate a foot from his chosen path to accommodate a practicing dancer either during his own work hours or after, and the spectacle of these heavy-hatted, opulently coated men, looking neither to right nor left, striding right through a rehearsal, was a usual one. They didn't mind performances nearly so much, because once the curtain was up, they could go into the basement and get at their pinochle. There, no dancer ever discomfited them.

As we were all constrained to work in the same space and at the same moment, apologies are probably due from both sides. The hammering got done, I can tell you, no matter what else was accomplished.

We counted doggedly, Trude and I, and tried to be spontaneous and witty. At eleven-thirty the dancers arrived exhausted and lay right down in heaps on the newly vacuumed carpet or among the cables on the stage. A few opened coffee cartons dispiritedly.

Fatigue began to tell. Ankles twisted, thighs went. Nelle Fisher developed a pain in her side and groaned whenever she was lifted. She refused, however, to stop work. I blamed it on the inexperience of the green boys, but I maligned the poor wretches. One night after performance, she fell to the floor of the dressing room and couldn't be moved. The doctor I called diagnosed the trouble as acute pleurisy. So for the next two weeks the girls and Trude took turns between rehearsals nursing Nelle and we divided her part up temporarily among the others.

I took Sono to my room at the Ritz. I was terrified lest anything happen to her. She had begun to develop pains in her spine.

A new finale to Act I, complete with dance, was invented and rehearsed. Sono's new solo was introduced. And when we showed it first to the cast, Allyn Ann McLerie burst into tears.

"It's too exciting," she blubbered. "I can't stand it."

Allyn was having a perfectly normal sixteen-year-old reaction to her first show. We kept forgetting that these hard-working drudges were children.

After each performance the staff held a council of war at which we reported what we felt and what our friends had said. Friends, lawyers, agents, stars and directors came to diagnose the show. Some liked one thing, some another. Even the very great experts canceled each other out by week's end. There is one matter they always agreed on: cutting the dances. A couple of balletomanes came to see me. They suggested cutting one or two of the songs. But I did not relay these ideas in executive session.

The girls fell ill; the girls got better. The boys fell ill. The cleaning women dragged their hoses and mops through our rehearsals and shouted. And all the time, every day and every night, I tried to find a better ending to the ballet. Version II was worked out, music composed and rehearsed. The staff arrived, looked, shook their heads, and departed with words of encouragement. Version III was rehearsed — on the stage behind the electrical equipment, in the men's room, in a rented hotel dining room with uncleared tables, stale coffee cups and crumbs.

Occasionally Cheryl Crawford appeared at rehearsals. "You need a good osteopath," she said to me once.

"What I need is a good idea."

"Oh, that will come," she replied airily and with what I felt was phenomenal optimism.

"Watch out for your head, Sono — the chandelier! Does that look like a Tudor lift?"

"No, it doesn't. The boy grabs the girl in the groin in a good Tudor lift."

"Well, this isn't different enough. Oh, what can a boy grab a girl by that's never been done?"

"Here — try this —"

"Watch out for your head, Sono. You'll be dropped."

"I've been dropped by the best men on two continents. Move those coffee things away from under me. I don't fancy broken crockery."

"Watch out! Oh, God, did that hurt?"

"Children," said Trude, rising from the dreadful piano. "Enough is enough. Try tomorrow after a night's sleep. We get it. Besides, it is my impression we are on the quite wrong track."

At night I tried to reach Walter. Not in his quarters — not in the officers' club. It was ten o'clock, his time. Surely he was not yet abed.

"Try somewhere else," said Sono, sitting up in mine, cold-creaming her face, her black silky hair like a tent over her shoulders. "He can't leave town. He's got to be somewhere. Try everywhere you know."

"He's mad at me," I wept. "I left him and he's lonely and mad."

"Goddammit," said Sono. "Perhaps he's asleep."

"Sono, you must sleep yourself."

"Oh, nuts."

"I'll take the phone down here under the bed and mumble. You'll not hear." I put a pillow on Sono's head.

"Operator — operator — you cut me off — I was speaking to Hobbs, New Mexico. Oh, yes, there is such a place. Get El Paso back."

A sleepy murmur came from under the pillow. "Do you know the numbers of any of his friends?"

Sundays we worked particularly hard because, there being no performance that night, we had two days in which to finish off scenes and dances. All new material is introduced on Monday nights. After a series of out-of-town Monday nights, a New York *première* seems relatively easy.

Version III was readied. Each one of these alterations involved music changes which had to be composed, copied, orchestrated, have parts extracted, be read through and then finally performed before the effect could be judged on a live audience. Each dance experiment therefore cost at least four days in time and many hundreds of dollars. Great sums of money can be wasted in orchestral changes.

My instructions to the dancers before curtain ran something like a series of football signals. "Do the ballet as rehearsed in New York until Sono's second entrance, then the Saturday-matinee version until the change into E major, then the sixty-four bars we rehearsed this afternoon but not the ending — that's not ready.

When Sono jumps do what we did last night. We'll do the last thirty-two bars tomorrow night the way we rehearsed them today." The dancers understood and never made a mistake. The members of the orchestra, looking at me dazed as they tuned their instruments in the basement, were not quite so secure.

The night of Version III I finally reached the lieutenant. It had taken five days to locate him.

"I'm a bust," I said.

"Well, you can't always be a success."

"Oh, Walter, I've only been a success for such a little time. I mustn't start being a failure so soon again."

A weary, weary sigh came over the line.

"Walter, how are you?"

"Bored."

"Do you miss me?"

"I did at first, all right. I couldn't stand it — so I stopped."

"Oh, you're teasing me. Oh, help. Oh, what shall I do?"

"Get some sleep. Finish up and come back."

"How long will you be there?"

"I have no idea. Anything can happen."

We were to show Version IV to Mary Martin just before the Saturday matinee. She sat in the middle of the empty stage with her hands clasped firmly around the handle of a dear little red silk umbrella.

"Now," I said, "you move slightly to one side."

"I move where?" Mary spoke with the flat Texas voice that was so notably carrying.

"To one side and Sono dances."

"Why to one side?"

"So Sono can dance."

"She can dance right here. I won't disturb her."

"But I thought you might like to rest."

"No, I don't want to rest. Why to one side?"

"At the end you go off with the gods and leave your abandoned husband standing alone with a bouquet of flowers."

"Who is on the stage at the end? Kenny Baker? Alone? Quite alone? Without me? I don't understand. I'm to be off stage while he's there at the finale of the ballet?"

"You've just made a magnificent exit."

"Well, never mind the exit — I don't understand. You and Sono act the whole thing out for me. And I'll see if I like it."

She didn't. The dancers got up off the floor of the stage where they had dropped and trooped off to make up for the matinee. We had a conference between shows. We had a conference around Mary's bed. Mary was too kind and sweet to say so, but I believe she thought that since I was being paid to do the thinking, I ought to get on with it. Something with herself, beautiful, center, possibly up in the air, and the whole cast on their knees offering gifts.

Other stars would have agreed more readily, would have accepted anything just to get the job done and then changed whatever they wanted later in our absence. None of Mary's previous experience, and it had been a relentless schooling, had conditioned her to give way easily. Convincing Miss Martin of what went against her protective instincts was a little like making Euclid back down. She was stubborn but she was fair. She wished it fixed to our mutual satisfaction — for she never thereafter deviated.

We invented Version V. The rapid flashing dancing had proved ineffective, so I composed a slow parade of suspended and floating goddesses. Mary had learned to walk and she now moved well. The staff arrived and thought "maybe." Kurt stayed up all night orchestrating, the copiers extracted the parts, the instrumentalists read through the piece, the electrician was briefed. The next night it was exposed before a full house — and this time it seemed right. Trude and I rushed into the ladies' room and howled with triumph. Nash, Perelman, Kazan, Weill and Crawford were standing in the foyer. They nodded, for a change, and smiled. I'd made it just in time. Two days later we were to leave for New York.

I ran to the hotel to telephone Hobbs, New Mexico.

CHAPTER VIII *Reunion*

THE show was a hit, and my notices much better than for *Oklahoma!*

"I'm glad you pulled it off, darling," Walter said from California, where he'd just been moved. "Now, for God's sake, hurry out," he added. "I think you'd better hurry. Our time may be short."

I was numb but happy; the thought of getting through a day without having to prove my value every hour or so seemed attractive. I looked forward to being cherished. I was so giddy at the prospect that I dreamed of social flippancies, of suppers, charming peignoirs and adorable hats, of good conversation and coffee, of meeting and entertaining friends. None of these images ever included housekeeping matters. As I journeyed West on the only available slow train, I took stock of my future with satisfaction.

To marriage I brought a good deal of skill in giving orders and a flair for comic acting. I also brought a warm heart and hope. But I couldn't cook. I couldn't clean or plan or shop. I could sew when I was quiet enough to. But although I was good with buttonholes and plackets, this accomplishment had been rendered obsolete by the invention of zippers. Emotionally, I was, as they say of little-known poisons, not proven. I had occasionally turned out to be a loving and loyal friend, but about romantic relationships I knew little, having bungled several with incredible perversity.

This time I hoped I would do better. No little girl ever rushed toward a doll's house with greater expectancy.

Once I'd put my mind to it, I was sure I could make my man happy. Would he make me happy? I thought so. I knew exactly what I wished and would make it very clear to him. I wanted someone who would love me and find me passionately desirable as well as droll; someone who would think that I was a genius and cherish my whims and preoccupations; and someone who would follow my rehearsals and wait backstage and take me out to eat when I was tired and applaud my performances with zest and delight and also, of course, with discrimination, but never with just discrimination alone. If I were late from rehearsals, he would, of course, cook dinner — or he would hire a maid to cook. He would consider my taste in household furniture and clothes sound; nobody ever had before, but he would. He would do work that interested him and I would naturally be interested in it too. After the war he would be free to take vacations whenever it suited me and we would travel and work and be enthusiastic together. If any of this seems preposterous or even pitiful, consider the attitude of any male artist toward his bride.

Opposed to these fantasies was the silence of this last month. I stared out the train window at the dull landscape and realized with fright, with terror even, that I had married a man, strong and willful, and that this man was now angry and quite unpredictable. He was appalled by the war, by the prospect of immediate overseas duty, and by the sample of marriage with a professional woman. He said he didn't give a damn whether I was a success or not. He wanted other things from me. Did I know what he wanted? He'd never said, or perhaps I'd never given him a chance to say.

In the short time allotted me I had been a selfish wife; and this was the memory he would take along to where the guns bit and jumped.

Mary Morris

Agnes de Mille

Lieutenant Walter F. Prude

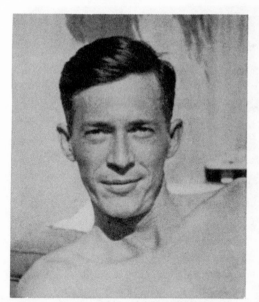

Walter, after tennis

With Pop, watching Walter play tennis

Djon Mili

Rehearsal of *Oklahoma!* for Walter: Bambi Linn, John
Butler, Erik Kristen, Maria Harriton, Kenneth LeRoy,
Katharine Sergava (lifted), George Church, Marc Platt
(on floor), Scott Merrill (in rear), me

Diana Adams in

The Nutcracker

Fred'k Melton

Sono Osato

Mary Morris

Ladies Salon,

11 every morning

Pearl Lang, Sono Osato, Kenneth Baker, Mary
Martin, Nelle Fisher

Scenes from *One Touch of Venus*

Kurt Weill, music copyist, Mary Martin, Cheryl Crawford

(*Left*) 3 every afternoon. Front row: Howard Bay, Kurt Weill, Elia Kazan, me, Trude Rittmann. Standing: Cheryl Crawford, (unknown), Ogden Nash, Sid Perelman, Maurice Abravanel

(*Right*) With Elia Kazan

Anton Dolin as the Prince
in *Tally-Ho*

Fred Fehl

Fred Fehl

With Hugh Laing in the opening scene of *Tally-Ho*,
photographed from the prompter's box during performance at the Metropolitan Opera House

Civil War ballet for *Bloomer Girl*

Trude Rittmann

Conference with Richard Rodgers, Jules Glaenzer, Oscar
Hammerstein II, Jerome Whyte

The "T'morra" song —

Joan McCracken

Sono Osato

Bambi Linn in *Carousel*

Graphic House, Inc

Bambi Linn and Robert Pagent in *Carousel*

What had I to give him? I had developed since girlhood a technique of isolation and could sit in the middle of a dinner quietly counting out a dance or a sonnet without the slightest social compunction. My ability to leave a situation and drift off became a family joke; I slept apart, I walked paces behind the others, I never played games. I had never shared a room with a classmate. It was my mother and Margaret who clung together; I walked alone. I refrained from casual greetings on the street or in rehearsal hall, not through unfriendliness, rather through unawareness. I simply was not there, until I consciously put a trained eye on the situation. Then I stared like an examining doctor. All neighborliness, all comradeship had been bred out of me. But this time, I could not walk apart. Whether I would or not, I had joined the human race.

We stopped at Needles, the sentry post of California. We stopped at Barstow, which had served early movie companies for desert location and which signaled to us as children the return back from transcontinental visits, the return to school and playmates. We stopped at San Bernardino, the turning-off point always on our trips into the forested mountains. Here Mother pulled back her dusty motoring veil and we left the car for a soda and to go to the bathroom. And here I now got out at six in the morning with my bags and Walter's foot locker and watched the dawn come up down the tracks. I was too nervous to sit or eat and as one cup of coffee was our ration, I paced the platform. And three hours later, the little north-bound train came and accepted me and started through the live-oak groves toward the great vine valleys of the central heartland. It got hotter and hotter although it was October, and the train could hardly creep up the hills, but finally, lost and far from anything that had ever touched my life before, the little town appeared on the plain — and we slid and gritted to a halt at the wooden station.

In the anonymity of uniforms, he made himself known and came to lift down my bag.

How odd but luxurious it was to hear him giving orders about my belongings! He seemed quite strange and detached and I prattled in a stuttering of excitement, picking up and putting down conversation as though I could not find a handle. We skidded around all the unimportant episodes of the past three months and edged closer or withdrew from the focal realization: that we had to start over again; that we didn't really know; that all values had shifted; that there had occurred an alteration.

As we drew up before a pleasant house, Walter apologized for the accommodations. They were not what he had in mind, he said, but the housing situation was desperate. They looked fine to me, I replied. And we went in.

That evening as we left our room, formerly the maid's — dark and airless and behind the icebox — the household, already at their evening meal, greeted the lieutenant's bride. The household consisted of the owner, a widower, his eight-year-old son, a tubercular-looking war bride of eighteen whose bridegroom was languishing in a psychoneurotic ward, and Lieutenant Bluntly from Florida and his 230-pound wife, Henrietta. He had been a garage mechanic and was currently an officer and Air Force instructor.

"Hiya, missus," he called out through tomato and mayonnaise. "Call that a hat?"

My hand went up protectively to the green brim with the little feather which I had mistakenly thought was unobtrusive and smart. (My hats had long been a family problem. My mother, after fruitless entreaties and warnings, had once appealed to the family doctor for help.)

"Lieutenant, you shouldn't let your wife wear a thing like that." He laughed hard as his little eyes fixed piercingly on me in a straight dare not to laugh back. "Sure you don't want to eat with us?"

"It's our first night," said Walter. "Thank you, but you know we haven't seen each other in three months."

"Well, maybe not your first night — but after that —"

What an astonishing thing it was not to have to think what I was saying — just to talk. And to be sure of friendly response — to stop being afraid. I was not going to be held accountable. Nobody was going to deprive me. He was on my side. Fatigue fell away.

The next day as I lay dozing in the garden, sleeping the half-drugged sleep of the convalescent, I waked to feel the hammock sag. Bluntly sat with me.

"My missus is cooking you a dinner tonight. She's some cook, I can tell you. Yum-yum. You and the lieutenant are invited and we won't take no." And smiling with firm coyness, he laid a fat strong finger on my nose.

"But, we have so much to say to one another. We've been apart. Please understand. Maybe next week."

"Oh, you'll get tired of talking to him soon enough. And you don't want to be alone every night! So six-thirty, don't forget. Then we'll sit around and just shoot the breeze. I know some real funny kids like to come over."

"But —" I murmured.

"We'll expect you. You need entertaining. Prude's the silent type. That can get you down. Oh, my! What have I said!" He roared with laughter.

That evening, three blocks from the house and, I hoped, out of sight, I waited for Walter's return. Finally the jeep appeared and I waved it to a stop. I explained our predicament.

"Certainly not," said Walter. "We don't start anything like that. Good God — our second night!"

So he made some trumped-up excuse about a previous engagement with the major, and Mrs. Bluntly rose from her baking with her enormous face all dewy from effort and looked at him, bewildered and humiliated.

"But I've got the dinner all ready," she said.

"My wife didn't know about our date," said Walter.

No one was fooled. They were very deeply hurt and thenceforth we were ostracized by the whole house. I was sorry about this, but that's how it was. This was my first test in the easy social life, my first test in arranging matters without giving orders. How well I succeeded became apparent in the undeviating silence that settled between me and my housemates.

Because Walter left the earliest, I was allotted the stove and sink from five-thirty to six-thirty. The red morning sun rose over the faucets in my face as I drew the coffee water and I stared into the growing light through milky eucalyptus trees. I used to look out over the roseate garden, the stock and asters and chrysanthemums standing acrid in the deepening mold and staining in color through the wet dew. I used to look out, as I carelessly measured the wrong amounts of coffee and burned the bacon, and say, "Beyond there is San Francisco, the beautiful city. We will take a suite at the Mark and have drinks with Alfred Frankenstein and Darius Milhaud and ride around the enchanted hills. What is the use of making money if I can't buy escape? I will somehow buy escape." And this is what we planned to do with the first leave. Walter came up behind me and murmured, "Not so high with the gas, darling. The toast won't hurry, it will just burn." And he turned down all the knobs like a trained organist at his manuals. He ate breakfast almost without speaking and was off with a hasty hug and a rush of overcoat to the honking jeep. I had the dishes washed and put away by six-twenty and my door shut and my head under the pillow as the chattering females descended for the second sitting.

Mrs. Bluntly was usually unloading groceries in the kitchen as I passed through on the way from my haven. She rarely looked up, but on the third day she said, "You left the coffee pot unwashed this morning."

"Excuse me. It won't happen again."

"And don't let your butter get mixed up with ours."

"O.K."

"I think your bathtub wants scrubbing out."

I went red to the roots of my hair.

"I'll lend you some Dutch Cleanser. You're not used to getting things clean, are you?"

Our house seemed to be equal parts clinic and corner barroom. There was never any privacy. Saturday was a particular saturnalia with troops of guests rollicking through all the apartments, but any night could be rowdy.

Flight instructors reported for duty every other day, and accordingly did not keep Walter's schedule. So at 11:30 P.M. a bunch of the boys and their wives would pile into the kitchen and whoop it up with whiskey, salami and scrambled eggs for a couple of hours. The icebox was directly outside our door and the walls were apparently of beaverboard. Everyone made free use of our bathroom. In fact, it was quite impossible for us to go from room to bath without crossing through fiesta. One night was rendered memorable by a young woman stepping on a mouse in the dark with appropriate sound effects. I believe she broke the creature's back.

I was absolutely and completely alone for twelve hours a day as the members of the household were not speaking to me, and in a kind of reflex, I began thinking about choreography.

A week gone with no barre exercises, a day spent with no creative study brought my restless nerves eating through the bottom of my mind. A dancer may rest after practice but never before —

never read, or talk, or play, never until after. The dancer's discipline of daily practice cannot easily be abandoned. He views the disappearance of strength and speed as a violinist might watch termites in his Stradivarius, and a choreographer, having no record of his past labors, is apt to be as restless and needful of reassurance. So, if I couldn't dance, lacking a barre and floor space, I hoped perhaps I could compose.

Accordingly, two mornings later I took the Paul Nordoff-Gluck score, his piano recordings and notes for my next Ballet Theatre work and went into the chintz living room, at this hour mercifully empty. I flew straight to the gramophone and spread my playthings on the carpet around me. I was deep in the seduction of an eighteenth-century marquise, humming, gesticulating and swooning, when what should I see but Bluntly's boots on the floor by my face. This was one of his days off from the air base and he was at loose ends.

"Now, whatever in the name of goodness are you doing?"

"I'm making up a dance."

"No kiddin'! Why?"

"It's my business to —"

"That right? Well, whaddyaknow? How do you do it? I'd sure like to watch you. Go ahead, don't let me bother you."

Apparently, he had decided to forgive me and make friends. And, by God, I tried to respond. The coldness in the house had been soul-chilling. He sat down and lit a cigarette.

I explained carefully, "I begin by listening to the music and I don't move for a long time and I try to think."

"Fair enough. Think away. Don't you get up and do things?"

"That comes later. First, I don't move and I don't talk . . . I only think."

"No kiddin'!" said the lieutenant.

I turned on Nordoff's remarkably inventive transcription of

Gluck's music. Bluntly examined his nails and began whistling very, very softly between his teeth an air not by Gluck. Nor by Nordoff.

"I think that music sounds all the same," said Bluntly. "Doesn't it ever get different?"

"Yes, it does," I said. "Don't you have to work in the morning?"

"Not all day Tuesdays, Thursdays and Saturdays."

"Good God!"

"Pardon?"

"Are you due for transfer anywhere?"

"Nope, never. I'm permanent. I stick right here. It's dull but it's safe. That's what I tell the missus. Seems funny to me, just sitting and thinking, if you have to make up a dance. I never heard of that."

"Everything about dancing is real queer."

We chatted on in this agreeable way for two hours. He sat with me all morning.

The next day I attempted to work in the bedroom, which had no light, no space and no music, there being no portable gramophone in the entire town for rent. So I took to sitting long hours in the public park. And throughout the waiting days, I attempted to get on with my eighteenth-century satire. I could not think of a step and I could not think of a name, but Hurok, who knew nothing of its story, was already advertising it as *Tally-Ho*. I found I had difficulty in keeping my mind on the plot, and nothing seemed particularly funny, but no doubt, I told myself, it would, directly. I also made notes for a possible book. These didn't seem much good.

In the park were wonderful roses and they were tended, beds and beds of them, by Jim, the gentle, slow-voiced, middle-aged gardener. He also took care of the children who played there without nurses, settled their disputes, washed their skinned knees, helped them across the streets and instructed them in ethics. They came to him in all situations and his word was law. I used to hear him administering justice out among the flower beds as I sat staring over my empty notebook. He always nodded as he passed, but he never disturbed me. We had, at my prompting, a few talks. His brother, first mate on a transport, had just gone down in the Mediterranean.

I spent the days brooding and walking by myself. I played games like counting all the different kinds of flowers in town, wild and cultivated. (There were 231 cultivated and 41 wild. After the rains, of course, there would be many more wild.) I told Walter this, but he was not startled. He could take it or leave it alone. The Germans had advanced another five hundred miles inside Russia. Sometimes I had my hair and nails done and that took up time.

"Oh, I know that girl," I said at the hairdresser's, pouncing with enthusiasm and companionship on a picture of Milada Mladova in *Harper's Bazaar*.

The manicurist said, did I?

"Yes," I said, "I know some actresses." But they turned out not to be the ones she hoped.

I shopped at extraordinary length for things like cold cream and shoelaces and ash trays. I saw by the headlines that my friend Leonarde Keeler was investigating the hideous murder of Sir Harry Oakes in Barbados. Thereafter, any horror details seemed almost like a friendly gay encounter.

I had brought Walter's old foot locker packed with wedding gifts and enchanting domestic appurtenances, and a row of new dresses hung in my closet. But there was, of course, no chance to use any of them. Nevertheless, it seemed a pity not to start practicing some sort of housekeeping even under these disconcerting and bizarre conditions, so I cut out of the *Ladies Home Journal* two recipes with colored illustrations and laid in a stock of ingredients.

The first called for meat and I went into the butcher shop to buy chops. "Loin or shoulder?" asked the butcher. I felt sudden sweat through my palms. I hadn't known there was a difference. Finally I found my courage. "Just bacon," I murmured. "I've changed my mind." Then I went to the grocery department. I knew nothing of amounts and had to purchase everything, including salt, because of my formal relations with the rest of the household. The supplies filled a small suitcase, which I kept under the bed, although I did remember to put the butter and milk, suitably initialed, into the refrigerator. I had in mind to make him a whole dinner, ending with a lemon custard pie. We would have to eat it in our back room, of course, but I had that figured out too, with the bureau as a sideboard and the foot locker as table. Also, of course, the entree was now to be fried eggs and bacon. I could see that I was going to have to achieve the ideal dinner by infiltration, but he was still in love with me and time was on my side. The vegetables would be easy, plenty of water, the gas high for hurry and only one burner of their stove borrowed at dinner hour. A single potato takes up little room in the baking oven. The pie could be made in advance.

I watched for a propitious unsupervised moment. It occurred two days later at 10:22 A.M., and profiting by the pause, I hastened to lay out my tools. Within fifteen minutes, I had involved nineteen utensils and was concentrating on the nice adjustment of stove, mixing bowl and sink, the one lagging behind the other by just enough time to necessitate the frequent addition of the garbage pail. When Henrietta entered the back door, she stopped and surveyed me without a word. After a while, she crossed the kitchen and went out, but she returned with a magazine and sat down in the breakfast nook. I gave her the expression which usually drove people from my rehearsal halls, but she continued blandly moistening her finger and turning the large crackly pages. She spoke at last. "Cooking?"

Flour and milk and butter can do unlikely things, as anyone who has worked with them knows — and there did not seem to be the same margin for correction as in a dance. Once they got out of hand, they kept working away at their own pace regardless of any intentions of mine. After what I judged to be a suitable time, nevertheless, with an air of unruffled satisfaction I popped the whole mud pie into the oven and turned the gas up high, the better to get on with the business.

"I won't be long," I said brightly.

"I can wait," she replied and turned another page.

I opened the oven door after a while and then quite efficiently and briskly, but still in silence, threw everything away and cleaned the pots. Henrietta mounted to her ruined legs, came steadily over, took the pie tin out of a drawer and handed it back to me. There was a scrap of something burned on the bottom. Steel wool helped that. She looked out the window and beat a little tattoo on her teeth with her mauve fingernails and waited.

When all was done, the sink pristine, the dish rag washed out and spread to dry, she began to move with unexpected speed and sickening proficiency, readying her own baking. My operation had taken just under an hour. I aired the suitcase out on the grass.

When I told Walter four days later, he said, kissing me, "Try a chop (I'll instruct you what kind), a potato and one green vegetable. The baking starts two years from now."

Every day I went the complete round of the real-estate agents. (There was a motel bungalow for rent down by the gasworks, but when I got there, three families were fighting over it.) Every evening at seven, Walter came home with a fistful of new addresses gathered at the officers' club. Some addresses did not exist —

some did but were not for let. None was ever available. "Have you investigated every abandoned railway tunnel?" he asked. I was also instructed to go every day to every likely shop and hunt for whiskey. "But every day, darling, every day. Don't neglect one single day. There are several thousand men and their wives alerted for our bottle."

When my hunts were over, I sat in the public gardens. The park was lovely and the weather was California and October. All the town gardens bloomed with a musky smell and in the gutters the few deciduous leaves crackled underfoot. The sky stretched high, and ringing blue, and against it the trees cut sharply. This was the clear-eyed season. The daily mists of summer had lifted — the rains not yet come — and so the country waited wide-open for the reaffirmation of winter storms. Around the town the great fields of grapes — muscat, Malaga and seedless Thompson — mellowed and dried on their miles of trellises, lending the air a winy bouquet and covering the earth with the luxury of rotting fruit and trampled leaves. The great cases of raisins stood stacked in columns in the open sun.

This was the California I had first seen as a girl, the autumnal brightness of the Pacific Coast, and as I looked into the endless shining sky, how many days, how many afternoons in the canyons behind Los Angeles came to mind! I seemed to stand again, a bare-legged child, and felt my heart jump to see the great yellowing sycamore boughs flung across the heavens, while at my feet tumbled the ice-cold water of some stream from mountains where the rains had already begun. In those hours, everything was possible. One met challenges in midmorning.

And for this reason I had my moments of rebellion there in the sun. Sometimes a kind of dragging forlorn terror engulfed me. Back in New York between Forty-fourth and Forty-sixth Streets and between Sixth and Eighth Avenues, a girl with my name was having a big run in the musical theater, everyone clamoring for me — but only for that month — never before and perhaps not later again. And here I was in farm country, lost in isolated vineyards, watching out the precious weeks when I should be back there pressing the advantage. Even now, a young dancer named Jerome Robbins was starting choreography on a ballet about three sailors. What if Robbins proved to be a real rival? What if — while I sat here waiting among the roses — he took the jobs that were marked for me and equaled or bettered my work?

I read that *Time* magazine thought my work in *Venus* pretentious and I raged to answer. I read that *Vogue* thought my style suggestive of Tudor's and couldn't eat my lunch. I read the four-day-old theatrical section of the *New York Times* and made lists of dances to do, and possible good steps, and the corrections I wanted to add to the current works.

Theater people pine and agonize constantly because they fear they will be forgotten. And they are quite right. In America, they will be.

All the tearing between ambition and love that a heart can endure I bore, exposed and frightened, during these hours. What business was it of mine to sit in this ridiculous household with these uprooted, ill-assorted, lost creatures who never could speak to me or I to them? Oh, how surprised they'd be if they knew who I was and what I'd done!

So what the hell had I done? Nothing that would interest them, to be sure! And who was I anyway? A young wife waiting beside a man who was shortly to risk his life. Black shame bowed my heart that I should hold myself apart, that I should ask special exemption for anything beyond the man I loved or beyond any other woman in these months of agony.

There was a great deal of time in the park to consider what I'd done in deserting my guy. There was opportunity to review the lost time, the time misspent, the time stolen forever from us. What lay ahead, no one could guess. Could I, I asked myself all day, in the weeks or even the days vouchsafed, make him realize that I would be a good wife, that I loved him as much as making up little dances, or earning a salary, or getting my name in dramatic reviews? He said he understood — but I knew, as I looked in his face or heard him speak, that he felt he had married a will-o'-the-wisp. Doubt had entered his heart. I watched with dismay his struggle to overlook it, to forget my delinquency, to pretend matters were just as they had been before. I thought of these things all day as I went about alone, with not a soul to talk to except, from time to time, the little thin girl, who shyly offered me coffee and who never had any good news from the P.N. wards. I seemed to be living in a slow-motion dream until six at night when conversation and thinking and noticing began again. At six-thirty Walter came home and we had a small drink in our cubicle, then sneaked out past the unfriendly cold stares of our housemates, to walk hand in hand to some hash house or chop suey joint. We stayed out as long as we could in the quiet of the streets, trying to find out what we thought about different things so that we'd know something about each other during the coming separation. I tried to tell him a little about my work. As I explained it, it didn't seem so important. The Germans were still strongly entrenched around Moscow.

We went shopping — I was looking for a good-by present.

"What can I give you? Whatever can I give you?"

He pressed his face against a glass. "That's a nice suit!"

"You can't wear that for years."

"I'm thinking of deserting."

We wandered on. "I know what you could give me — a money belt."

"That's a horrid present. Have you much money?"

"No."

I had found him a fine fitted toilet case. "No, no. Take it back. I have to carry everything I own on my shoulders. I only need a toothbrush, comb and razor. Take it back."

I had knitted him a khaki muffler.

"I have one, *maestrone!* Same color, too, strangely enough!"

I had brought from New York a knitted pullover.

"I don't need it, darling. And you know I have one."

"What did you do with those wonderful great socks I knitted you?"

"I gave them to a girl."

"Oh, what can I give you? Whatever can I give you to take away to remember me by?"

"I'll remember."

We celebrated Armistice Day, the old Armistice Day, still a holiday, although a kind of shamefaced one, with chop suey and a movie. It was a Russian documentary about the siege of Stalingrad.

The Russians have a sterling attitude toward death and its concomitants. Martyrdom for them, it seems, is guaranteed with mortification and they are not squeamish about emphasizing this point to wives and mothers. It struck me that afternoon that the heroes of Stalingrad were particularly mature as they were regarded by their fur-hatted colleagues with gravity, clenched fists and soul-reaching oaths that puffed in white breath out over the poor frozen cadavers. It made for peculiarly apt Armistice consideration by a bride and groom.

"I don't think I could be very good about wading through frozen water in subzero weather," I said.

"Nor I," said Walter. "I'd just shut my eyes and go down to the black bottom."

"You know something?"

"What?"

"You've never seen me in evening dress."

"What has that got to do with my drowning?"

"I'm pretty lovely."

"I believe you. When this is over, what shall we do in evening dress?"

"We'll go out to dinner and I shall be very, very, very beautiful."

Walter had friends; we were not entirely alone. There were Major Dr. Richard Evans and his wife, who took us in like stray dogs and helped in every way possible. There was the bluff divorcé who kept telling Walter he was a fool to have got married and eloped himself two weeks later. There was a sergeant named Noggle who was more than kind about bringing rumors, often reliable, about stray whiskey. He drove us far afield several times in a cross-country search. He was gay and wry, by all odds the most amusing creature around, but, because he was noncommissioned, untouchable. Our social life had to be carried on, therefore, secretly, far from town. We used to sit in his Ford after a successful hunt and toast our efforts in paper cups. Noggle had plans for coming out on top of the war. He had put all his pay into Mum, the deodorant. His foot locker was full of jars of Mum. "When we get to the South Pacific the boys are going to need it bad. They'll pay anything."

"Provided," said Prude seriously, "there are girls."

"Eventually, there are always girls."

One night Noggle said to me, "You're sweet."

"No, I'm not," I said. "You just ask my housemates."

"That's all right," he said. "You're sweet, but you sure need handling."

"She thinks she's a serious-type girl. It's foundering. No more drinking, my dear. You will be thick of speech when you say good night to Bluntly. Mrs. Bluntly intimidates my wife," Walter explained, pounding the cork back in the tiny bottle with a triumphant sense of possession. "Mrs. Bluntly has been able to do what the organized theater has not. She has reduced my wife to a whimpering neurotic."

Walter alternated his social, or scherzo, mood with dreadful bouts of moodiness. I got to know the pattern well: a cloud presaged rain; a clear blue sky was a trap and a weather breeder; sharp storms would not, as hoped, pass over, but must endure or possibly augment to hurricane; anything might follow a fog. This tendency of his may possibly account for the weather-forecasting corps's shifting him with all possible dispatch to ordinance, where any amount of foreboding might be thought in order. His views on the war did not bear considering, and here he truthfully had grounds for depression: Japan held the entire Pacific except Australia and Hawaii, and California still momentarily expected submarine landings. But I began to realize that his pessimism was a dodge, a propitiation to fate, as though to forestall the surprise of calamity by making a great show of counting on it. Oh, the wicked Texan teasing I was regularly subjected to! It had me denouncing and raging. "Don't raise your voice!" he would say. "You're too little. It will do you no good to object. Poor sawed-off thing!"

And I always believed the monstrous fantasies, the dreadful charades. I never learned. "It's almost not fun with you," he sighed. "You're too easy!"

"Do you ever tell lies about anything important?"

"That's rude. You're too little to be allowed to be rude!"

As the WAAC drove him home one evening, I said rather peevishly and throwing her an acid look, "You're late! What keeps you so late?" "Don't scold me, *maestrone*. You're fresh as a daisy, but I'm exhausted from bending all afternoon over a hot secretary."

When we could, when we had time off, we escaped with a picnic basket and books and sat out all day far from the town in the

crackling fields and watched the white tossing boughs of the syca-
mores and the gilded vineyards. Birds flew high and there was a
restlessness in the sunburned grass. Autumn was ending. He read
me George Moore, Evelyn Waugh, Dorothy Sayres and E. M. For-
ster. We stayed out as long as possible before returning to our bur-
row behind the icebox, where warmth, light and communication
waited like the quiet in the heart of a hurricane.

When we walked at the end of the residential section we felt
dirt suddenly under our feet and smelled pungent weeds in the
dark — sage and sunflower and the grapes of the surrounding farm-
land. The evenings were sharpening up. We came home under a
blaze of stars with our coats buttoned tight.

And as we walked, gradually the sense of well-being came back,
the perception of zest in trivia, the lovely realization of every moment being the prelude to something vital, the timid and expectant withdrawing before certainty, the surprise of certainty, the
languid waiting, the heightened perception of matching and com-
plimenting all experience, every kind of experience, food, or a
silly sign on a window, a remark overheard, the storytelling of
reminiscences to the long-awaited audience, the nonsense that was
not nonsense but a veil across the unspeakable, the idiot games
that held the magic and excitement of childhood, the silence that
was a path under our feet.

But the clocks kept ticking. We were locked into our tight little
time as into a cell and told to solve everything quickly because
very likely it might prove to be for always.

One morning I had returned to bed after making his breakfast
and was well into my second nap when Lieutenant Bluntly beat
with his fist on the door.

"Get up. Get up. Your sweetie-pie is on the phone."

I leaped to respond.

His voice was quiet. "I'm coming home."

"Oh, what luck! We can have a picnic!"

"No, dear. I've got to pack. I'm being shipped out."

"Well, for heaven's sake! I must pack too."

"Dearest, you don't understand. I'm not changing bases. I'm going overseas."

"When?"

"Tomorrow."

"When can you get back here?"

"In a couple of hours. Don't go too far from the house."

"What's happened?" asked all the people sitting around the kitchen where the phone was.

"He's being shipped." As I closed my bedroom door, I heard the lieutenant address his wife. "Haven't I told you how lucky you were? Don't you ever complain to me again about being stuck on an air base. At least you miss this —"

After a while I washed my face and got dressed and went out among them again to make a pot of tea. They watched me without speaking, their eyes following my every move. They almost forgave me, my punishment was so excruciating.

"Would you like a piece of my chocolate cake?" asked Henrietta and mounted to her poor overburdened feet and fetched it herself. I took the tea and my cake back to my room. It was very good cake, but it took me a long time to eat it. I washed the plate, and the cup, and the spoons, and the fork, and the teapot and put them back on the shelves. "Thank you," I said. "You cook very well."

"Not at all," she replied. "You can have another piece when you want it."

I made the bed and straightened up the room. I looked at the clock. I went into the street and looked up and down. Only thirty minutes had gone by.

I ran down to the public park. Jim was way in back on his hands and knees weeding pansies. "Jim," I said, "my man's going out. Can I have some roses for our room?" I tried not to let my voice embarrass him. I looked hard at the gravel at my feet and thought about not embarrassing him.

"Sure, yes, sure," he said and took his clippers from his back pocket. "Any special kind?" I shook my head. "I don't suppose it matters what kind. Hold out your skirt." Later he said, "Come around to my house. I have nicer roses."

"There's not time enough."

"There's time. They don't get off the base so quick. Papers and things. It's a twenty-five-minute drive, too."

I put the roses in every receptacle I could find — glasses, jugs, bottles, vases. The room, the whole house was fresh and delicate with them — and when a window curtain stirred, a breath of white rose perfume or pink rose moved in the stillness. The essence made itself known like the deepening color when a cloud passes.

He came home in an Army lorry driven by a WAAC, at six-thirty. I was sitting where I had been sitting for three hours, on the curbstone, my feet buried in the dry leaves of the gutter. I jumped to meet him and he lifted his foot locker and me together into the house.

There wasn't much more to explain. A captain had been scheduled to go but had developed an abscessed tooth and was in the hands of the base dentist. Walter stood next in line.

"So what happens to the captain?"

"I guess he'll stay on here for a while."

"Where are you going?"

"Jefferson Barracks, St. Louis. Here are the orders."

"I'll follow."

"You can't. It's against strictest regulations."

"I'll follow."

"See — look — here it says 'no family or dependents' may accompany. Go to New York and wait."

All this time he was packing. He finally looked up. "Do you think you could manage to stop crying for a minute?"

"I don't think so. No."

At the bottom of the foot locker were some wedding presents we'd never had a chance of using — a teapot from Cousin Jane and an embroidered tea cloth from Arthur Kleiner.

"I'm going to make us tea," I said, spreading everything out, "in our own household if it only lasts half an hour." I bustled about in the kitchen. Henrietta gave me two more pieces of chocolate cake.

"I don't like chocolate," said Walter.

This I didn't know. There were things like this I hadn't had time to learn. "Goddammit," I said, "you're going to eat this chocolate cake if it's the last thing you do in town. Oh — my dear — oh, my dear — help —"

Later we met Jim on the main street. He shook Walter's hand and wished him luck.

"I understand you've been kind to my wife. I want to thank you."

I was wearing my blue and scarlet dirndl, the one my sister Margaret said was unsuitable to my position and age. I'd pinned a rose in the bodice for gaiety. Walter was, of course, in his khakis. I wondered if Jim saw how handsome he was, how straight, how slender, how quick for life. I perceived that he did. He said, "Whenever you want more flowers —"

"I'll be going away myself tomorrow. But I'll never forget how kind you've been." We shook hands again and he went back to his gardening.

At 5 A.M. the C.O.'s limousine arrived. We loaded up and we were driven to Fresno. I was to be permitted to accompany him that far and no farther. I had bought a little address book and as we swung around curves and slipped down the highway, I tried to recall the addresses of all the people I knew in England in case he was sent there and not to the Pacific.

As a matter of fact, on learning that he was to be detailed to Jefferson Barracks, he was fairly assured of the Western theater as his destination. He was greatly relieved at the prospect, for although a bullet was a bullet anywhere, the Pacific offered additional nonmilitary horrors of climate, bugs, disease and loneliness not so prevalent or aggressive in Europe. Europe seemed in any case like going home. He knew it and loved it, and he had many friends there. No matter how painful this departure was in some ways, therefore, it brought action after months, after years of inertia and stupefying waiting and a certainty less fearful than what had been dreaded. I could not help noticing the brightness in his eyes, the latent anticipation clearly seen in every soldier's once the first shock of abrupt withdrawal has been accepted.

We loafed around and then we had dinner in the grillroom of the hotel, which was decorated to look like Amalfi. We had veal cutlets and I think we had wine.

Then we drove out to the airport and waited until at last the plane was ready. Men all over the waiting room detached themselves from silent knots of women, shouldered their bedrolls or bags and moved toward the exit. I don't remember what Walter said to me, but I know I laughed. People were startled. They looked at us almost angrily. He kissed me once hard at the gate and then marched straight to the plane and entered without looking back. All the windows of the plane were covered. The man that followed him left two women and a little girl and boy. He literally staggered with grief and was so shaken by sobs that he had to place one hand on the railing of the steps to steady himself. I waited with my fingers locked in the iron mesh of the gate. The engines roared to frenzy, the plane bumped and taxied to the end of the field. Not a curtain inside moved, not a light showed. The engines crescendoed again and the plane rose and soared away over the mountains. I waited until the last twinkle of light was gone — the last vibration of sound. The moon took over, still and cool, and November mists rose milkily along the runways.

At my elbow stood the sergeant. "We'll go now, ma'am, if you're ready. I'll take you home. Why don't you sit in front with me? I can answer all sorts of questions and it will be easier for you."

When I got home I found that my room was full of smoke. Walter's socks, which I had washed and placed on the radiator to dry as a last demonstration of housekeeping, were blackening and the newspapers under them smoldering and flaking to the floor in ashes. The coffee-drinking wraith was the only one up and she was alarmed by the clouds of smoke pouring from under my locked door. We threw out the ashes and opened all the windows. Then I had some coffee in the kitchen with her. Wretched, lonely youngster — she was the one person in the whole house to wish me good-by. She lent me her alarm clock, showed me how it worked, and then stood gazing at me under her thin hair in her little cotton dressing gown with the butterflies. Suddenly she threw her arms around my neck. We clung together, shaking.

I left a note for the others with the money I owed for my share of the butter and coffee. I went away at dawn, bag and baggage. Nobody waved. The house sat stolid on its lawn and looked at me under lowered lids.

As I passed Jim's rose garden, I saw the blossoms glowing in the brightening day. But no one in the whole town was up. Three soldiers with duffel bags were sitting silently at the station.

CHAPTER IX   *In Broken Times*

I arrived in New York very weary. Mother was waiting. Regularly whenever I had come home from adventure, broke, sick, heart-worn, Mother had been waiting. She offered household continuity, pleasant meals and a clean bed — my own. She offered lack of surprise. I sank between fresh sheets and heard the dull humming of New York, which is its unique sound, and the phone ringing as Mother kept track of everything she possibly could. And when I had slept off the first shock of return, I woke to see her sitting sewing quietly, a tea tray spread. She always began the healing process by relating cheery messages from friends and neighbors. I had learned over the years that as long as I could take a cup of tea, could listen to the needles click, could ask who just had telephoned, and hear without concern the reply, could note the energy and balance of daily living, that then I could survive. It is not only sleep that knits up raveled sleeves, but the sound of household industry, unobtrusive and performed with zest. Continuity is a woman's magic, and in its practice my mother was an artist. Now, as she sat waiting for me to wake, she was knitting mufflers in dark blue for the merchant seamen whose canteen she helped manage.

It was to be Mother's job for the next two years to run a home for two bereft women, to listen to letters from Africa, Italy, England and Germany, to keep careful track of our exact hourly where-abouts in case of emergency, to go through a darkened movie theater with the usher and a flashlight, find a daughter sitting alone and put into her hands the cable announcing a safe arrival some-where dreadful, to receive messages from abroad and translate them into anniversary gifts and first-night flowers, to try to keep conversation going when all talk failed, to finish dinner alone when nerves snapped and she found herself suddenly with empty places and the knowledge that her girls were walking up one street and down another, seeking solace from house fronts and traffic, to see hope in bad headlines and a termination in what seemed inter-minable, to find her own replenishment by helping those in need.

There were always packages for sailor and soldier friends at her feet, and her desk at home was littered now, not only with Single Tax tracts, letters to fiscal reformers in every part of the world, and copies of the *New York Times* addressed to friends in Parliament, but with peanut butter jars, slabs of chocolate, tea bags, chewing gum, boxes of nuts, novels and soap, in answer to requests from young friends in literally every war theater. Mother was a personal, individual, but by no means small, U.S.O. headquarters.

Walter called on Thanksgiving Day. Suddenly, there was his voice on the phone. The operator was careful not to indicate whether or not it was long distance.

"Are you in New York?"

"No."

"Where are you?"

"Honey, there's an armed M.P. on each side of me expressly to see that I don't answer that question."

"Are you all right?"

"I think the security regulations will permit me to state that I'm fine."

"Will I see you?"

"Saturday night, and all day Sunday. I ought to be ringing the bell at five o'clock."

So the next day, Friday, I called a four-hour rehearsal of *Oklahoma!* and drilled them as they'd never been drilled in their lives — and then I went to the orchestra rail and told them why.

"He's never seen a thing of mine. He doesn't know what I do. If he's disappointed, my heart will break. That's the simple truth."

"Don't worry," said McCracken and Bambi Linn.

"Will you tell the singers also?" I asked.

"I'll tell every bloody pit musician and grip," said Marc Platt. On Saturday I rehearsed *Venus* the same way.

And on Saturday afternoon, I palpitated between the hairdresser and my mirror. The bell rang at five exactly as he had said. And he bounded up the stairs as he had done so unforgettably so long ago — and there he was, standing in my studio, "our" studio now, in his great army coat. His cheeks were cold with the November frost.

There was a fire on the hearth and the drinks were ready. I wore a dress he liked.

We dined at Charles restaurant with wine and then we proceeded up Eighth Avenue to Forty-fourth Street and the St. James Theatre. The doorman knew me, the ushers knew me. They looked Walter over and winked. The back of the theater where I usually stood was, as always that year, three rows deep with uniforms. This night, knowing the circumstances of Walter's departure, and as a wedding present, the Guild had made it possible for me to buy two good seats. The conductor, Jay Blackton, and the first violinist bowed to me. The overture began.

I do not think there has ever been a performance of *Oklahoma!* quite like that one. The cast still included Alfred Drake, Howard da Silva and the incomparable Celeste Holm — and the dancers numbered Joan McCracken, Bambi Linn, Katharine Sergava, Marc

Platt, Margit DeKova, Ray Harrison, John Butler, Scott Merrill, George Church. Every nuance of the show had been worked through. The performers were freshly rehearsed and that night they tried their hardest. For me. Tears came to my eyes as I saw how they were trying and how really exquisite was their skill.

In the smokehouse scene, Walter grabbed my hand and said, "But this is opera. I've never seen anything like it."

We went backstage at intermission and held a reception. The dancers were all waiting in a group to be introduced. Katharine Sergava is fairly reserved, but she kissed Walter heartily.

In the middle of Act II, we slipped out. Walter gave our stubs to two astonished standing WAVES and we ran to the 46th Street Theatre, arriving at *Venus* in time for Mary Martin's lovely solo, "That's Him," and the following ballet. And there, too, when we went backstage, another bevy of beautiful women were waiting. Sono threw herself on Walter's breast although she'd never seen him before. Mary Martin, a fellow Texan, was equally exuberant and gracious.

So then we went home. Walter had loved *Oklahoma!* but he said not one word about the dances.

I stood it as long as I could and then next day at lunch my pride buckled. I ventured to prompt him, naming over possible virtues. Yes, he liked McCracken; yes, he liked Bambi. But he still didn't mention my work. And of course he liked Sono but not the *Venus* ballet. In fact, he liked nothing at all about *Venus* except Mary Martin and Sono.

"Can't you please tell me if you like anything at all about my ballets?"

"I do."

"Oh, but say something!"

"Look, dear, you're professional. You're good. I can't see your work as though it were someone else's. I just can't."

"Weren't you moved at all?"

"As by music? No —"

"Or as by Martha?"

"No — of course not. Darling, really!"

"I hoped you would be, a little."

"Maybe at some other time."

As I later watched men prepare for immediate overseas duty, I grew to recognize this strange inability to respond. Life for the soldier was where the men were, and where the plannings and the daily disciplines and involvements. For Walter the whole of living had become centered in the camps, in the harnessing for the trip toward mortal combat. Our little shows seemed cute as store windows and just about as important, fit to keep the civilians busy and out of trouble, but related in no way to the vast, the momentous and quickening impulses in which he now lived. Music could still reach him, music always, and certain books, but not dance charades, the path to his nerves never having been through his eyes. Since he had seen so little dancing, he was peculiarly unprepared for this exposure which took place under operating-theater conditions. I believe that night he literally saw nothing, but I had not the wisdom nor the imagination to understand and my feelings were hurt.

But there the matter rested.

So we talked of other things and made what plans we could for the week that was probably left us.

When he bade me good-by, he handed me his laundry and promised to rejoin me in two days and "Don't," he said, "don't go anywhere for longer than forty minutes without letting your mother know where to find you."

So I delivered his wash to a Chinese laundry and spent some more futile hours hunting for a portable gift. Mother had been smarter: she had contrived him wrist warmers and a chess set he could hold on the palm of one hand (they kept a transoceanic chess game going throughout the war) and an extraordinary hot-water bottle that worked with chemicals.

She also contributed advice. Mother always found appropriate advice. "If you get cold, Walter, remember that newspapers under the coat serve as insulation. Just put newspapers under your military jacket. And if you get hot, put wet leaves in your hat. That's what the Australians do. Wet eucalyptus leaves — but any leaves will do. I used to beg my husband to do this during tennis tournaments — but he wouldn't." Walter promised. I gave neither advice nor tokens. I could find nothing.

I was not to see him until Wednesday, and there seemed to be little to do. So I turned, as always, to the practice barre, and buried myself in Carnegie Hall. There, in the animated decay of that compost heap, amid the rotted, the forlorn and the germinating, once again I warmed my heart. I didn't have to explain to dancing colleagues. I could say, "Stand further back," or "After you," or "Which leg?" and much had been exchanged in the way of brotherly endeavor and encouragement.

When class was done, there was still the rest of the afternoon to be got through, so I went into the Carnegie drugstore and began writing a letter — an important one which was to say everything I had not yet made clear and was to last through the war and be carried in his knapsack. I phoned Mother as requested and she said no news but to come have dinner with her and not to mope, a suggestion that struck me as sheer impossibility. There were, I figured, forty-eight more hours to be got through somehow before we met again.

I found myself standing and talking to emptiness in all sorts of places, frequently the open street, until at last I slipped into Aunt Clemmy's, the restaurant below my studio, and had a lugubrious meal, swallowing hard on the soup and blotting the magazines with bad tears. Around nine the place shut up and I was forced to leave. And so, wearily, I went upstairs.

Someone seemed to be inside talking.

He was there, in greatcoat and muffler, sitting at the phone.

"Never mind," he said into the phone. "My idiot wife has just come in," and he hung up. Then he stared at me without moving. "My darling," he said, "we had two hours. Now we have twenty minutes." All the while I had been downstairs weeping, he had been upstairs over my head, phoning every number in my telephone book. He had reached the *M*'s — Motley and Mainbocher. In those two hours, my mother, who had been working at her house on the other end of the alphabet, cemented a friendship that was to last with deep sympathy until her death.

He lay down on the bed without taking off his coat. He was not even smoking. I sat beside him and held his hand.

"How long?"

"Two years, probably."

"Mightn't you have a furlough sooner?"

"No."

So then the time came and I tied a handkerchief around my head and went with him in a taxi. I did not get out at the Pennsylvania Station. He shouldered his heavy bags and became a khaki back and went through the doors.

We had had in all — in broken times — just ten weeks.

It was not until two nights later that I heard the great ship calling all through the dawn as the convoy put to sea. For two days and two nights it had lain in the river. He was within sight of my house and unable to send a message. How many men lined those rails, staring at the dimmed lights of apartments and hotels while the ships around them silently and invisibly gathered? And the women within the city listened and listened and then they heard it, and when daylight came they phoned one another. This was the pattern throughout the war: the cessation of all news and the waiting and then a sound or a radio message and the women phoning at dawn.

Martha Graham called in the morning. "We must now love him with all our hearts. I'll be over later."

With the morning came an unexpected visitor. I received him in my bathrobe, too listless to dress, an admiral, the husband of a lifelong friend. I gave him the paltry little bottle of Scotch I had managed to find, and he sat down genially.

"Now, what do you suppose I did last night?"

I shook my head.

"I went to see *Oklahoma!*"

"That's nice," I said.

"And whom do you suppose I was with? Don't try to talk. I'll tell you. The skipper of Walter's convoy — and I called to explain that he is one of the best admirals in the fleet and one of the most experienced and careful — a brilliant seaman — and his war record is splendid. Walter could not be in better hands."

I was breathing again.

"And I'll tell you more because I know you'll keep your mouth shut. He's going to the European theater and not to the East, and he's going to be stationed first in a not too exposed position."

"England?"

"The Admiral liked your dances very much. And now don't you open your lips to anyone, not even your mother or your sister, or anyone at all. And thank you very much for the whiskey."

My sister Margaret, who was a veteran in the experience, said to me that day, "Now you begin living in the future. You'll plan and arrange, but whatever you plan and whomever you meet will be held in trust. You will experience nothing fully at the moment. But you will not lose it — it will be there for you later."

Martha Graham came, as she said she would.

"As long as you have him, nothing ever again will not be fun," she said. "It will always be more fun because of him, away or here."

"Marriage is difficult, Martha. I didn't do very well. I want a chance to do better."

"Of course it's difficult. What's easy?"

"And I'm afraid for what will happen now. I'm not pretty and no housekeeper at all."

"He loves you."

"He's going to whole continents of women."

"He's a Southerner and of course he flirts."

"He said he didn't like my work and I can't bear this."

"Now use your imagination! If the last week has been hard for you, think what it's been for him. Dancing is a difficult medium in any case, and he doesn't understand it too well — and you're his wife."

"He understands your dancing."

"Ah — I'm not his wife."

"He understands other artists' songs and writing."

"But not his wife's. He cannot consider anything of hers impersonally. No husband can, ever — ever."

"I don't understand."

"You put your mind on this! This is the way men frequently are. Oh, I've met one or two in my time.

"But as for you, you keep your head up as an artist and never mind anyone else — anyone — and that means your husband also. Or me — or even you, yourself, sometimes. But it does not mean you cannot love him."

"Men are not very understanding always."

"No, not always. But, oh, my dear, he's gone to dreadful things! Love him. This will help him even in danger, in physical danger,

I mean. Hang on with all your hope. You can, I believe, actually protect him. I feel this. I feel he will not be hurt: he has not yet done his work." She went down my little stairs and, looking up from the bottom, said softly in her breathless rusky voice, "He loves you, you know."

"The dancing doesn't seem so important now."

"Ah — but you've done it. You've proved yourself. If you hadn't, it would have eaten at your heart always. When you are able to stop work, you will be able to — that's that.

"All of this is hard," Martha continued. "I'm not going to try to tell you that it's any easier for knowing that millions of women are suffering in the same way. That doesn't help. Nothing helps, really. But would you like to live outside the passion of your time?"

"No," I said and entered the waiting with my sisters.

Two weeks after he'd gone, it seemed he had been gone six months; a year later it seemed the same, neither more nor less. It never got worse, it never got better. It stretched.

The women developed instinctive means of communication among themselves. Compulsions seized us to talk about our men, quite as though they were new babies, to strangers, to anyone, to read snatches of letters aloud, hugging the personal sections to our dresses in secret gloating and brooding; needs to have their luck toasted at table (even by strangers), to seize on any little token, a chocolate bar, a tin of peanuts, chewing gum, a book, to snatch it and mail it, explaining carefully why and naming the man by name; a need to compare situations with any woman — saleswoman, waitress, bus conductor. We met and knew one another, utter strangers standing side by side, reading headlines at the news stalls; we met waiting at the post office, holding our packages; we met in the grocery shops, weighing Christmas boxes (five pounds' maximum for each man) and watching one another, deciding what could be afforded and what not, and recognizing the look that anything could damn well be afforded, even the very poor deciding this.

This is not the way the history books will tell the war story, but this is the way we knew it.

Soldiers were given definite psychological training and preparation and when they were sent overseas they were more or less ready. But no one prepared the women. We were given orders, though. We were told that the least we could do for the folks who were really taking the brunt was to be gay and to write only that life progressed vigorously back home. On the other hand, we were urged not to let them think they were not missed hourly. This imposed a nice balance in style.

We were told that what we who were left at home could do in the name of shared suffering was to live the best possible common-sense lives, tell the truth, mind our business, and keep ourselves in order for the weary ones. But we woke in the night frightened. We woke so frightened we were amazed. We stopped in the day and bit our lips with anger and helplessness. There were sudden tempers and tears, there were unpredictable shortness of speech and collapses of energy.

Any sign of emotion or tenderness unmanned us instantly, any kindness or any cruelty. A Christmas carol was just damned well unbearable and when the turkey was carved, every woman avoided every other woman's eyes as she fought not to make a spectacle of herself. The sight of a new baby stopped us cold. There were idiotic scenes of no dignity, as, for instance, the time I discovered that a picture of me was going to be published in *Life* and that it was highly unflattering and I rushed to the editor's office and wept and explained that my husband was handsome and overseas, that we'd just been married, and that I could not risk having such a picture of me broadcast, and I wept so hard, the editor tore the negative in front of me.

Again, there was the first wedding I attended after his departure, two members of the Ballet Theatre company, and again my silly uncontrollable weeping started, Lucia Chase, who was a widow, and I clinging together until Antony Tudor pulled us apart and kissed us and made us laugh. As a bereft mother explained it, "There is a knife standing in each heart and it needs but the careless touch of a finger or a breath to twist the blade."

And some of the touches were not so careless. For dark, personal reasons, many people could not resist this chance at cruelty. There were the intellectuals who demanded aggressively if we believed in war and asked across our dinner tables did we relish the idea of being the widows of dead heroes? There were men of peace who fulminated against destruction and argued that no idea was worth fighting for that leveled Casino or Dresden. There were the men that wrote pornographic books and sold them as exact campaign experiences. There were the newscasters who, after the fourth Martini, swore with something akin to professional pride that the war would last another eight years. There were our consciences urging us to throw up everything and join the forces, accepting any routine job at all, and the ensuing nightly struggle for wisdom and sanity.

There was the constant obscene and morbid curiosity as to just how we were managing to bear up. Many a wife has hung up the telephone or walked away on an indecency — mainly from other less involved women. We who were in it never, under any circumstances, violated one another's privacy. This much we could do for one another.

The loss was total — one part of it was not more unbearable than another, whether one lay frightened in the bankrupt bed, wondering as the great nights stretched open all around, or whether one heard a passing remark in the street and realized there was no one to share the joke.

How the months rolled by! How the months stood heavy! Every morning I adjusted the little headache that was the token of my loneliness and his proxy. It lived in my brain like a mouse. It was a very little headache, but it was almost never absent and it nibbled on the string of my life.

I spent what time I could alone. There were many hours to be alone, in hotel bedrooms, in restaurants, walking in strange streets, in churches. Sometimes I reread my marriage lines.

I remained throughout this progress snappy, hysterical, changeable and frantic. Learning to love is difficult for some, particularly to anyone who had put such a reliance on hating. Anger demanded nothing but energy and was replenished in manifold ways, with brilliance of speech, bright cheeks, flashing eyes, racing blood, and adrenalin to the heart, and always with action antic in spite and the quick battle laugh. The fever engendered was almost like ecstasy — almost, but never quite. Work withered, friends fell off — and when the great need arose, I could neither trust nor give — not wholly, not enough, not without caution or asking for a tallied account. I kept saying, like a litany, "All the world's a mirror, and all the men and women merely me." I'd been, it seems, too long before the ballet glass. I had broken the glass and, like the girl in the fairy story, I was frightened.

Sometimes I perceived clearly and sometimes I raged. The adhesions of habit make bitter breaking; it is a tearing of the mind, tissue by tissue, a ripping to exposure, and one returns and returns to patch up the hurt ends into the old web. I think this is what is meant by being reborn and there is nothing less likely or harder come by.

It seemed to me that I had devoted years to running away, lashing through time, fitful and ambitious, and here I was, ringed by death, swung out in catastrophe, with another life in my keeping. If I fell this time, both fell, and as we dangled between lives, we tried to weave, as though with breath and by will alone, a cord of perceptions that would outlast time. What we were was of no account nor in what ways we had failed, but what we hoped to be: that was the power. And that was still the mystery. There had been no time for a gay manner of learning, for doing things together, for sharing work or play, for meeting friends. Perhaps, somehow, this lack would make the suspension easier, there being for us no daily patterns to rupture. But, oh, how bitter was the deprivation of first experiences! Never to have seen a job of work through or shared any neighborly experience. There were going to be no little jokes and no daily teasing, nor any physical kindness to ease the learning of our roles. We were going to have to make a marriage by faith, to become seasoned and experienced partners while we had forgotten the sound of one another's voices. And so we tried.

It was only at night when I was quiet and listening to the war news that I knew peace, as I sat with my glass of sherry, writing to the A.P.O. number. Only then, and when his letters came.

The message of arrival was delivered three weeks after departure on Christmas Eve. I was in Chicago with Ballet Theatre. The mail clerk and the porter and a bellboy all called together as I entered the hotel lobby from a long rehearsal. I grabbed the desk and fought for breath and they said, "That's fine, miss. That's all right now. That's fine. You can have your Christmas." The message was from an unknown place and read simply, "ARRIVED MERRY XMAS." That was all.

The first letter came two weeks after and the postman climbed the stairs and beat on my door in Greenwich Village. "Wake up. There's news!" Thereafter, he always did just this when there was such news or sometimes he ran after me down the street calling and waving and I would turn and race to meet him — and there, like water in the desert, was the beloved handwriting — and I would look forward to the unknown message instead of the already memorized ones.

The first letter said, in part:

> I read the letter you put in my knapsack. I was sitting up on deck looking out over [deleted by censor] in the cloud-strained moonlight. Men lined the rail the length of the ship. There was a little space between each man, enough to show how profoundly alone he was and how private he wished to be with his thoughts. I could almost collect those thoughts in my hands, they were so palpable. At night when my boys are all asleep, knotted into strange, deformed shapes in their too-short bunks or spread around grotesquely over duffle bags and blankets on the deck, I look at them in the unearthly glow of the blue emergency light, hear them moan and mutter in their sleep, and I wish them very well indeed.

When I came into the house after work, there was a stillness, the sound of no one. The mechanical punctuation of a telephone meant only that I was not out of communication, but when it stopped, the stillness settled. Sometimes a soldier's cap, passing down the street, brought a reflection of excitement. I recalled how it had been. I recalled with my senses as when memory rouses to smell or sound. Occasionally, very rarely because there had been so little time for the depositing of clues, I came upon a tangible hint, like a cigarette, or a button, or a telephone number on the back of an envelope — and I marveled, as I always do, how the shell remains when the unique life is gone.

But an unexpected neighbor moved in to bear me company through this trial and to fill the loneliness; and it was music.

In the flat directly overhead a young man, then unknown, Grant Johannesson, began practicing for his Town Hall debut. So now when I came home I heard, as I stepped into the closed emptiness of my rooms, the stern and hearty reminders of endeavor. There were scales, all kinds of scales, in octaves, descending, ascending, chromatic, arpeggio — the tones one after another in logical miraculous sequence. They rose like steps and there was never an ending; beyond was always the possibility of another. His hands were strong, his touch firm and kind. No radio can do this — no recording of any kind. The living sound was clean of all electrical insistence. It was personal and temporary and it would pass away and never be repeated. And there were mistakes, thank God. It was a human performance.

He played Brahms, all the great Intermezzi — the Brahms that Walter so loved — and I sat below in the first chair I had bought as a start toward a permanent home and listened with tears of gratitude and benison slipping from my tight eyes. Then I went upstairs and slipped a note under his door to thank him.

The war raged in every quarter of the globe, but life seemed to be stilled inside my studio as I sat alone with the chain up. In the daytime working, at night with the curtains drawn, the fire lit, the traffic quiet and no phones. I sat writing my long letters, which were my only moments of vitality. And I fell asleep with his letters spread over the coverlet or in a packet under my hand. I got so I could recognize which was which by the touch. I fell asleep planning what it would be like when this trancelike state was over, when the suspension would be ended, this strange death in life with all decisions postponed, all conclusions and developments arrested.

Book Two

I struck the board, and cried, "No more;
  I will abroad.
What, shall I ever sigh and pine?
My lines and life are free; free as the road,
  Loose as the wind, as large as store.
    Shall I be still in suit?
    Have I no harvest but a thorn
    To let me blood and not restore
What I have lost with cordial fruit? . . ."

But as I raved and grew more fierce and wild
      At every word,
    Methought I heard one calling, "Child!"
    And I replied, "My Lord!"

                              GEORGE HERBERT
                              (from *The Collar*)

CHAPTER X *Children's Games*

AT the time of the *One Touch of Venus* rehearsals, Ballet Theatre wanted a new work from me. I wrote out a scenario and handed it to the young composer Paul Nordoff. It was to be a gay and bawdy romp, in the style of Watteau, to a composite selection from Gluck. Nordoff went away with six or eight Gluck operas under his arm and came back in two weeks with a thirty-five-minute score, complete with overture, which, although only one third original Gluck, was so perfect in style and vivacity that the musicologists detected no forgery. I could not possibly keep pace with this accomplishment. Whatever I suggested Nordoff do, he did that night and came back the next morning to play for me. Since I couldn't keep him sufficiently occupied, he asked to do another ballet while I was busy with *Venus* and studied the scenario of one of our young soloists who had announced his intention of trying his hand at choreography. He was a bright enough dancer, and a good comedian, but of course no one could be sure he had any talent as a choreographer. He was sure himself and somehow he wangled the chance to try.

"I've just spoken to this boy, this Jerome Robbins, about his script," said Paul, "but he's already given it away to a guy named Leonard Bernstein."

"Who's he?" I asked.

"Protégé of Koussevitzky."

"Oh, I remember. He's the young man our ballet master threw out of class for playing Shostakovich during *pliés*. He plays well. Can he compose?"

"Who knows? The scenario is damned good."

"It is?" I said with a certain uncontrollable dismay. "I wish mine were! So Jerry's come up with a promising scenario, has he? What do you know! These youngsters!"

"Yes, his synopsis is charming and simple and logical," continued Paul. "Supposing we try to fix yours."

I got on doggedly, as I had to, with my Broadway chores, throughout August and September, and now Nordoff's finished score awaited me. Ballet Theatre panted for rehearsals. With Walter gone and my private life in abeyance, I decided to throw in my lot with the touring company.

In the course of its nineteen-year history, Ballet Theatre has had but one inspirational motivating voice: Lucia Chase. It has had several impresarios. In 1943 the role was filled by Sol Hurok, a world figure in his own right.

He has long thought of himself as the last of the great impresarios. It is not clear to any of us why he was to be the last, but I've no doubt that his intuition was in this, as in so many other matters, infallible. And it is certainly doubtful if there will ever be anyone who can follow his performance, for it presents an amalgam of Caesar, Bishop, Tycoon and Patron Grand Style, Balzacean in its furor either of praise or rage. His manner is at once florid and blunt and it is always noticeable. His personal style overwhelms fashion and situation, for although dressed by the best tailors he always somehow contrives to appear in costume. His coat hangs in folds from the bull-like shoulders. His square neck supports the broad flat head with its friarlike fringe of white hair and the fedora (Borselina felt) set banditti style over one eye.

His smile is wide, wicked and lusty. There is something extremely virile and challenging in Hurok's smile; at his laugh nerves dance all down Fifty-seventh Street. His shrewd eyes see everything, squinting in concentration, see not only what lies within normal vision but behind him and inside steel vaults. He can appraise at a glance, subtract the percentage, tote up the profit, and reject or accept while kissing a hand. His undeterred feet punish cement and marble as his ebony stick stakes out the earth before him, stabbing like a rapier in a flourish that sets his diamond finger ring winking.

His hands are ferociously strong, which is good for clapping his artists — and only his artists — and Hurok has always been shameless about this, standing at the back of the house and beating up response. "Bravo!" he would cry. "Bravo! Bravo!" And nudge and beam around until the cue was taken up. Seeing Hurok get a house started was like watching a giant with his shoulder to the wheel. It moved. It damn well moved. He saw that it did. And when the triumph was accomplished and the clamoring had died off and the flower petals been swept away, he would progress across the empty stage to his hero and the approach would be like showers of gold falling on the happy and deserving subject — not literal showers, of course, but spiritual and emotional replenishments, and Hurok would open his huge arms and embrace the chosen one, and with his head high, he would look around like a master craftsman taking a Cellini out of the oven to the wonder of the workshop and the whole world. And then there would be a party with absolutely every well-known person in town present — not one absent — and Hurok, the smiling host, standing before the groaning boards and circling the tables, ordering more and more with only an occasional muttering among the spies at the telephones as to what exactly was going on in the pressrooms of the *Times* and *Tribune*.

He has always moved in a Renaissance atmosphere of intrigue

and machination. He would as lief have set aside his trousers as his wariness. What big-league baseball is to most native Americans, intrigue was to Hurok and his colleagues. It never palled. The very small area bounded by Carnegie Hall on the west, Columbia Concerts farther down the street, the Hurok office on Fifth at Fifty-sixth, and Ballet Russe wherever it was had long since become a network of espionage conducted by heavy-hatted and accented men with Slavic faces who patrolled the beat and came to formidable conclusions at the Russian Tea Room, where they met daily for lunch. In the same area the objects of their debates, with hat boxes of practice clothes knocking at their knees, circulated rapidly, paying no mind to the negotiators, not recognizing them probably, and dining sparsely at drugstore counters.

Transactions reached periodic climaxes at the tearoom until Hurok received the red button of the Légion d'honneur and retired to more suitable state at the St. Regis or, better still, at the Pavillon when entertaining unusually worthy clients. His rivals continued in modest *bistros,* gnashing their second-rate teeth over less rewarding plans. The dancers remained at the drugstore counters.

He has made two or three fortunes, and lost as many. When disaster strikes, he pays up and he shuts up without a whimper. But as the first fresh note of violin or bagpipe or castanet sounds through ruin, he rises ebullient from the wreckage, adjusts his assistants and his fedora and goes forth without the memory of a doubt or a rebuff, without the smallest reluctant twinge from the last scorching, to preach once more the perfect gospel. "Well" — he shrugs wryly — "now we have to think of next year. Anyway, I don't want Columbia should get this new soprano. I'll fly over tomorrow. Or no — better you go. Tell her she deserves the best. Tell her she should be a Hurok attraction. Don't let You-Know-Who speak to her." As some can divine hidden waters, he gauged popularity. He was a success dowser. What sixth sense informed him of exploitability and readiness? His rivals would love to share this secret wisdom.

When he pronounces box-office totals, everyone attends with eyelids suitably lowered; this is canon law.

"It is great art," says Hurok. "The American people love great art — I want to bring art to the people."

Happily for Hurok this wholesome and high-minded attitude has in no way confused ambitions of a less altruistic nature — and the highest art has been coaxed to pay off quarter millions. Minyamum! He hasn't always understood it, what he brought, but he chose it and even sometimes went against his own personal taste to obey the Voice. He might have dealt in other commodities with equal profit and less risk — in almost any business certainly. He knows politics, history and political science and speaks publicly with knowledge and force. By conviction, he is a liberal, an old-school, free-thinking socialist. And certainly he could have had a political career. He chose music because he loves music and because he loves ballet. He loves ballet as few Americans have ever loved it, with his entire delight, with the belief and satisfaction of his whole heart and mind. When he hears Tchaikovsky, wine pours through his veins, and when he sees the impeccable line of Swans — ah, then the snow is cold on his lips, the droshky bells ring, and Holy Mother Russia beckons under her diadem and streaming satin ribbons. All the glory of the imperial court, red and gold and sable-strewn, rises again, all the glory he as a poor boy was shut out from but which as an immigrant kid with twelve dollars in his pocket he set forth to establish in a wilderness across the world.

He speaks with the cadence and accent of Russian colloquialism and while deferring to nothing so picayune as grammar, manages to make himself pungently and memorably clear. His remarks have become maxims in the business: "If the people don't want to come, nothing will stop them," and, with his sudden chuckle of conspiratorial camaraderie, "Don't worry. Whatever happens, we aggra-vate more people than they aggravate us."

Perhaps his greatest gift of all, perhaps next to his unerring instinct for success, is his capacity for inspiring loyalty and enthusiasm. His staff workers implement his notions with skill and invention. They are, whoever they number at the time, a fighting corps of skill and undeviating cohesiveness, on call fifteen hours a day, seven days a week, and subject to emergency strain most of the time. They never balk. He has imbued them with the belief that their work is creative. They give without stint and he can always expect them to. This is an attribute of great leadership.

The only balletomanes comparable to Hurok were Lucia Chase and Lincoln Kirstein. Kirstein fell in love with ballet when a Harvard undergraduate and has dedicated his life and his inheritance to found the American Ballet (later the City Center); he is responsible for the presence of Balanchine in this country. Lucia Chase formed and owned the Ballet Theatre and was, as she styled herself, the "behind the scenes driving force." She has served this company with her personal fortune and twenty years of unbroken effort and has given to the American theater more artists in choreography, dance, musical composition, orchestration and conducting, costume and scene designing than any other theatrical institution in a like period. This is a contribution of dimensions.

She is a New Englander, quiet of manner, precise of speech, girlish in demeanor, and with the resistance of granite. Because she is extremely feminine, she dodges and flirts and adjusts with grace and quicksilver diplomacy. She does not yield. This inconstancy, this seeming caprice, has always reminded me of the technique of Queen Elizabeth, who drove men frantic while preserving England. Lucia has had one object — the maintenance of Ballet Theatre. It has survived for eighteen years — a long period for a costly private theatrical enterprise.

She and Hurok differed radically in professional background and in all superficial ways, but on certain fundamentals they agreed, however unconsciously. He had made his money fighting step by step, finger by finger; she had inherited hers. But she did not, for this reason, underestimate it. To both of them money was power — and power was vital to achievement and therefore life. Money to both meant influence and companionship. It also, to both, spelled out loneliness. Each had great courage, enormous pride and boundless energy. Each had a dream, he his blueprint of proven international success, she her vision of a newer and possibly more American way of doing things. They called themselves collaborators on this venture, but they met head on in irreconcilable contest for domination. No one yet, fourteen years later, has decided who won.

Tally-Ho should never have been the name of the new work, but as I could not think of any proper title until after Hurok's exasperated press department had contrived one, *Tally-Ho* it was called. I have always suspected this was chosen because of the long O's and the horsy connotation, as a possibly profitable confusion with *Rodeo*, then in the repertory of a rival company.

"What do you think *Tally-Ho* means?" I asked one of the Russians in charge of exploitation.

"Children's games," he answered promptly.

"Well, possibly you're right," I acceded: the ballet dealt entirely with adultery.

Because of recent distractions, professional and emotional, I began rehearsals without a clear plot. I began anyhow. I traveled with the company from Chicago to San Francisco to Los Angeles, where the *première* was to take place with me in the leading role.

Ballet Theatre at that time boasted a remarkable repertory including seven of Antony Tudor's best works. Tudor was at his composing peak and the most influential and effective of all younger

choreographers. The classic stars and box-office names were Alicia
Markova and Anton Dolin, but its great performing strength lay
in its roster of soloists, a group that has never been surpassed by
any company, not even excepting the Diaghileff troupe and the
first fabulous Ballet Russe de Monte Carlo in 1934. Altogether, it
was a traveling organization of very considerable fascination and
prestige.

But they lived and traveled then, as they live and travel now,
in the simple camaraderie of the gypsy wagon. The company that
entrains for a Broadway out-of-town tryout or for an opera tour is
well dressed and gay. They carry beautiful handbags and snappy
make-up kits and, beyond that, they carry almost nothing. A ballet
troupe, on the other hand, is dressed for disaster. They wear Tyro-
lean winter coats with hoods that can be slept in and will guarantee
warmth no matter what breaks down or gives out (during the war
many a night was passed flat on station floors). These troupers
are apt to be covered with genuine Canadian woolens from the
skin out. They are studded with cameras. They look like an expedi-
tion of field workers sent out by the National Geographic Society.
Since they have no money for tips and must carry unaided all they
need, they are slung with heavy German and Italian leather cases,
at that time prewar and terribly battered. And since they are home-
less and lonely, many of their cases contain small pets, animals or
birds, trained not to make a sound when the conductor goes by.
Five minutes after tickets have been collected, the car becomes a
pet shop and everyone, man and woman, knits quietly among the
barking, hopping and chirping; traveling poker games of formidable
duration and intensity resume. Not for these performers the frivolous appearance of the trippers who think of the hour and a half
ride to New Haven or Philadelphia as adventure. A ballet tour
lasted then eight months at least and covered about twenty-six
thousand miles under difficult conditions.

Traveling great distances and changing program every day while at the same time rehearsing new substitutes and new choreography in hotel lobbies, local dancing schools, opera-house basements, dark stages and hotel bedrooms can be bone-breaking. Ballet Theatre was rehearsing two new ballets, mine and Jerome Robbins's. All the dancers worked without surcease, but only now and then on my bit. I was granted regular hours in Chicago, all over the city, one hour on Thursday in St. Louis, two hours Tuesday in Kansas City, nothing in Denver because of the altitude, an hour in Seattle ten days later, and steady time in San Francisco. But by then, most of what we had done in Chicago was quite forgotten.

"How is Robbins coming along?" I asked Muriel Bentley.

"Oh, God," said Muriel. "The counts! I don't know what this guy Bernstein is thinking of. Jerry is on the phone every night begging for simplifications. He won't change a bar and Jerry asks the impossible from us. I tell him I just can't — and his temper!"

"Is it good, Muriel?" This is a question asked regularly of all new works by those shut out of the rehearsal halls, and in ballet companies everyone is shut out except the dancers specifically involved. It is not an idle question. We are all bound up together and our interests are interdependent in many ways. We rise or fall as a group. "Is it good?"

"Hard to say," said Muriel. "It's unlike anything you've ever seen. It's brand-new. He's busting with ideas. I'll say that for him."

At night I sat in my hotel or Pullman and tried to solve my own choreographic problems. I needed the bodies of the dancers, floor space, and time, but we all had to share these among us and human strength was not limitless.

To these circumstances, a constant in traveling repertory troupes and bad at any time, were added the restrictive difficulties of war and the extreme mutual distrust of the two factions, the classic and the modern wing. My leading man, Hugh Laing from the Barbados, and Anton Dolin, born Sydney Francis Patrick Chippendall Healey-Kay, from Slinfold, Sussex, were not on speaking terms. They had long maintained an attitude of hostility which they never before had found satisfactory opportunity to express. Dolin had been, since the days of Diaghileff, an international star, had worked under the supreme masters of his era, Fokine, Massine, Nijinska, Balanchine, and now, as Alicia Markova's partner and choreographer, was a figure to reckon with. He had revived, edited and choreographed with great success several classics for Ballet Theatre. Laing, on the other hand, although younger and considerably less known, was the leading performer in Antony Tudor's ballets and Tudor, we recognized, was the first creative talent of our own epoch. Hugh was therefore powerful too and he had decided that now, thanks to my folly, was the moment to discipline Dolin. He chose my rehearsal hall for this exercise not knowing when such God-given opportunity would again offer. Thereafter I did not choreograph; I refereed.

From time to time Dolin suggested courteous reconciliation, but Hugh stood his ground; aesthetics forbid compromise. They were both right in their way; their styles were irreconcilable. I began to devise the scenes so that they never appeared jointly. Inasmuch as the story depended chiefly on their interrelation, this proved a drawback of consequence.

When the emotional weather was favorable, Hugh could be helpful, and he was always an actor after my own heart; he had been my partner for five years in England. But the weather was not always favorable; he was then moody or raging, depending on events. He was also absent for days. Dolin was, as a rule, present, at least for some of the rehearsal hours, but he had a disconcerting habit of departing suddenly for lunch with the mayor of San Francisco or Elsa Maxwell or Sam Goldwyn. But even when present and willing, he was not always tractable, for he looked on pantomime as a time for recovering breath and straightening costume. And rhythm he had never got around to.

"Pat," I said toward the end of one exasperating rehearsal, "can't you stay on beat?"

"Well, ducks, it's not my speciality." (He pronounced this English style in five syllables, which made the statement all the more conclusive.)

He was, nevertheless, one of the most skilled men in the ballet world, probably the finest partner, and he cut a memorable figure in his particular style of nineteenth-century high-schooled gesture, the method of purple portamento grief with velvet cloak, drooping lily, silk tights, and fist to the heart. For the tremendous wrung-out gesture, there was no one in his class, and it was precisely this flamboyance I wished to exploit. Hugh played with understatement and reserve. Their scenes together became like dialogue written jointly by Bulwer-Lytton and Chekhov. In between, I trotted and stamped, barking suggestions and hoping to achieve liaison between two historic periods of theater; but I was not subtle enough to catch up with the styles so successfully canceling each other out, nor with the moods and bafflements of rehearsal vapors.

Anton (Pat) Dolin is basically kind. Wherever there was any genuine trouble he was always the first to help. He labored for years to try to make it possible for the insane Nijinsky to find asylum in America. He succored Spessivtzeva in her lamentable illness. He has helped innumerable young artists with money, advice and jobs, but he could never resist wicked Irish mockery. He could never resist taunting Hugh.

I had heart-to-heart talks with Hugh after each session. "Postpone! Postpone!" roared Hugh. "It's Dolin's fault. You can't get it done. You've got to postpone."

Of course it wasn't Dolin's fault. It was mine.

We kept moving about the country, fiddling with rehearsals. Hugh grew moodier and moodier. Harold Lang was in the corps de ballet; he was pretty moody quite often too. Jerome Robbins and Michael Kidd were moody, but at a distance. They had each begged off because of their own choreographic responsibilities and were just as nervous and bothered as I was. They watched from the boundaries with the alert eyes of terriers.

Lucia Chase herself was moody enough. She had expected a part equal in size with the other three and it wasn't working out that way. Rehearsals on the whole were in a terrible state and got quite soppy with tears, relieved only by rages.

These are the common ballet rehearsal conditions in America. The exorbitant demands of all theatrical unions so drain the treasury that there are never funds enough to pay for a quiet, adequate period of rehearsal at home base.

Every so often Robbins took me aside for pep talks. "How are you coming?" he asked.

"Oh, Jerry, I get so tired of the quarreling. How's yours?"

"I can't think of another step. I've done a solo for everyone and they're pretty good. But there's nothing left for me. For the life of me, I can't think of a single thing for me to do."

"You will."

"I'd better — and, Jesus, the music's hard! We spend hours counting out each sixteen bars. Bernstein won't change it, though. He likes it."

"Don't you?"

"Sure, it's driving us nuts!" He gave his characteristic giggle of sardonic appreciation. "You're brighter. You chose Gluck. He can't argue."

"He's the only one who can't around my rehearsals."

"Don't let the boys upset you. They're not the only smart

ones," he counseled. "Other people have talent too. Hold your head up. Shout them down."

But I was tired. I wasn't sleeping nights. There were too few letters. And the ones that came were full of cut-out holes.

During all this silliness there was a war going on, untold numbers of men were being ferried across nameless seas, the wounded were being returned every week, the spoiled and the broken ones. Montgomery fought across mile after mile of hot sand. The Mark VI tank appeared. There occurred Salerno and the furnace of Anzio. When we stopped to think, it seemed impossible to continue to care whether a leg beat came on count 3 or count 4. And yet we had to care. Either we chucked everything and delivered ourselves over to the heroic tests, or we held together somehow the fabric of our lives, no matter how shoddy; a fabric which included right counts, not poor counts, right arm positions, proper words, fine tonalities. We returned to our hencoop peckings and tried to summon the energy to keep caring. We had to say over and over if life continues it matters, one day it will really matter again, it must matter again; no purpose is served by accepting second-class work.

There was Myra Hess quietly playing Bach in the empty National Gallery at noon every day for whoever wished to come in and listen. And that mattered. There was Toscanini pouring forth courage and majesty over the air waves weekly. We might not be of this stature or material — we were a bunch of quarreling dancers — and what we achieved reached far fewer and to less effect — but that is what we were — and we must be that to the top of our bent and never stop minding about the wrong foot. Like smoke in the air, hung the grief over our heads as we rehearsed our little runnings-around and prancings.

At the time of the San Francisco season, the government decided to release the full details of the Bataan death march and accompanying newsreels of the terrible fighting in the South Pacific. We, the ones left behind, went into shock. We found ourselves raddled with hate, fear and great shame that we could learn to hate so abominably — so quickly. It was impossible to go to movies without seeing documentaries of bits of G.I.'s being dredged up from some mosquito-infested South Sea bog. I remember rushing out of one, leaving behind Loia Cheaney, my companion, unable to bear even her company, a WAVE, and one of Walter's loyal friends. I spent the night writing one of those letters that lay in the morning in the wastebasket, and at seven I went downstairs to meet the lady lieutenant again for breakfast. I realized then the valiant function of her uniform, the clean white, the businesslike blue, the hat, as reassuring as a nurse's cap, and the insignia that bespoke discipline and expertness and knowledge, the mark on her brow that was the sign that the government had noted my lousy night and was taking steps. Her starch and cleanliness, her quiet manner were like a hand at my back. But what she said in her soft Texan drawl, as dulcet as a dove, was, "Rough time, honey? We all have them. I think they were wrong to release the details; but then, they didn't ask me."

She walked with me to the Opera House, talking about Walter. One of the unendurable aspects of the separation was that I never heard his name mentioned from one week to the next. Inside the Opera House my companions were screaming and yelling about a spotlight that had gone on the wrong dancer the night before and about the color of a new sash. So I went in and swelled the chorus. It was good to be able to scream about something.

Then suddenly there were only five hours of available rehearsal time left. Not continuous, but spread over five days. "I'm warning you," said Hugh. "You'd better postpone."

I addressed Sol Hurok, just arrived from New York, and begged for a postponement. "Certainly not," he said. "We've already sold out. There is six thousand dollars in the house. Minymum!" I then announced that I could not be ready to dance myself; that Janet Reed would have to create the role. "In that case you can finish the ballet easily," he said, beaming. "Dancers are all crazy and tarrrible unreliable." He diverted my attention with a superb salad named for him by one of the city's best chefs, and current Ballet Russe box-office figures, learned informally but authentically from sources unnamed. He then boarded a train for Los Angeles.

Hugh said at lunch in the drugstore next day, "I am perfectly willing to eat eight bananas at once. That ought to bring them all to terms."

Hurok alone could postpone. I gave chase to Los Angeles, arriving at midnight in pouring rain. At Union Station soldiers leaped into all available cabs and drove away. So, after an hour's wait, I walked the two miles to the hotel in a subtropical deluge. The porter did not wish to let me in on the Biltmore rugs, but I insisted, and learning that Hurok was in the bar, I entered and stood in a puddle and dripped at him. He was terribly unnerved, just as I hoped he'd be. My teeth were chattering and I began to shake. He jumped up, pulled my hat off and wiped my head and face with table napkins, tablecloths, fine monogrammed handkerchiefs, clucking like a hen in Russian all the time.

"Calm yourself," he said, patting my wet hand. "Dear madam, dear miss, calm yourself. The choreographer of *Oklahoma!* should not despair. You always have triumphs."

"Mr. Hurok, the last scene is no good. The costumes don't fit. We have no seamstress here. The dancers —"

"You can fix all," said Hurok, giving an order, but he surveyed me carefully. Although I believe he had thought up to that moment hysteria was a Slavic prerogative, there was a glitter in my eye that foretold an unpleasant fifteen minutes and possibly even a decision.

"You will pull it off, won't you?" he suddenly asked quite trustingly, like a child.

I had him. He was listening. And he had the power to save me. "Mr. Hurok, I knew you'd understand. You're a great professional."

Jerry Robbins suddenly stood with us. He was dry. He took in my appearance and, removing my sopping hat and gloves from a chair, sat down. "Been out?" he asked. "Mr. Hurok, can I speak to you about orchestra rehearsals? I've just had Bernstein on the phone and he insists —"

"Certainly, Jerry, certainly. Have something to eat. What can I do for you?"

There was to be no more nonsense about postponement. Sol Hurok had grown so inured to balletic shenanigans that he did not know any longer the difference between real need and opening-night nerves.

He pinched my cheek hard. Hurok pinches the way Napoleon is said to have done, giving a sense of glory together with loss of all physical sensation. The choreographer of *Rodeo* and *Oklahoma!* and *Venus* couldn't fail. He departed next day for New York, prophesying triumph.

He left behind him chaos. The costume situation was desperate because the costumes had been made while the company was on tour and nothing fitted. I think we could not have pulled up a curtain had it not been for Mitchell Leisen, the moving-picture director, who for no reason that I can name, except goodness of heart, turned over his personal atelier on the last Sunday, hired seamstress and sewing machine, and devoted the entire day and night to revamping, fitting and adjusting. Friends like Mary and Dennis Green rallied round (the sight of six-foot four-inch Dennis tirelessly pasting spangles on a lady's fan is something I shall not soon forget). When people speak unkindly of Hollywood and its artists, I ask them to consider Mitch Leisen, a high-priced and busy executive, sitting all Sunday on the floor with basting threads in his mouth so that a bunch of traveling dancers could get on with their job.

Each time we rehearsed we changed the story line. The crucial scene was restaged the day of the opening at three-thirty, not just a regrouping of steps, but an alteration of denouement. The last rehearsal took place at seven-forty in full costume and make-up on the stage with the audience out front. I was working like a somnambulist, Hugh dragging me through.

"Duckie, this is the absolute ruddy limit," said Dolin, trying to warm up his legs and learn the end of the play at the same time. The dancers stood about in their pastoral Watteau suits, looking as though the French Revolution had already got well under way.

I watched the *première* from the back of the auditorium with Jerry Robbins's arms about me, holding me up. The audience yelled with laughter. Charlie Chaplin, in the third row, was reported to be convulsed.

There were seventeen curtain calls. I alone took three bows. But I was dubious. It was left to the aged local manager, L. E. Behymer, to encourage me. "Well, Miss de Mille, you've got another hit. I've wired Hurok. It was pure Gainsborough, pure Gainsborough. And in the orchestra I could hear and remember things I knew before you were born, 'London Bridge Is Falling Down,' and it's a good ballet, nice dancing and fine posing. Enough of each. And natural. Through all the posing there is that fine Shakespearean quality. I've wired Hurok."

Never mind what he wired Hurok; the stage-starved audience in Hollywood had been kind.

I returned to New York ahead of the company and plunged into revision with dancers borrowed from my Broadway shows.

The speed of composition depends on many factors. All the

dances in *Oklahoma!* were composed in two weeks and never altered. Not a step of *Rodeo* was changed. The Waltz and the "T'morra" dances in *Bloomer Girl*, the funeral dance in *Brigadoon*, the "Mamie Is Mimi" jazz solo from *Gentlemen Prefer Blondes*, and the "Whores' Goodbye" from *Paint Your Wagon* were to be devised in single short rehearsals. But it is the preparation for these felicitous sessions that tests the intention of the composer and his skill. Sometimes months and weeks of discarded work lie behind what seems to be spontaneous improvisation.

I got along much more happily in New York. Everything was easier with my own dancers, because they trusted me, and because there was no jealousy or tension in the rehearsal hall.

By and by, Ballet Theatre worked its way back across the continent to us and my brilliant dancers taught them the revisions. Hugh was astonished at the caliber of the Broadway girls. He was particularly taken with Diana Adams; he married her.

I wrote to Walter on the eve of the New York opening:

> The rehearsal this afternoon was ratty, exhausted and bad-tempered. I've never once had the company when they were not tired to the point of lassitude. Dolin, for a variety of complicated reasons, has lost interest in the work and his indifference is now total. [One of the reasons was not so complex: I had cut his part down and built Hugh's up.] He's a wonderful partner but I'm not a classic technician and he's bored with my inefficiency. If you were here I think I'd be having a drink, and then I'd have a hot tub and you'd rub my back and feet and then maybe you'd read me some poetry and put me to bed and hold my hand. This is not an important work, but it had a point, or I believed it had. I wonder how much shines through?
>
> It's the night before and I should say something cosmic, I suppose, but like you on the eve of our marriage, "I've said I love you and that covers everything and I'm dead beat." I can only repeat I wish I'd done better and leave the whole matter right

there. I'll dye my tights now and figure out a way to retrieve
a comedy point someone else should make.

The next afternoon the one-hour dress and orchestra rehearsal
(all the time we were allotted on stage) was a disaster. "This is
dull and much too long," came a ponderous voice from the stalls
where the management was watching me dance. "Cut your number. It's boring." Then they filed across the stage in a great gloom
without speaking to me or wishing me luck. One of them kissed
Lucia and said she was a genius. She needed reaffirmation. She
was carrying fearful financial and managerial burdens. And she
was, besides, damn good in her role. Nobody said anything to me
because I was supposed to know better.

Six-foot-three-inch, red-haired Oliver Smith, hovering around to
supervise the sets for *Fancy Free,* which was to be *premièred* four
nights later, alone of all the group personally wished me luck.
He handed me an orchid. "Wear this for me. The ballet has style
and wit."

I went to the theater that night certain I was facing a fiasco.

Lucia sat at the opposite dressing table, thinking God knows
what. The ballet had brought her small satisfaction. Her part had
been shortened brutally, the bills were high, the turmoil great.
But she is game at the moments of testing and can summon her
forces without rancor. She cheerfully wished me good evening. I
stood, unable to take my coat off. Finally I sat down dully and
stared with distaste in the mirror.

On my dressing table lay a box of violets. There was a card in
Walter's hand. "Why, it's from my husband," I said, astonished.

"From your husband?" said Lucia, turning around, her eyes
wide with wonder. Then they overflowed. "Your husband," she
murmured and bowed her head. Lucia was a widow.

Sono Osato arrived in complete *Venus* make-up so that she could stay to the last possible moment. She had come to make me up. She didn't think I did well enough by myself. "Could you keep your cheeks from shaking until I'm through?" she asked.

"No," I shuddered.

"There," she said, throwing down the pencil. "That's better. Now you look lovely. I, at least, think you do. Try to keep your face still." She kissed me. "Give them hell!" She rushed to her waiting cab.

Well, Dolin didn't drop me as I had feared, but due to the unending changes he had confused the counts — never his specialty — and missed his first entrance. He was brilliant nonetheless. Hugh was excellent, Lucia extremely funny in the remnant of her role, and the company absolutely wonderful. Harold Lang, now a Broadway star, drew screams on two stage crossings.

I got my laughs. I kept going until the end. As I staggered off stage with my arms full of flowers, a phone was put in my hands. It was the whole dancing cast of *Venus* at their stage-door phone.

"Well?" they said. . . .

Leonard Bernstein and Nora Kaye escorted me back to Mother's supper and discussed corrections until dawn, and then between them dragged me across the street to my studio. I opened the door too tired to care longer and stopped dead still. Beside the bed stood a young apple tree in full bloom, its arms spread out over the quilt, the blossoms pallid and clear and unmoving in the breathless room. On my pillow lay the lieutenant's card.

Still shaken from my own *première*, although somewhat reassured by the audience response and John Martin's encouragement, I went four nights later to Jerry's *Fancy Free*, choreographed, composed and designed by three young men under twenty-five. For the past week Jerry had been walking about the Opera House like one risen from the dead. He did not attend my opening through sheer nervous inability to sit still and watch. I understood this perfectly. But now, with my ordeal behind me, I could look on his serenely, and so I went in excitement and curiosity, wishing him luck with a clean heart. No one, outside the six performers and Lucia Chase, had seen one step of the ballet. There had not been a single advance word in the press. A month before, Bernstein had replaced Bruno Walter on a half hour's notice on the podium of the New York Philharmonic when the great conductor was suddenly taken ill, and the following morning the young musician had been accorded front-page acclaim in every metropolitan paper. And just the week before, his Jeremiah symphony had received the Critics' Award for the best American piece of the year. So Bernstein was known. Oliver Smith had designed *Rodeo* but nothing else of note. Jerome Robbins was totally unproven. Except with regard to the score, the audience assembled with nothing beyond normal anticipation. They assembled to witness a *première* without parallel. The great red and gold auditorium rocked with explosions of laughter usually heard only in popular theaters. Halfway through, we realized we were watching a hit put together with the craft of a Broadway success. Not one gesture was wasted or repeated or lost. It was enchantment, thirty minutes of it, from curtain up on Oliver Smith's set of a murky bar on a New York summer evening with the barkeeper asleep beside his radio, to the last tearing exit of the three sailors after a passing skirt.

Although the story is slight — three lonely sailors on shore leave in New York — it proved robust enough to become the plot subsequently of a musical comedy (*On the Town*) and a movie. The comment is truthful and poignant, the humor superb, and the style altogether fresh. It is in the vernacular, the contemporary jazz idiom, but superimposed on the discipline and cleanliness of classic technique, and it has inaugurated a new choreographic style. A generation of dancers has borrowed from it liberally. It was obviously the expression of a new original and first-class talent derivative from no one. Our urban life had found its poets. Three historic careers were guaranteed that night.

While the audience gave itself to applause, I rushed backstage and discovered Robbins sweating and startled, leaning against a wall. His eyes moved about almost in terror. His mouth was open. He kept giggling in short mirthless gasps. I don't think he could have taken in what I said, but I kept talking anyhow. I held him tight. I told him he was safe and need never be frightened again, because with such humor and tenderness, with such a grasp of form, he could do whatever he intended to. I kissed him. He still shook. I bade him remember what I said in times of disappointment and failure. And then he was inundated.

It was the finest first work I have ever seen in the theater.

The next day every management in New York and Hollywood wanted him.

Robbins had been a poor boy, coming from a hard-working and humble household. What his parents thought of their only son taking up dancing as a career I cannot guess — nor what arguments and prayers they had used to turn him toward more profitable and businesslike pursuits during the eight years that preceded that night at the Metropolitan. They held High Holiday afterwards and for days following. The doors of his home stood open and his mother and sister and aunts never left the stove. Everyone in the apartment house came and stayed; everyone in the street went in and out at will. It was too much. Robbins ran away and very quietly in humility and terror in the arms of friends sought privacy and a chance for revaluation and peace.

CHAPTER XI Rhythm in My Blood

THE ending of *Tally-Ho*, or the lack of it, haunted me then as it still does; I intend one day to put it right.

I find it hard to make up my mind about endings; beginnings are, for me, somehow easier come by, as they are for everybody. Fokine, I believe, began frequently at the end and worked backward. Doris Humphrey always composes the end long before she gets to it, about the middle of the work or shortly thereafter. An ending has to be a summing up, the logical total of all that precedes, the final statement; in other words, the point of view. And this was seemingly so difficult for me to achieve I thought it wise to pause at this moment and consider why. And so I set about reviewing my work, its characteristics, patterns and methods, as another choreographer might.

Every worker recognizes his own devices. I can name mine easily. I cannot always control them, but I can name them: I have an affinity for diagonal movements on the stage, with figures entering at one corner and leaving at the opposite, and unless I watch myself, this pattern recurs tiresomely. Why in one corner and out the other? I am not such a fool that I don't recognize the tendency, nor so starved for invention that I cannot think of other geometric directions. But this particular arrangement moves me and releases ideas. Could it be because the first fine choreographic design I ever saw was the *Sylphides* mazurka danced by Lydia Sokolova with the Diaghileff ballet? And when I think of her great leap and the lines of still and waiting women leaning in a kind of architectural wonder for the next cross flight, I understand. That was the path of the first comet and it blazed a mark on my brain. That track spells ecstasy. But behind this reason, there must be more.

I use a still figure, usually female, waiting on the stage, side or center, with modifying groups revolving about, always somehow suggesting the passing of time and life experience. Why does the woman waiting seem to me so emotionally pregnant? One woman standing alone on the stage while people pass until a man enters upstage behind her. Why upstage and why always behind and why the long wait? I cannot be sure, but I remember waiting for years, seemingly, shut away in my mother's garden. My father was absent most of that time and I longed for him to come home to release me from the spell. Possibly the answer is somewhere here.

Why is my use of circles, open or closed, a constant? The avoidance of symmetrical design, with the exception of the circle, my acute difficulty with all symmetrical design, even including square-dance pattern, which one might think was my native language? My repeated use of three female figures, a trilogy which because of plurality takes on symbolic force? And the falling patterns — the falling to earth, the swooning back, the resurrection, the running away always to return to a focal point — seem also to be insistent; and more important, more gross and unbearable, the breaking of all lyric line with a joke, as though I could not trust emotional development but must escape with a wisecrack.

It must be obvious even to people not familiar with dancing that these relations are individual, that they are to some degree sexual, and that they reflect a special personality pattern. I speak of my own work because I have a right to, but these observations apply to everyone. Consider, for instance, some of the recurring idioms of Balanchine: the single male figure embroiled with two to six females, one of whom either blinds or strangles him; the entanglement of either male or female bodies in endless ropes or chains (the lines are seldom made up of both men and women); the repetitive use of the grand reverence, or imperial court bow, as part of the texture of movement; the immaculate discipline of traditional gesture; the metrical, machinelike arrangement of school positions as unadorned as the use of unmodified scales in a musical composition; the insistence on two-dimensional symmetrical design; the superb but classic relation to music. One might build an interesting picture of Balanchine, the man, from these points of style. They are as natural to him as his sniff.

The characteristics of Jerome Robbins are very different. There is above all his free-limbed and virile use of the body, a complete spontaneous release as in sports, an exuberance, a total employment of all energies. Whether the gesture is gay or anguished, all resources are put into play and the strength and vigor of the movement communicates with the gusto of an athlete's. This in part may explain his enormous popularity with all audiences. The gesture is manly, it is keen and bold, and it is complete. Briefly, it is exhilarating, and it brings to the spirit the satisfaction that a yawn or a stretch brings to the muscles. Women choreographers are less released, their movement often blocked or broken, or modified by reticences, not shyness of content but carefulness in physical effort. The difference is equivalent to that between a man and a woman throwing or jumping. Her gesture may be exact and serviceable; his will be total. Robbins enhances this quality by quoting literally from acrobatics and stunts.

His skill in rhythmic invention is the greatest in the business, according to Trude Rittmann, who has worked with all of us. Robbins is besot by rhythm, visual and bodily rhythms as well as auditory, and when he gets hold of a gesture he continues inventing out of the core of the matter until he has built an entire design and must wait for the composer to catch up. His rhythms will then work in counterpoint to the musical pattern. It is thought that if he had turned his attention to music, he might have been a first-class composer. Whereas Balanchine's rhythmic sense is spatial and linked to the music, Robbins's is independent. I, on the other hand, am totally derivative and lean and grow on melody. I cannot move without melody. May there not here be revealed a subtle sexual distinction? The men work free and on their own; the woman must wait for the lead.

But Robbins's most easily recognized trait is, praise heaven, his humor. In its grossest aspects, it takes the form of straight gags — very good ones, but bald and outrageous. In its more sophisticated manifestations, he introduces surprising and impertinent conclusions into his pattern, deliberately leading one on to expect a certain resolution and then insolently offering another, untraditional and slightly rude, though always logical because he is never foolish. He jokes with rhythms, with space, with relations of bodies, with light, with silence, with sound. These are all elements of style.

The grosser emotional fixtures of theme and content are plainly manifest — fixtures such as, in the case of Robbins, a preoccupation with childhood and games, with the bewilderment of growing up, with the anguish of choice. The unexpected, the joke, in this field seems to turn back on the choreographer and sit hard; each love story splits into three or more people; each romance spells destruction or transcience; all repeats over and over. There is no resolution. In short, life turns out not to be a joke.

For my part, I seem to be obsessed by an almost Henry Jamesian inability for hero and heroine to come together happily, and by that other bedeviling theme, the woman as hunter. These are easily read. But the impregnation of abstract pattern with personality adjustments is, I find, far more subtle and more interesting. A great deal has been written about the kinesthetic transference between audience and dancer in the actual muscular technique; the field of spatial aesthetics remains, however, almost unexplored.

We know much about emotional symbols. They have a history and a science, iconography. Those used by the medieval and Renaissance painters were understood by the scholars and artists of the time — but, more wonderful, they mean to us today spontaneously just what they meant then; they seem to be permanent. We dream, Jung tells us, in the terms and symbols of classic mythology. Moreover, primitives shut away from classic learning dream in the same terms. Is it not also likely, then, that certain space relations, rhythms and stresses have psychological significance, that some of these patterns are universal and the key to emotional response, that their deviations and modifications can be meaningful to the artist in terms of his own life experience and that these overtones are grasped by the spectator without conscious analysis?

Doctors are aware of this and utilize the knowledge in diagnosis. The significance of children's manipulation of space in writing and drawing is carefully studied, and the insane are observed for their relation to and use of walls, floor, doorways, heights, and so forth. Obviously these matters are basic to our well-being as land and air animals. And as plants will turn to sunlight or rocks or moisture according to their nature, so we bend toward or escape from spatial arrangements according to our emotional needs. In the diseased mind, the reactions are overwhelmingly overt. But look around any restaurant and see how few sane people will sit at a center table unless the sides are filled up. Yet formerly the king always dined dead center and many times in public.

The individual as a personality, then, has his own code in space and rhythm. It is evolved from his life history and from his race memory or, as Jung calls it, the collective unconscious. It is just the manipulation of these suggestions through time-space that is the material of choreography.

Take, for example, a simple daily gesture like walking forward and shaking hands. There are in this, first, the use of a separate limb common to most vertebrates, the upright position of the spine and head characteristic of man, the instinctively recognized expression of friendliness shared by all species as opposed to the instinctive expressions of fear and distrust. With animals, when approaching a friend, the hair lies flat, the ears are relaxed though alert, and all enlargements and ferocious distentions subside; breathing is normal. So with man. Heart, pulse and lungs are easy, the eyes alert but neither distended to see danger nor contracted to pinpoint a target; the mouth is closed or smiling because no unusual demands will be made on hearing (to hear extraordinarily in times of acute danger, the mouth is opened and breathing suspends). And since no unusual effort will be necessary, the muscles neither brace nor tremble. The sum total of all this will be spelled out in the rhythm and position of the reaching hand.

But let there occur the slightest rebuff and see now what happens; hackles rise, hair bristles, lips curl to bare incisors, hearts pound, lungs fill, and on the instant all muscles prepare for attack. In ordinary intercourse, this naturally is not visible on full scale. But it needs only the slight widening of the pupil or nostril, the barest flicker of finger tip, to give the signal; the enemy has been recognized and addressed. Further subtle and meaningful modifications take over when the passage alters by the tension of a specific situation — when, for instance, someone who is often frightened of encounter meets a friend, or one who is never frightened meets someone not to be trusted, or two trusting friends meet under dreadful conditions, and so ad infinitum. Within each of these circumstances the body becomes a totally different chemical organization and yet retains the stamp of its own life habits.*

It is the actor's art to mimic exactly with a full awareness of all the overtones and significances. The dancer, on the other hand, explodes the gesture to its components and reassembles them into a symbol that has connotations of what lies around and behind the fact, while the implications of rhythm and spatial design add further comment. Of course the choreographer is no more troubled by all this than is the businessman by the enormous anthropological heritage he puts into play every time he casually tips his hat.

Coleridge says of portraiture: "A good artist must imitate that which is within the thing, that which is active through form and figure, and discourses to us by symbols . . . the universal in the individual or the individuality itself — the glance and the exponent of the indwelling power. . . . Hence a good portrait is the abstract of the personal; it is not the likeness for actual comparison, but for recollection." Every gesture is a portrait. Behind it lie the histories of the race and the individual as well as the comment of the artist.

When I, as an artist, am moved, I must respond in my own instinctive way; and because I am a choreographer, I respond through my instinctive gestures. I may come into the pattern with conviction and the excitement of fresh experience, but this must also reflect a personality habit. It cannot be otherwise. Somehow, as in the grooves in a gramophone record, the cutting edge of my emotion follows a track played deep into the subconscious.

There is a further personal identification in choreography because most choreographers compose on their own bodies. Certain recurring steps can be explained simply by the fact that the choreogra-

* A primary school teacher told me that she knew that children were beginning to trust her when they touched her with the palms of their hands; at first they only poked. It is only at moments of intimacy, possession or pity that an adult will touch with his palms.

pher performs these steps well and has a tendency to use them when demonstrating. Martha Graham has a kick and a particular skip that have stood her in good stead for twenty years. The explanation is simply that her left leg kicks straight up in a split, 180 degrees — a very spectacular feat. The right does not; hence the single-legged pattern. (It has been very interesting to observe over the years that Graham pupils who began by imitating her mannerisms have gradually eliminated the personal idiosyncrasies and maintained the great style unblemished. In *Diversion of Angels* and *Canticle for Innocent Comedians,* Graham's gesture has been purified of all subjective tricks and stands in the keeping of her disciples as abstract as the ballet code. It is overwhelmingly beautiful.) I am right-legged and right-footed, and most of the sustaining and balancing work in my choreography is done on the left leg; many of my dancers have complained bitterly. A dancer with short legs jumps in one manner, whereas a dancer with longer ones performs the same jump in quite another. So with composing. And identical pattern problems take on the modification of the composer's physique as well as his character adjustment, for it is always the choreographer who has to start the moving, and naturally he does it his way. If there were no instrument on which a song writer could work except his own voice, unquestionably his vocal restrictions would shape the melodic line.

The choreographer is also influenced by his performers. If I were to work, let us say, with a soloist whose arms and back were the strongest in the dance world and whose phrasing of legato lifts the most beautiful, but whose footwork, on the other hand, and allegro were weaker, quite obviously my composing style would adjust to his needs. Were I to compose with a man of enormous elevation and brilliant *batterie* but less dramatic force, my approach would then be necessarily different. And it must be noted that one works with the dancers at hand. One cannot summon from outer space a dream body capable of anything — or even exactly what one wishes. In the matter of one's own body one has obviously even less choice and must make do.

Furthermore, all artists, including choreographers, are influenced by their peers as by their antecedents. This is the way of organic development. Late Beethoven and early Schubert, for instance, are almost indistinguishable; while Brahms took certain themes, note for note, from Beethoven; and Shakespeare stole nearly all his plots — all the good ones certainly. Had they worked as contemporaries in the same studio, as do choreographers, with the same performers, the tie would have been closer yet. Furthermore, most choreographers, like the apprentice painters of the Renaissance, get their initial experience studying under the personal influence of a master, taking part in the actual creation of his works, and spending years — the formative years — under constant artistic domination. The wonder is that any individual expression develops at all.

But it does develop, and with it the deviations and mannerisms we call personal style. Usually the artist is unaware of the process, as he is unaware of his other spontaneous modes of expression. Few willingly believe the insistent repetition, the catch phrases, the special idioms we use in conversation. Who among us has recognized a first recording of his own voice? We prefer to think of ourselves in terms of universals shared by all mankind — by all the ways, in short, in which we resemble or possibly surpass others. Our neighbors, on the contrary, distinguish us by our oddities and crotchets, and it is just for this reason that a cartoon when effective strikes everyone but the subject as revealing.

If idiosyncrasies of expression constitute a key to others' understanding, they serve the artist in much the same way, as a means of self-revelation and a technique for reaching his emotional reservoir. They determine his work habits and of course the character of his expression. But whereas each worker will develop his own combination, his own formula, so to speak, he will have virtually nothing to do with its choosing and can use his critical faculties only to shape and correct. The emotional key, the kindling spark, lies beyond the reach of his mind deep in instinct. When we find these habitual patterns pleasing, we say the artist has developed style; when they appeal to our taste less, we say that he is repeating himself.

But the great repeated constantly. How do we, for instance, recognize Bach in any two measures of his music? Obviously because it sounds precisely like him and no one else. It is a question, I believe, of what is basically present and not how often the devices and tricks are employed. Indeed, if variety were all, one could compose with a slide rule. There is great style and lesser style, and style altogether to be condemned; but none of it has to do either with repetition or derivation.

It is difficult for the individual to evaluate his own strengths and characteristics, and the theater is strewn with lives ruined by unwarranted determinations to sing, or write, or act. No guarantee goes with desire, and there is unhappily just enough genuine talent neglected to confuse the issue. Nevertheless, granting a modicum of true ability, one must not be afraid to fail now and then. It all depends on the reason why.

One may, of course, fail because one has chosen the wrong kind of work.

One may fail because one has no discipline either in work or the handling of emotional problems.

One may fail because one wishes to fail — a hard tendency to detect, but a history of avoidable catastrophe indicates a need for medical help.

One may fail temporarily because of grief, harassment, or exhaustion and, in the theater, from lack of time.

And then one may fail in trying new and unknown ways of expression. A creative life without failure is unthinkable. All physical growth and emotional change involve discomfort and a good bit of highly unattractive transition. Consider any adolescent, for example, taken at face value and with no thought of what is to come.

This fear of defeat haunts the creative worker uncomfortably, and there are fat days when all of us long to be left alone. But the first moment we permit ourselves to feel safe, the first moment we save ourselves from exposure, we are in danger of retreating from the outposts. We can be quite sure that this particular job need not be done, for, in all probability, it will have been done before.

"One must risk one's career every six months," says Elia Kazan, "in order to stay alive and effective in one's work."

But although work will never be safe, it may happily sometimes be easy and quick. Very frequently the best work is the easiest. But the rhapsodic release comes only infrequently and the professional must learn to compose at will — to employ aesthetic aphrodisiacs. For a young artist, this is perhaps the hardest task. Each person must learn his own path through the labyrinth of escape and idleness. Anne Lindbergh speaks of a technique of "acquiring grace": "Most people are aware of periods in their lives when they seem to be 'in grace' and other periods when they feel 'out of grace.' . . . In the first happy condition, one seems to carry all one's tasks before one lightly, as if borne along on a great tide; and in the opposite state one can hardly tie a shoe-string. It is true that a large part of life consists of tying the shoe-string, whether one is in grace or not."

To translate this into terms of the working artist, the state of

"grace," or inspiration, occurs when an idea is both clearly perceived and deeply felt, when circumstances do not block realization, and when technique waits ready and almost unconsciously
available. The last is the controllable factor, a technique ready and
available at the needed moment. Behind this lies a life's ordering.

For three weeks preceding any big job Jerome Robbins works
himself into a lather of excitement on studies, all of which, he
explains, may very well be discarded once the dancers are assembled, but without which he cannot begin. These preliminary exercises furnish him with momentum and conviction. They are a
warming-up process. Hanya Holm, on the other hand, never pre-
pares this way. She studies and thinks, but when she walks into
the studio, no plan has been determined on. It is between her and
the dancers and God, she says. But God, I have found, cannot
be held to a schedule, and any kind of composition that involves
a finishing time — and this is the essence of all theater — makes
definite demands on inspiration. Inspiration has to be on tap as
long as the components of design are living bodies paid by the
hour.

But we may be grateful that very seldom are circumstances
propitious and that the work fights through hard and slow. The
moment one knows how, one begins to die a little. Living is a
form of not being sure, of not knowing what next or how. And
the artist before all others never entirely knows. He guesses. And
he may be wrong. But then how does one know whom to befriend
or, for that matter, to marry? One can't go through life on hands
and knees. One leaps in the dark. For this reason creative technique reduces itself basically to a recognition and befriending of
one's self. "Who am I?" the artist asks, and he devotes his entire
career to answering.

There is one clue: what moves him is his. What amuses or
frightens or pleases him becomes by virtue of his emotional par-

ticipation a part of his personality and history; conversely what neither moves nor involves him, what brings him no joy, can be reckoned as spurious. An artist begins to go wrong exactly at the point where he begins to pretend. But it is difficult sometimes to accept the truth. He has to learn who he in fact is, not who he would like to be, nor even who it would be expedient or profitable to be.

He may think he cannot afford this risk, but it is equally evident he cannot afford hackneyed success. For this is no success. And everyone instantly recognizes what has happened. The breath of life has gone; the workshop has become a morgue.

The real failing, the killing off, is not in taking risks but in choosing some work beneath his capacities and in doing it in a slick and routine fashion purely for recompense. This hurts the whole field of work, dirties and dulls down the audience, and destroys the individual. In the disreputable suburbs of each art form flourish great fortunes made just this way. I do not for one moment wish to imply that first-class work does not also bring in money. God is good, and it frequently does. But let us be sure in our hearts, no first-class job was ever achieved without a good deal in view besides the check.

The folks who think only of money may cynically pretend they do not care, but their stomach ulcers and their alcoholism prove they do most dreadfully. It is not so much a matter of what work is done but how it is done. It is vital to everyone to know that work is necessary and done to the best of ability whether making soap operas or washing floors, and it is only when the dust is swept under the rug that the process of disintegration sets in.

Far better than succeeding regularly is a good tough falling-short of a challenge. All work — one's own and everyone else's — benefits from this effort, successful or not, just as all science benefits from each difficult experiment — even the ones that seem not directly to bring results.

Louis Horst said recently at a testimonial banquet tendered him by the dancers of New York that he wished to thank all the dedicated and devoted artists with whom he had had the privilege of achievement; and he wished also to thank those who had tried and failed, because without them, the great could not have gone so far.

It is not for the individual to demand a certificate of quality before starting. He cannot and he may not. He has to work on faith. And he must listen only to his conscience, which will be stern enough in truth. He must listen to no other voices. For to listen is to be lost — to listen to critic, or friend, or business interest. He can pray only that his tastes and passions will be common to many. But he must suit himself first, himself before everyone else. He must, in other words, marry the girl of his heart despite the family or he will bed down for life with a wench not of his choosing.

I know now how the *Frail Quarry* should end, as I know that this should be its rightful title, but it has taken a deal of living and shaking down to come to terms with my instincts. The ballet was essentially a wry piece and not at all the romantic comedy I had hoped. It had, however, an honorable enough life; poor maimed pretty little thing, it had six years of performing. But today it lies in limbo waiting for a great comedian and waiting for the finish that burns in my brain.

CHAPTER XII *Consolations*

JUNE 7, 1944, was the day the American Expeditionary Forces crossed the Channel and invaded the northern coast of Europe.

During the spring we had felt the excitement quicken. The month of May, we fancied, would be the mighty one. Then we looked toward June.

Suddenly there was a cessation of mail. Not one letter, not one V-envelope got through. The radio broadcasters marked time and were palpably noncommittal. Only Russia kept reporting inhabited places, retaken or lost. But at dawn on Wednesday, the seventh, the radio began to tell. The Channel had been crossed; the invasion was begun. Newscasters stayed at their microphones all day. Households were reluctant to move from the radio even to get a cup of coffee. All over the United States the phones started ringing, the women asking, "Where's yours? When did you last hear?"

Church doors stood wide open for us to come and go and come again. All big shops closed. There were block-long queues at the blood banks. We regarded each other in a kind of wonder. Friends met and touched without speaking; indeed, that day there were no strangers. There were no strangers anywhere in the world that day. There were, it seemed, not even enemies. Each individual walked through fire according to his own circumstances and acknowledged formally fellow suffering. One could not hate or rage. One went to one's knees and reached for one's neighbor's hand; one would have reached for one's foe's. Over a stretch of beach shorter than Malibu, the play beach Proust had written about, the skies rang and flesh and will forced decision. We waited and opened our mouths breathlessly.

Those days were without match. Everything seemed bigger, louder, deeper, more resonant. Every trivial action, such as eating breakfast or riding on the subway, seemed somehow connected with Normandy. We lived from moment to moment without plan.

There was no news to write. There would never be any news here again. All the news had gone away.

Letters came through a week later. And the casualty lists.

But work had to go on — and living of sorts. I was offered a show about the Civil War by Harold Arlen and E. Y. Harburg and I thought I saw an opportunity to do a ballet which would embody the almost universal feeling of sacrifice of those at home. The score contained one rhapsodic outburst, a colloquial Hymn to Freedom, "The Eagle and Me," and eight or ten of the loveliest songs I'd ever heard. When Arlen first sang "Eagle" for me, I found I could not speak for some seconds. (It is a remarkable song and he is a movingly fine singer.) I quickly agreed to do the show, thankful that I would have a chance at last to put on the stage what was in my heart. But would they accept a serious ballet about women's emotions in war? I asked. About why people were willing to go out and die? About why we were willing to let them? Yes, yes, they said. Of course they would. They hoped this would be a show with significance, seriousness and poignancy. Broadway and Hollywood writers are very reluctant to use such words. They are easily embarrassed by the thought that they might be trying to do anything but make millions of dollars. However, in spite of their indirect and diffident manner, I gathered that, in this group, the ideas of freedom, patriotism and brotherhood might be considered and even mentioned, albeit, indirectly. I signed for *Bloomer Girl.*

So, delighted and enthusiastic, I began rehearsals, working under what I suppose could be called inspiration. From the first rehearsal I seemed to be acting under a compulsion beyond myself. I commenced with a few tentative notions and a scrawled diagram, and of their own accord the dance sections rushed together. It was as though I saw a design blueprinted in the air over the dancers' heads and as fast as I could speak I pushed them around, not just in pantomime, which is always easy for me, but in formal design, which is not, and in two hours I had blocked out a double square set of intricacy and power. The dancers, fired by my frenzy, began to feel they were engaged in something important. In four days the ballet was roughed through to completion. In four days a strange and unassimilated company had become a unit and had completed a twelve-minute work.

I was helped in this rapid accomplishment by the high quality of my soloists. Into my auditions had walked James Mitchell, a youth from California, without apparent disability, although the back which kept him out of the Army proved a problem. He had strengthened himself for his craft by lifting and tossing full crates of grapes and oranges on his father's fruit ranch. I gave him a small Latvian brunette with whom he had no trouble at all. He has had a number of brunettes to throw about since, including Nora Kaye, Alicia Alonso and Gemze de Lappe, and done very well with all. The grape and orange conditioning gave him probably the strongest arms in the business, and the adagio style developed by him and his partners has become since a valued addition to ballet vocabulary. He had not then what he has since acquired, strong ballet technique, having performed exclusively in Lester Horton's Modern Group. He proved a remarkable actor, and was also modest, observant and astonished at finding himself in a Broadway show. In three days

I entrusted the captainship of the troupe to him; he was more surprised than ever.

His partner was Lidija Franklin, whom, as Lidija Kocers, I had known in the Ballets Jooss — her nobility of manner and of deportment, her phrasing were the kind only great stars develop. She had also a gift for tender pantomime.

Trude Rittmann was, of course, at the keyboard.

Five days after commencing, I showed the ballet to the bosses with self-satisfaction and the complete pride and belief of the whole group. I have never felt so smug in my life, delighted to find such tragic strengths within me. Hitherto I had been only wistful or comic.

At the end of the showing there was not a sound. The silence did not, however, betoken awe. The men were all just as disappointed as they could possibly be. Harburg found voice first and, stepping over the bodies of three prone, sweating girls, addressed me. "No. No. No. This is all wrong. Where is the wit? Where is the humor?" I was naturally taken aback and a little short in my answers.

"Humor? In war?"

"But this is tragic. Where is the courage? This isn't real de Mille. This isn't what we bought."

"How the hell do you know what real de Mille is? I think this is the realest thing I ever did. It is not *Oklahoma!* if that is what you mean. If you wished to buy *Oklahoma!* you're a little late."

The dancers, hollow-eyed, sat nursing their pulsing feet, watching with fixed and silent attention to see if I were going to lose control over my work. Everyone began making suggestions about women waiting for their husbands, buoyant and humorous. Arlen suggested that we end with a peace celebration and all the boys coming home alive. Everyone alive. There should be no worrying or depressing intimations. But he did like the ballet. Some others hoped to drop the whole idea. I finally found voice. "I took this show in order to do a ballet about women in war — and we don't find the war funny. A frivolous ending would not be true to what everyone in the whole world is feeling."

The next day I invited a group of my friends, including Eugene Berman, to see the ballet behind locked doors. They confirmed my opinion that it was the best thing I had ever done in my life. I then threw it away.

In another week I'd whipped up a happy ending in which everyone returned from war unscathed and there was great rejoicing. All the company seemed delighted. All but the dancers and Trude and me. "Which version do you like best?" I asked them.

"Are you kidding?" they answered morosely.

Neither they nor I could believe that we would not be permitted to do something meaningful even if sad — especially in these times. Everyone was feeling too deeply. Belittling seemed like blasphemy.

Arlen walked the floor with me, trying to help.

"Is he all right?" the dancers queried as they eyed me in conference with one of the bosses. "Is he on our side? Or is he on theirs?"

Obviously, we must start afresh. I sent the company home. I sat alone in the rehearsal hall with Trude and hit my fists on my head. "Never mind," said Trude. "We have dinner and then we go back to work and stay six hours if you want. All night. Quietly. Alone." We went back. Not an idea presented itself. Not a gesture. It is one matter to think up a new variation when you find you have not said what you intended. It is another to have said exactly what you intended and then, under duress, try to force a fresh version.

I thought of Walter. I wondered if he'd changed. If he would only walk into the room right now and put his arms around me. If I could look in his face again right now. Tonight. This night, in this dirty studio. In all this mess. I found I was weeping very hard.

I put out my hand to him. Trude suddenly cried, "Aggie, what are you doing? Do that again. Get Jim. This is it." I rushed to the phone.

"What are you doing?" I asked Jim.

"My laundry," he replied simply.

"Can you come here? Hurry!"

So it was done between us. And Trude snapped the lid of the piano and said, "Now bed." It was midnight. Jim was again astonished. "How is this possible? After you'd absolutely given up?"

Next day we showed the company and those wonderful sore-boned people took fire all over.

But the bosses had another opinion. "Oh, my God," wailed Harburg. "Can't we get rid of this somber, dreadful ballet?" John C. Wilson was extremely nervous and brittle. He found himself in an awkward position. The kindest and most sympathetic of producers, he was reluctant to break my heart, but on the other hand, he felt a genuine repugnance toward including anything dreary that might cut down attendance. The wives and the lawyers and the backers were plainly frantic.

"Look," said Harburg. "Women will faint. They'll weep. They'll leave the theater."

"You don't know women," I countered. "They'd rather have their grief talked about and shared than made light of."

"Well, it doesn't go in. Not this version. That's final."

There were other dances in the show and they were all very funny and were received with shouts of laughter. (Joan McCracken had the men gasping and shrieking in "T'morra" and "When Grandma Was a Lady," and nothing more delightful and romantically elegant had been seen than the Waltz with which Jim Mitchell and Lidija Franklin closed the first act.) So the staff knew that my lack of humor in the war ballet was deliberate and stubborn. They kept clamoring for "the exultant side of war." The rehearsals had become known around town as "Three Versions and a Devil." By and by, when one has worked under these tensions fourteen hours a day for seven weeks, all sense of proportion or good humor or friendliness disappears. One gets just hellbent. I got glassy-eyed, incapable of talk with outsiders and prone to falling asleep during dinner. My skin itched from inflamed nerve ends as though ants were walking all over my body, and I got fat.

It was possible during these years for some women to work among older men, serious and concerned with the great conflicts, men of dedication and principle, and it must have been comforting for them. My sister Margaret was working among such in the O.P.A. It was stimulating to her, for she felt she was doing something helpful, although she described her office as "a warren full of insane rabbits" where she battled night and day to keep the manufacturers of ladies' handbag clasps and fur linings from wrecking the country's economy. "But don't get me wrong," they always said to her when asking for a release of restrictions, "I've got one son in the Pacific and another in Italy. I'm for the war effort."

"So am I," said Margaret, "and the answer is therefore 'No' to all requests."

"Then I can't go on making handbags of this quality."

"So? In view of the world situation?"

At night as I sat writing, as I sat planning the next day's dance steps, I asked myself if I were doing anything beyond insisting on quality handbag clasps? Maybe not. But it was what I could do. "One must proceed," Martha had said, "as though one were going to live."

Where I worked the bickerings and rivalries dragged at one's spirit and the odor of futility rose like miasma, all day, every day. I justified my presence there by one hope, that I could do something good, something better than I ever had done before. That the situation, that the tensions of the time would use me, would pull something out of me beyond my talents or understanding. And I came to believe this dance might have the reason and the passion *Tally-Ho* lacked. I came to believe this dance might have value.

Whenever one of the bosses was in the theater, I showed the version they liked, but at home, at night, I tried to rework the whole matter on paper. And in the mornings, with dancers posted at the doors to give warning, I secretly rehearsed a fourth version. I had composed four ballets in four weeks. I don't know how the dancers stood it. But by this time they were as mad and as determined as I was. Every time I gave way on a point they despised me. Every time I stood fast, their approbation shone in their eyes and they silently changed shirts and shoes and waited at attention for the next set of orders.

Harold Arlen had been let into the secret. "I hope to God it stops the show opening night and shuts their clamoring mouths. It's close to being great. Let's fix what's wrong."

There were by now three directors and six writers all demanding authority and assuming no effective responsibility. The long rehearsals were conducted without rules of order, protocol, or artistic plan. Vilification was rampant, as the wrangling staff raced in full cry up and down the aisles. "I'm going to have your paranoids removed," yelled one author to another at the close of a gala rehearsal. "Homo, Sweet Homo," sang someone under his alcoholic breath.

The night before we left, there was a council of war to which I was not invited. There must be some way, they thought, of stopping a dance director from doing what they had not hired her to do. There were union sanctions, but they were loath to invoke them. Instead, they directed Mainbocher to reason with me. Mr. Mainbocher was connected in no way with the production, but they knew I would listen to his persuasions with respect. And listen to him I did for two hours on the phone just before entraining for Philadelphia. He concluded by reminding me of what I had to gain financially by the show's success. He begged me seriously to consider my own business interests and throw away the ballet.

In Philadelphia that night, after rehearsal, at two in the morning, Wilson let me have it straight. But, as always, he was kind. He put a glass of the very best Scotch in my hands first. "Out?" I asked meekly.

"Yes, darling, it's beautiful, but it's going to ruin our show. The whole War Ballet in its entirety has to be deleted."

"Well, then," I said, "you've got to have something in that spot on Monday. Let it open and then cut it, but don't make me do anything cheap in its place."

He promised not to. He even gave me the ballet material for my own property to perform elsewhere later. He promised to replace it with a singing chorus for which I would not be responsible.

I did not tell the dancers. I wanted them to have their single performance with joy and hope. I told Jim. "You mean," he gasped, "they're just throwing it out without a fair showing? All that work? That moving, fine work? Why, it's like the death of a child! It's like killing something."

I told Trude. I suggested that it would really be becoming of me to give way. They were all men of established achievement. Some of them were extraordinary talents. Maybe I was wrong. Maybe my stubbornness was just conceit. She looked at me quietly; and then something monumental happened. Trude gave battle. She pointed out that I was being paid a very large sum of money for my opinion, not for theirs, that it was my instinct as an artist they'd contracted for and nothing less. "Do you believe in this work?" she asked.

"With all my heart."

"Well, then, stand by it. Besides, tonight in the theater I had a feeling about it."

At the opening performance we did the secret, or fourth, version. That performance, which was to be the only performance, was superbly lit by Ayers and most wonderfully costumed by Miles White. "But why," said the staff in incredulity, "did no one tell us it would look like this? It always seemed so dreary in practice clothes!"

White-faced, the dancers performed with a tension that tightened the exchange between stage and audience to the point of agony. Their gestures that night were absolute, their faces like lamps, and in the hush when Lidija Franklin faced Mitchell, looked into her returned soldier's eyes and then covered her own because of what she saw, no one breathed. In the stillness around me several women bowed their heads.

I stood at the back holding Trude's hand. At the end, there was no sound, but as Mitchell and Franklin returned for the hallelujah parade, there was cheering.

As the people filed out past me, one woman, recognizing me, stood for a moment with her eyes covered and then quietly handed me her son's Navy wings.

At the party afterwards, Yipper Harburg put his arms around me. "Goddamit! I've begun to like the dreary thing. To think that a lousy bit of movement can make people weep, and me among them! A lousy bit of movement!"

Terry Helburn grabbed my hand. "It's been all around New York that you were ruining the show by insisting on the impossible, putting a tragic ballet so late in the evening, close to the end of Act II." Terry grinned with demure maliciousness. "And it is impossible, but you've done it. The argument's over."

Wilson said, "Darling, it gives me great pleasure to state we were quite, quite wrong."

"Hurrah!" said Arlen, and kissed me.

Jim Mitchell and Lidija Franklin said very little. "We knew," they said as they went home quietly to start on their laundries.

And Trude said, "You see, dearest, if you stand fast, if you have the courage —" and then she broke into a giggle. "Of course it's just as well to be right. There's always that —"

In spite of Walter's repeated admonitions that I must not on any account attempt to follow him, that I must not go overseas, that he had to know I was at home safe, I kept plaguing the U.S.O. offices with requests to use what skills I had and let me go to Europe. Two days with him would be well worth a six-month battlefront tour, but this was not to be easily arranged. A meeting between us could, of course, not be guaranteed. The chance that I could find him in Europe was one in five thousand. But, I figured, with one less ocean between us, I could have at least that chance. In any case, I would be able to share a little of what he was living through.

Richard Pleasant, who had projected and organized Ballet Theatre, was now an artillery major and in charge of U.S.O. troupes leaving New York. I poured out my heart to him repeatedly and he promised to do what he could, explaining, however, that there could be no guarantee of Europe. I might very well be sent to the South Pacific. In fact, if it became known I had a husband in the Western war theater, it was certain I would be detailed to the other ends of the earth. Had we not married, I could have reached him with far greater ease. And every month Walter wrote, saying, "Stop trying. Quiet down. I won't have it."

In January 1945 a moving-picture director came to call on me. His name was Wesley Ruggles and he had made his fortune with some of the better-known Mae West pictures. He was going to London and, in spite of bombs, fire and rationing, was intent on making a musical movie in the most lavish Hollywood style. "There is no reason why the British cannot be taught how to make big Hollywood-type spectacles — and there must be pretty girls over there somewhere. I'm going back to have another look." He wanted me to help.

I'd accepted, of course, before he finished the first sentence. I accepted without reading the script or checking on his reputation, his style, or his habits of working. We parted most cordially. He flew back, promising to obtain a labor permit, an entry visa, a Bank of England currency release, a tax waiver, passage, and my salary deposited in dollars in an American bank, a tremendous list of undertakings.

Arthur Lyons, my Hollywood agent, had fits. He was on the transcontinental phone within twelve hours. He told me it was sure to be a bad picture, that Ruggles had a name for being difficult, that I'd damage my reputation and let myself in for more heartbreak than I could imagine. I replied simply that any wife in America would submit to a public hanging to get the chance I was about to have. He thereupon stated that he had private information that the war was about to end; he declined to name his sources. But the Irish LaMarr, who had been trying to keep up my courage during this period, had walked the streets and sat in endless restaurants talking cheer, and offering drinks, understood better. "It may not do you much good professionally. But you've got to go. I'll explain to the Coast." So I cabled Ruggles acceptance and reassurance. Thereupon Walter began writing that he had special particular reasons for wishing me not to come. He was referring to the buzz bombs, of course, about which he'd heard prophetic warnings, but he could not be explicit. I took a dim view of his caution, jumping to the conclusion that his ardor might be cooling off. I cabled Ruggles to persist. January turned into February, and February into March.

Meantime, I organized troupes for Army camps, hospitals and staging areas. That winter of 1944 was the first in which I had three musicals playing at once — *Oklahoma!, One Touch of Venus* and *Bloomer Girl* — and these furnished a nice choice of songs and dances with which to make up little revue programs. We had the full complement of girl singers and dancers from *Oklahoma!* and the dancers from *Venus* and we did the hit numbers from both shows in costume. I supplemented them with comedy scenes from my old concert repertoire which I taught my best soloists (Lord — what a cast that was! Allyn McLerie, Sono Osato, Diana Adams, Bambi Linn and Janet Reed) and just for the hell of it, I added a couple of Bach and Mozart pieces which I did myself. Somebody besides me might be pleased, I figured, and the rest could endure them; they lasted only two minutes each. Once *Oklahoma!* in its entirety was performed at Camp Kilmer, and later, *Bloomer Girl.* On another occasion Ballet Theatre sent all its stars. They presented various famous *pas de deux* and, over-looking Army injunction against provocative sex, Antony Tudor's *Judgment of Paris,* to the astonishment of all.

The men responded strangely, particularly at the embarkation centers. It was a response not always expected or previously experienced, sometimes manic, sometimes morose, sometimes impertinent and smarty. ("That's rotten!" yelled a boy after my Bach Gigue with such promptness that I burst out laughing and the whole audience yelled.) But the reaction was neither true nor connected with us. They were all emotionally suspended as though with shock. Many of the men had never seen live performers before and therefore had not learned to clap as a mark of pleasure. Most of them had never seen dancing beyond a tap time-step. I wrote my mother after one performance at Camp Shanks, "They laugh and holler at all sad, tender, quiet or romantic moments. They don't even see the comedy. They call out at anything unfamiliar quite as though we weren't alive and able to hear, and sit dead-silent through what we think is fun, the Post-Card girls in *Oklahoma!*, for instance. However, they sat last night without moving or leaving, which stupefied their officers, and toward the end they were laughing where we intended them to. The officers rushed backstage to ask for a repeat as soon as possible." Usually at the end of the evening we had won them over. We were thanked for this. One officer said to me, "U.S.O. sends them hotcha numbers and sometimes a good comic, but beauty has simply been withdrawn from their lives."

The men in the hospitals were, of course, quite unpredictable, particularly the psychoneurotics. The girls had necessarily to show some leg, but we were forbidden to do anything that suggested sex, a drastic restriction. Here Bach, always so prophylactic, came in handy. But it was extraordinary to see the men seated in patient rows an hour before performance began. In the hospitals the mobile patients were rolled down the aisles almost two hours early and watched us get ready with unflagging curiosity.

When not dancing, Sono used to go sit among the boys. "Aren't they pretty?" she said of the *Oklahoma!* girls as they stood singing in their starched dresses and ribboned hats. "They sure are, ma'am," one replied. "I wish the guys in the wards could see them." So we went into the wards and improvised and invented whatever we could between the beds, while a tiny minipiano was pushed around for us. It wasn't very good dancing, but the men sitting up in their harnesses and pulleys didn't seem to mind this. The girls were charming and friendly and they stayed singing and joking until the very last moment before being loaded into the Army buses to return to their evening performances. On Sundays, when there were no theater shows, we could perform all day and stay until late at night. The dancing boys worked hard doing anything they could, packing and hauling costumes, chauffeuring and helping as messengers. Boys like Peter Birch were putting in four to five hours every day in hospital duty, as assistant nurses or stretcher bearers. There were several in the troupes fretting bitterly at the disappointment of an Army rejection and they clamored for any chance of helping. Later at night I stood in the theater basements sorting out my own costumes from the *Oklahoma!* and *Venus* outfits. We had to have union wardrobe women to care for the Broadway properties, all paid full-scale wages by individuals and the theater managements. The shopping, hauling, packing and unpacking and refurbishing were done by dancers eagerly and freely.

We usually had a beer party afterwards at the club base, and made G.I. friends to write to. I gave Walter's serial number to everyone just in case, and the kind and gay men would promise to tell him that I had danced nicely and that he would be proud. Always I paid a visit to the PX and grabbed chocolate bars and peanuts and Kleenex, which seemed to have vanished from the United States. "This," I would say, snatching and clutching, "so help me God, is for a soldier overseas. It's not for me."

"She's blushing," said the soldiers around. "She must be telling the truth." And so I was allowed to buy an extra two or three Hersheys for him. These I took as my payment together with the comfort of being with men in their last days here or of staying with them through a part of the awful nights when they returned. To them it could not have meant more than a curious and pleasant diversion. But to us it was profound reassurance. Being with the soldiers even in such a glancing and superficial way kept us somehow in flesh-and-blood contact with all we believed in and loved.

The memorable performances were Mary Martin's. She used to go in her Mainbocher lace negligee and take a chair to the footlights or possibly down onto the floor among the men and there she would talk to them quietly. Radiantly beautiful and sweet, she explained that popular singers were always yowling about how men were two-timing them or beating them up, or cheating them, or leaving them, but that she didn't think men were really like that at all. She thought men were nicer than that. "Listen," she said gently and leaning forward over the back of the chair as Lotte Lenya had taught her to do, she began delicately and intimately the Ogden Nash lyrics from *One Touch of Venus*, "That's Him."

> *You know the way you feel when there is autumn in the air?*
> *That's him. . . . That's him. . . .*
> *The way you feel when Antoine has finished with your hair?*
> *That's him. . . . That's him. . . .*
> *You know the way you feel when you smell bread baking,*
> *The way you feel when suddenly a tooth stops aching?*
> *Wonderful world, wonderful you,*
> *That's him. . . . That's him. . . .*
> *He's simple as a swim in summer,*
> *Not arty, not actory,*
> *He's like a plumber when you need a plumber,*
> *He's satisfactory.*
>
> *He's like a book directly from the printer:*
> *You look at him — he's so commenceable,*
> *He's comforting as woolens in the winter,*
> *He's indispensable.*
> *You know the way you feel that you know you should conceal*
> *The way you feel that you really shouldn't feel?*
> *Wonderful world, wonderful you,*
> *That's him.*

It was a moment of enchanting intimacy and the soldiers looked at her with the trust of little children. They stopped smoking. They stopped shuffling their feet and fidgeting. They stopped whistling and calling out. They forgot that tomorrow they were being shipped. They forgot the last camp rumors and privations.

They lifted their faces like babies and listened. It was the final message from their sweethearts, delicate and humorous, and brought to them by this most lovely of ladies. She whispered her last remarks and it was as though she had her lips to each man's ear and had kissed him Godspeed in token of the woman who could not.

A dancer named Bill Blood came to see me and, sitting on my newly upholstered grass-green sofa, told me what he had been learning. He was in a sailor suit and had just returned from the South Pacific.

"On the whole, men enjoy war," he said, sipping my tea. "It gives them a workout, a release, something they know only a few times in ordinary life. What does the ordinary man have emotionally? Graduation, marriage, the birth of his first child, the death of his father, and that's it. But on our boat we had the equivalent of an opening night every two weeks or so. The day before a landing we were tense as hell, but busy and keyed up. The hour before was agony and the fighting itself we can hardly remember. But afterwards! If it had come off — it was lousy for the ones that got hit, of course — but the others! They were beyond themselves, almost manic, as though drunk. But they were not drunk; they were in a kind of ecstasy. They did things they didn't know they could, they sang, they danced; they were without restraints or inhibitions of any kind, bigger than life — heroes! They almost never know this at home and they miss it. Actors and artists meet enough tests. They don't need wars."

It is this, I believe, and the freedom which war brings, the disruption to galling daily patterns, that prove so attractive, that explain why wars are endured.

I remembered the groups of freshly enlisted men I had seen climbing on trains all over the United States, the white-faced tension of the first couple of hours giving way to dawning alertness as the first cigarettes were shared, the first exchanges of information over coffee, the awareness of comradeship and freedom.

Women do not need these artificially contrived challenges; their own physical pattern and child-bearing bring them quite normally to total involvement. But they, too, have profited from the freedom. The First World War got them out of the kitchen and into business offices from which they never returned. The Second gave them moral and financial independence and, strangely enough, brought the men back into the household as sharers of domestic burdens in a way that has never been approximated in our culture by the educated classes. These two wars precipitated women's natural evolution toward equality and freedom.

The emotional release of war has been by no means restricted to the individual; war uses the whole community, binding individual to group as our life does not often permit. The perception of purpose more vital than a single life, the feeling of fragile flesh and brotherly interdependence — how large and reassuring a vision this is to us who live so split off from each other, individual from family, family from neighbor and community. Only at times of disaster can we lose ourselves in common emotion and we find it so liberating an experience that we will suffer dreadful things in order to know it. For we must have periodic Dionysian release, and if we cannot come by this through regular channels, we will have it through gang adventure, lynchings, witch hunts, revival meetings and, most cathartic of all, large-scale slaughter. War for a good many people means less loneliness, less uselessness, most futilely and dreadfully the first recognition of brotherhood.

By way of private life I waged a series of shattering campaigns with my old and greedy landlord and the young and greedy upholsterers who redecorated my studio. This constituted one of the strongest emotional bouts of the interim but was brought off triumphantly at last. Battle maps and diagrams were sent regularly overseas and final colored photographs of the victory. It was easy to refurnish the studio because I started with no furniture at all except a bed and a table and eight large mirrors. The rooms were repainted and piece by piece was found in junk shops and auction rooms and described minutely in letters with small explanatory drawings. Ivy-printed curtains were purchased for the great French windows that lined one wall. One closet contained our wedding gifts, unused and waiting the master's coming. I had a hoop-skirt chair in green and white striped silk, a very old Swiss corner cabinet and a good reproduction of Branwell Brontë's portrait of Emily; also two original Oliver Smiths and two Motleys. The floor was bare but revarnished and it reflected back the firelight. He kept writing, "Don't buy any more. One chair is enough. No more furniture please." I think he wanted, on release, to grab me by the hand, put two or three books in a knapsack, and run to the ends of the universe. But we could do that, I explained, apologizing for the next purchase. Everything we owned would fit in one packing case and could easily be left behind. Nearly all the money was banked. I wasn't spending much. We could do anything we liked. I continued in my white rooms, with the fire snapping on the hearth, writing and describing and walking about between sentences, putting my hands on the furniture and touching and studying the pretty dishes. And then I would tell him in detail what it would be like when I opened the door and he entered, for the first time, his home, ready and prepared for him.

I succumbed to the urgings of my mother, sister, agents, soloists, best friends and doctors, and bought a mink coat. This seemed like thumbing my nose at history and I wrestled for a week with my conscience, but I very soon found that if the fur was rich enough, the face did not matter, and the congratulations on my improved appearance quieted my scruples. I hoarded my money. I planned.

And I ran down the street to see Martha.

CHAPTER XIII *The Milk of Paradise*

ALL during this separation I told myself as I wrote my husband that later when he returned I wanted to quit the theater and rest. But deep in my heart I knew I wanted nothing of the sort. Was it likely that under the stimulus and joy of his return I would suddenly bank my fires? Men have always been able to experience family and work together. It has been assumed that because of the greater emotional demands made on women, they could not have both, and they have hitherto been constrained to choose. But I was in a new century and I was greedy. I wanted wifehood, motherhood and work. I wanted all.

There were two thousand years of domestic history dead against me and against me were the race memories and traditions I had myself inherited. But there was in my blood something else, another need, as deep and as old, and this urged without respite or peace. This would not let me be.

I had drunk the Milk of Paradise and known power. I could not think to give this up. I could forfeit my life, and my comfort, riches and convenience, for love — but not the magic release of work! This was my identity.

The fact that for millennia all such desires have been arbitrarily suppressed in women proves nothing but the brutality of convention. In primitive and ancient cultures women were thought, because they were women and because they gave birth, to have special powers and were the preferred celebrants vital to certain life and death occasions.

Mastery in any field is attained by practicing what is valued at times of recognized importance. No genius, no matter what the field, is an unprecedented accident. There must be a need, an expectation and trust. Behind Sappho was a long line of honored female poet-composers, the last supremely great female composers in the history of music. She was the culmination of a tradition* and it is instructive to note that Sappho was not only by contemporary accounts (which is all we have of her, since the music has been lost) the greatest of her profession but that she was a good wife and mother and that her social reputation within her community and during her lifetime was exemplary. It was a century later that the boys in Athens started a whispering campaign of personal defamation which reinforced a growing legend: that any woman who dedicated herself to art must be a freak, that artistic creativity was compensation for lack of creativity in more natural and suitable functions. This myth was not based on fact, or on any larger understanding of women's capacities or happiness, but directly on men's convenience. Women have at last, to their terrible cost, come to accept this view. It suited their men. And they understandably wanted to suit their men.

As the conviction took hold, and woman began to think of herself as not only different but inferior, she gradually lost her function of a necessary ritual voice in the community. Where is she, for instance, in the Christian Church? In the Hebraic? The Moslem, Hindu, or Shinto? On her knees with her head covered up and her mouth shut, removed at a prophylactic distance from the high altar and all sacred vessels. In our church women have been considered from Old Testament times unclean, a moral and ritual-

* There were similar priestess-musicians in Egypt, Assyria, Babylonia and India.

istic hazard. The very functions and powers that primitive religions cherished here betray her. Women from the end of the first century A.D. have not been allowed to officiate in the church, build or design the church, compose or write for the church, perform in the church,* nor even for some hundreds of years sing as lay members of the congregation. "Woman was represented [by the early Church Fathers]," writes Lecky, "as the door of hell, as the mother of all human ills. She should be ashamed at the very thought that she is a woman. She should live in continual penance, on account of the curses she had brought upon the world." †

Consecrated women, that is, women whose every female function had been exorcized, neutralized and spayed, were permitted certain holy or clerical offices but always secretly, and behind bars. At one period the unsterilized were forbidden by papal edict to sing anywhere at all, even over their slop pails and washboards. But this restriction could not long prevail. Women's natural rejoicing while scrubbing floors and cleaning out the garbage was not to be restrained and they gave tongue to their enthusiasm. But only domestically. The church doors remained shut except at a most terrible price: the dedication of her entire life, private floorwashing and all.

And many thought the cost slight. For among other attractions the church provided the only art experience the average person, male or female, could know. During the Dark Ages its vast projects exploited all the talents available in any community. Throughout eight hundred years of endowed scholarship it developed the many arts it could use. But the arts it could not use — chiefly dancing — withered. No ecclesiastical or ritual choreography was composed nor was any method of dance notation evolved,

---

* Women have been admitted to Protestant choirs only within the last three hundred years.

† *History of European Morals,* Vol. II, pp. 357-358.

as unquestionably would have been done had the holy fathers wished to preserve any visual ceremonial. The artists the church was permitted to use, that is, men, achieved great works. The artists it was not — what became of them? Barred up. Barred out. Wasted. Lost.

Stimulated by religious sanctions, the average husband and father placed even harder and more cruel blocks in the path of women's imaginative expression. By persuading themselves and their wives that no woman could devote time to anything but her husband and household without moral treason, they managed to discourage undomestic yearnings. Men wanted their wives womanly; by that was meant, we gather, they wanted them steadfast, attentive, enthusiastic, enduring — most certainly enduring — and serene; and by serene was meant that the women were to have no doubts about men's judgments and no disturbing inclinations of their own, a concept successfully implemented by a child a year — usually a convincer. Sixteen children without benefit of pediatrician, nursery school, or corner drugstore guaranteed attentiveness.

The women who were at the head of a great household were in a position of considerable influence: they administered battalions of servants; they supervised the many domestic industries which supplied virtually everything used in daily life, and which had to be made on the premises; they ran dispensaries for whatever medicine was needed; they arbitrated and organized and instructed. They did not, therefore, have much leisure and any free time there was they devoted to husband and children and not to idle flights of fancy.

The women had no doubt great satisfaction in being necessary and effective and may well have been both serene and content; we have not heard otherwise. The important point is that we have not heard. They were speechless. The experience of rearing up families, which was the universal lot of all lay women, did not find in seventeen centuries a single authentic female statement.

Nor did any of the men speak up. Men have sung about acres of pearly breasts, snowy throats and bee-bruised lips, but about the service, companionship and character of his helpmeet, not one word. Until the Victorian era the sharer of bed and bosom remained "my wife, poor wretch!" Consciously or unconsciously, women have lived for hundreds, for thousands of years with the belief that their happiness lay in serving God wholly or in serving husband and children wholly. Thus by religious sanction and matrimonial reinforcement the great taboo was fixed in our mores.

For over a thousand years woman's chief creative expression was restricted to the statements of saints and visionaries locked behind walls, special in nature, in no way representative of ordinary woman, her passions or fate.

Outside the safety of the church most transgressors against the social code paid dearly for their defiance with loss of caste and with cruel personal restrictions. Only lower-class women were permitted to embroider or paint, the two being considered of an equally artisan nature. Certain pretty outcasts were permitted to sing or act, although there were long periods of interdiction against even depraved women doing either. But within and without the cloister the usual price of self-expression for intellectual or well-born women was the forfeit of sexuality.

As late as the eighteenth and nineteenth centuries, when gentlewomen began to have what we would consider professional careers, the majority remained spinsters. The married few took husbands late when the pattern of their minds had been firmly set, like Elizabeth Barrett and George Eliot. The exception that leaps to mind is, of course, George Sand, but it must be remembered that if she had many lovers, she found by her own admission lasting happiness with no one; she remained ill-mated and lonely throughout.

And as one considers the great names of the last two centuries certain facts become apparent: many worked semisecretly under male pseudonyms; few married, fewer still bore children; very nearly all were sick, flat on their backs as often as not.

And what kind of art did these rebellious lonely people produce? Except in two fields, not the best. There were among them a few lyric poets not comparable to the greatest men, a few second-class painters, no architect, until very recently no sculptors, not one single first-rate composer excepting the nuns Kassia, Mechtild, and Hildegarde, whose work their church did not think fit to preserve but who left a tremendous contemporary reputation.

This is a fairly frightening history. It matters not a whit how you educate a girl, what techniques or attitudes you teach her. If she knows that her men will not welcome her talents she is going to proceed timidly. Put any gifted child at the keyboard, train her, exhort her six hours a day, but let it be borne in on her that there never has been in recorded music a first-rate female composer, that no man will consider her work without condescension, and, worst of all, that within herself she may provoke conflicts that she cannot hope to surmount, and you may get results, but they won't be Beethoven.*

This has been wasteful for art, cruel for the women, and unhelpful to the men because they have been persuaded to build up their pride of manhood on assumptions that were bound to give way the moment women found the restraints served no good purpose and need not be endured.

---

* It is interesting in this connection to consider what educators have found in regard to the schooling of Negro children: that they show no inferiority of endowment or application until about the eighth year when the full realization of their social status and lack of opportunity becomes clear to them. Trauma frequently cripples further development.

Today women know almost as much freedom as in pagan antiquity and turn eagerly to the arts, but to only three with promise of supreme success:

First, now as before, and always, to the performing careers, where in spite of long periods of interdiction and censor they have managed consistently to excel. Second, to creative storytelling and prose, in which they hold their own with the best. And third, to choreography. In this field they have practiced without restriction. No man ever barred the way here because no man thought highly enough of the business to keep women out, as he had done from so many august, holy, or honorable occupations.

The Christian Church had proscribed dancing and it was utterly without dignity, cut off from all serious motivation, the sources of ancient meaning and glory. The Christian Church was the first great church to do this. So strongly had dancing been involved in all previous worship that it took more than one thousand years to root it out of the Catholic service (a good deal longer than it took to root women out). But it was at last eradicated and there remain now only vestigial remnants in the Mass. The church is poorer for the loss; the effect on dancing has been disastrous. For two thousand years dancing and dancers have struggled under religious and social censure more formidable than that placed on any activity, except sin itself — and sex.

Dancing nevertheless remains the germinal art, the mother of theater and all other arts, in an anthropological sense the mother of the church. And it is in this ancient medium that those members of the community debased from proper participation in more honored practices have served a quickening purpose. The rejected art and the rejected artist meet here in apt congress. Here woman is despised for her trade and not for her sex, and there is all the margin between success and failure in this differentiation. It has been the women who have transfigured not only the art, but the

point of view and purpose of its practitioners, its status and relation to other arts and to the community. Dancing is the only art
where women have functioned to such crucial purpose, but it is
the only art where they have not worked in the teeth of universal
doubt.

There have been great male choreographers — Noverre, Bournon-
ville, Petipas, Fokine, Massine, Balanchine, Ashton, Tudor. I think
one must truthfully report that the greatest have been men. But
there has been no artist in a class with Michelangelo, Shakespeare,
Goethe, or Bach. Indeed, to rank any choreographer with these
seems like impertinent hyperbole. Nor have there been any male
figures comparable in dynamism and originality to Isadora Duncan,
Martha Graham, or Mary Wigman.

The very handicaps and limitations which have frightened away
gifted men work to woman's advantage. Here her training and
habits stand her in good stead. Here even her body is helpful.
Anonymity has been her history. She is at home in an art without
literature, without past or future. She has never hoped beyond today and tomorrow — or much beyond the door of her house. Are
not her daily efforts spent on evanescence? Cooking, washing,
watching, caring, each day erasing the labors of the day before as
each gesture erases from the air its precedent? And as every day's
work must start afresh in endless repetition, so each dance begins
clean with no record. The dancer enters space without a guiding
mark and the pattern is rehearsed and leaves no sign — no sign except the exchange between living people, the relationship established, if only once and never again. The patience for this is
woman's special endowment. She is aware that there is no substitute for the breath of life; that it is unique and personal; that the
unduplicated action, the unrepeated speech, the gesture or word
thrown away or heard by few or only once may be as important
as any public message. She remembers that the source is inex-

haustible; that it is the moment of life that counts, the rebirth; that again and again and again the dancer jumps and runs, and when he falls, another, by vital invitation, leaps out. This, woman understands. This is the stuff of her life.

Women today comprise nearly one third of our total working force — many thousands of them in the arts — but the ones that turn to dancing do so still for the antique reasons — power and Dionysian release on their own terms.

Dancing ranks with women's oldest professional careers, religious dedication and prostitution. It is inextricably related to both. First as priestess, then as prostitute, then as theater performer the dancer found a way of winning fortune, an excuse from household slavery and enforced seclusion.

Dancing has always been fruitful in its effects of direct fulfillment and satisfaction, and today the appeal is, as before, spellbinding through the body. It is not the concomitants of theatrical success that draw young girls so much as the vision of becoming generically DANCER in the permitted dress, exposed legs, free and floating arms, aerial skirt. I think they want this because it produces effects of transformation as recompense for all they find insupportable in woman's traditional lot.

Dancing inflames and exercises the senses of the viewer (hence its long connection with prostitution) and of the performer (hence its long connection with religion). It is a physical release as no other performing art can be, because it is practiced on the whole body; the body is the instrument, the medium itself, and the exposure is total and voluptuous. Therein lies the clue to its compulsive lifelong hold. It can become more frequently than not a substitute for physical sex and it has all too often been chosen as a vocation because woman's life, sexually speaking, has become in our civilization unsatisfactory, uncertain and expensive to the individual.

In what way, then, is dancing a solution? Briefly, it guarantees satisfaction and control to people who are afraid they will not otherwise know them. A dancer can do more than pray or hope; she takes matters into her own hands.

Every girl has known from time immemorial that she had better have a dowry or looks, and if she possessed neither, there was usually nothing for her but to be family drudge or enter the church, where God could be counted on to overlook what husbands would not. On her appearance still depends in large measure her chance for a good marriage and children, for a continuing sex life, for a high income. Numbers of ill-favored women have succeeded to the physical rewards of life, it is true, but it is in spite of handicap and by exercising faculties not demanded of the more handsomely endowed. Age and appearance, therefore, are important, particularly in any situation where women outnumber men.

Doctors assure us that any feeling of inferiority induced by physical appearance, short of mutilation, is in reality a symptom of a deeper conflict, and that the truly beautiful are as capable of self-doubt as the plain. This may be so, but it is not the prevailing popular understanding.

A woman's age has always been important because her value has been reckoned chiefly as a breeding animal and fecundity determined her economic status. This is happily no longer so.

Youth and physical beauty, nevertheless, are still held up before us as a promise, and have been in legend, story and song. We are told, and we believe, women more than men, that to win love, but, more imperatively, to retain love, we must be beautiful. It is a terrifying threat. And it faces us on every billboard, magazine page, screen, stage, shopwindow and, yes, even on the pages of every nursery picture book, because the princess was always beautiful or became so. And as we grew up, we accepted the idea more and more. Mother's friends always spoke of "the fine little boy" or "the son," but it was "the pretty little girl," and if that adjective was omitted and the word "dear" substituted, we became sensible of something hurt or slightly damaged and needing special tenderness.

Woman's best approach to happiness, we learn on all sides, is the quick rousing of men's erotic interest, and the advertisements are explicit as to what rouses men. It can be bought in a bottle — and it is quite expensive but well worth the price. Five of the largest businesses in the United States — cosmetics, ladies' clothing and accessories, furs, jewelry, both real and false, women's magazines — have sprung from the premise that romance follows beauty and that beauty can be purchased. The young woman is advised to make herself lovely and then lie around like a kind of bait, and she is warned that only after the trap has successfully sprung can she satisfy her own inclinations.

Now, for many young people this is a dismaying proposition. A girl may very well feel she cannot make the grade; she may also feel fundamentally outraged in having her life controlled by someone else's tastes, implying, as it does, a passivity which she may interpret as helplessness.

The fact is many women do not favor being passive, are downright frightened by it, having witnessed centuries of results. Young girls see quite a lot of women, particularly mothers, and often they are not enchanted. They see mothers tied to housework who would prefer not to spend their days sweeping and cooking. They see mothers and older sisters doing jobs and chores which are considered more menial and less important than fathers' jobs and that bring in no money. It is father who has the cash for his freedom; mother must ask. Indeed, mother has almost no freedom at all to speak of. Mothers are always at the call of other people's needs and desires. Their daughters find little charm in the pattern. They would like to be free to please themselves, forever children, unless they might grow up to some of the freedom of father. But growing up for a woman, as they observe, seems to mean less freedom, and no guarantee of happiness. And so some of them, the dancers, never grow up.

Very few dancers develop the bodies of mature women; they keep lean in the hips and flat-breasted, a phenomenon remarked on by all costume designers. It is also a fact that the greatest performers, the women best capable of communicating sensuous satisfaction, are in their bodies least sensual. In effect they have sacrificed all organs of personal fulfillment and maintain and cherish only the means for public satisfaction, the system of bones and sinews for levitation and propulsion. The ballet foot and leg, which when used to its full capacity can evoke an almost physical response, is in repose as tight and straight as the leg of a mule. Certain great soloists have been lacking in even primary sexual functions and are known to have menstruated rarely in their lives. For the rest, very many, possibly a majority, are partially frigid and most tend to be, in spite of legend, more chaste than otherwise. I do not mean to imply that they are not passionate and gallant, but that certain deep rejections and fears prevent easy sexual release. The majority of American women are, it is claimed by medical statistics, partially frigid, and perhaps dancers no more than others. In any case, the dancers have evolved a substitute expression and do not mind the state so bitterly. This, of course, is no good answer to the fear of life. But it is an instinctive and practical one.

Even Isadora Duncan, who clamored the loudest for love, was no exception. She was a true sensualist and she seems to belie in the richness of her experience all I have argued about women's substitution of dancing for life. But consider her point of view repeatedly expressed: she vowed when very young never to submit to woman's usual fate, never to marry, that is, never to put herself or her fortune into any man's keeping, to bear children if and when she pleased, to leave them or look after them at whim, to be absolutely free and to remain so. She wished to have the freedom of a pagan as she imagined it, for she recognized love as a transient ecstasy. The communion on which marriage is built she never, I believe, envisaged, nor constancy, security, fruition, these being the rewards of the female life she scorned. She followed a dream, power without responsibility, release without cost. And her way of attainment was the cultivation of her body. The littlest ballet pupil in first position before the mirror is starting on the same historic path.*

For in dancing the face matters least and the body is beautiful if it functions beautifully. It is not the shape of the leg, but the use of the leg that tells. Furthermore, and most felicitously, the beautiful use changes the flesh and corrects all manner of imperfections. Contrary to maxims, one can by taking thought add a cubit to stature. When a dancer stands before a mirror, she no longer sees what her big brothers see, but a promise. If her nose turns up or down, no matter: men will gasp at the carriage of her head. If she is fat, she will get thin. If she is thin, the muscles of her back and thighs will enable her to move like a voluptuary. And who is to say or who cares what she is, whether this or that, if she stands in the center of a stage in the revealing and beautiful uniform of her trade, escorted by the best cavalier in the business, who has forfeited the right to refuse her and must take her if she is the best, not the prettiest, mind you, but the best and the most skillful. And there for all to see, in public, she will perform with him the ritual of romantic courtship. More than in any other art, there are enor-

---

* I would like to interject that very few daughters of contented mothers have become ballerinas. I cannot name a father who urged a dancing career on his girl unless he was himself a dancer and looked upon the matter as one of natural succession.

mous rewards as regards direct attention, admiration, emotional release, and they remain always under the performer's command. She never surrenders her will. She gets her rewards directly by her own effort. There need be no intermediary — and for any female who doubts her powers this is a temptation of frightening persuasiveness.

Dancing represents sex in its least costly form, free from imprisonment and free to a great extent from emotional responsibility, and, above all, as a sure thing, independent of someone else's pleasure. In other words, it means freedom *from* sex. The forces which impelled women to the austerity of the church operate to form the great dancer. In a strange transmutation dancing is a form of asceticism — almost a form of celibacy.

Is, then, the aesthetic impulse rooted in neurosis and unable to develop except under the compulsion of pain? Are these brutal disciplines and forfeits necessary to creative effort? The ancients did not rely on any such goads and, notwithstanding, their art flourished. The restraints we place on women creators could well be accidental to our culture, of no great profit to the individual or the work, but, rather, destructive to both. I believe this to be the case and that the genius with which certain women write or paint or compose or choreograph derives from faculties and needs beyond any mere act of compensation. I believe that talent is compounded of the entire personality and is as much a sign of exuberant health as of sickness. But the bewitchment of hundreds of thousands, of millions of girls by the dream, by even the discipline of dancing cannot be called creativity, nor even vocation. It is escape, it is protest, and it is, in large part, hysterical protest.

For a time it serves the art form well, but only for a time. In the working conditions of our world and theater the dedicated ones are forced under emotional whips to greater and greater effort.

But there is a limit. The personality ceases to expand, ceases to breathe, in certain aspects it withers and this is reflected in a stunting of the art. The audience is always aware.

An act of suppression that cancels out emotional or imaginative life, the one at the cost of the other, is obviously wasteful. With either choice a major section of the personality is wrecked and all human relations, in marriage and out, must suffer.

A dancer's release, like most magic, is transient and won each time by renewed and arduous effort. Dancing has become consequently a kind of sexual limbo whose inhabitants identify their own flesh with their purpose, a confusion not equally true for women artists whose bodies are not their lifework. Dancing is, in a deep sense, the only physical union many of these women know, a sort of automarriage. And as with all such narcissistic unions, there develops an aura of melancholy and the promise of death. Many a young dancer has drowned in the mirrors before which she spends her life. The others live only when the reflection from the audience fans breath back into their emptying spirits.

Whatever rewards the dancer knows in place of the usual emotional and sexual associations, she is frequently assailed by doubts in her late twenties or early thirties. Even the very great know these morbid spells. The needs of the heart cannot be cheated forever. The dancer grows frightened. The dancer realizes suddenly she is a spinster and aging, no matter how fast she gets around the room. The life of merciless effort, the dimming chances of permanent fame, exhaustion and the growing comprehension of what old age means to a fading athlete without family or home suddenly terrify even the stanchest. The conviction grows that the sacrifice has been too much and perhaps not necessary. There is many a *volte-face* at this point and a marriage with at least one child in a frantic effort to put life back on balance.

But our theater is not set up for family life; dancing in particular is conditioned by world-wide touring, uncertain irregular seasons and precarious pay. Dancers today do not inherit the career dynastically as they used to, like the Vestris, the Taglioni (five distinguished members and three generations in this family), the Grisi, Elssler, Karsavin clans. Our dancers are not protected wards of the state with guaranteed salaries and pensions. The married dancer is called upon to relinquish jobs that would further her career and settle for domesticity against professional interest. Many do this serenely and good-naturedly; this is nothing more than the problem of reconciling life and art, which is present with all workers, but in a dancer's case, particularly for women, it is final. She may consider the exchange worth the price either way. She may not and live in perpetual conflict.

It is astonishing under the circumstances that none of these factors deters young girls one whit. Five million of them in this country alone are studying to be professional dancers.

Perhaps this is so because women today, even dancers, cannot bring themselves to accept these conditions as permanent. They see no reason why they should not have both work and family, what with Deepfreeze, Waring mix and diaper service. They believe also with all their hearts and hopes — because it suits them so to believe — that sweet reasonableness and a sense of fair play will dissolve the major block to the double life: their husbands' attitude.

Marriage is difficult with any artist. "A man does not love a woman for her genius; he loves her in spite of her genius," writes Maurice Goudeket, the husband of Colette. Marriage is perhaps hardest of all with a theater personality because the work is not wholly under the control of the individual. Dancers above all do not make easy wives. The union has to run a gamut of conflicting loyalties. A dancer's husband has to share his wife's discipline. His life is as curtailed as hers and quite literally by hers. Most

men, particularly men outside of the profession, find such conditions onerous.

But the unrest is general and pertains to all careers and all
classes of society. Preachers, doctors and teachers warn; magazine
and newspaper editorialize. The women's magazines are particularly
explicit: if the wife has to work outside the home she must never
let it impinge on her husband's schedule, and if inside the home
she must see that it is finished and put away before he comes back
from his own work and she must never for one moment let him
think that hers is important compared with his, or his interests
and hobbies and needs. And for this reason and because it will be
construed as a direct reflection on his virility, she must not earn
more money. He will develop ulcers, sinuses, abscesses, tuberculosis. He will borrow the classic symptom of women's frustration,
the bitter, black headache, and although women's magazines do
not care to name this, he will add one of his own, partial or total
impotence, which is a form of suicide and just as unanswerable. He
may in the end leave her.

If the women do not depend on their men as their grandmothers
did, the men similarly manage to do without them. It has become
a game of mutual attrition played out on a level where both are
pitifully defenseless. Medical statistics and divorce courts list the
ruin. The suicide rate among men, the alcoholism, the excesses of
sedation and narcotics, the growing overt homosexuality, the juve-
nile neuroticism and delinquency attest to the monumental cost of
the emotional adjustment. This is the "furious and lamentable
region" that Conrad speaks of, "the dwelling place of unveiled
hearts" where there is neither right nor wrong but only human
suffering.

Woman has always accepted with grace, with pride and satisfaction, her husband's interests and achievements, taking joy,
taking not in any way a sense of diminution and shame. Can

the husband endure to learn this? Does he wish to? Will he not rather attempt to put things back as they were, stuffing all hopes, ambitions and zests not centered on himself into the family cupboard and setting his back to the door? Indeed, indeed, things cannot go back. Pandora's box is opened. The girls are earning money.

It is of no consequence who works better — men or women; it is important that each work differently and that each be allowed to try without penalties. "Never destroy any aspect of personality," said my grandmother George, who had no career except caring for her family, "for what you think is the wild branch may be the heart of the tree." Not all women want a double life. But those who do should not be denied on the grounds of sex. It is not easy to be a devoted wife and mother and a first-class artist; it is equally hard to be an artist with no root experience in life. It is impossible to be a good wife or a wise mother, embittered, balked and devoured by inner energies. Creative exercise can be disciplined to a household schedule — not easily, but women everywhere prove it can be done. For when all faculties are exercised the enormous releases of strength and satisfaction more than make up for the extra attention demanded. Extra attention? No, rather, elimination of waste and repining. The alternation of diaper washing and composing spell one another in mutual refreshment. Ask any responsible working mother. And the children will reflect the zest and energy of the parent's life — and as to the work, how it flourishes! How it flowers and expands! Even under discipline, perhaps particularly under discipline, because it is voluntary and joyful, because the sources of life are fulfilled and replenished and because, as in all things, the greater the range of accomplishment, the greater the capacity for more.

I think this is what Isadora Duncan meant when she spoke of founding a new religion: the total release of women's hearts, the total use of their gifts.

Women have bent to the yoke and the scars of their durance are upon their children. But with the lessening of all social and religious restrictions, with widening economic opportunities, with practical invention bringing ease and leisure, there stands between woman and whatever life she yearns for only one barrier: her husband's good will. Failing this, she fails all. She must have his blessing, his pride in her achievement. Let him dower her with this and there will come the great works for which we have waited so long. But beyond and beneath there will come happiness.

It is an act of recognition that is needed, an act of love.

CHAPTER XIV R. and H.

IN March 1945 Rodgers and Hammerstein once more collabo-
rated with the Theatre Guild management, Theresa Helburn and
Lawrence Langner on a musical version of Molnar's *Liliom* to be
called *Carousel*. The staff that had produced *Oklahoma!* reas-
sembled, Reuben Mamoulian, Miles White and myself. The only
addition to our group was Jo Mielziner replacing Lemuel Ayers
as scene designer.

I had had the barest acquaintance with Dick and Oscar when
I signed up for *Oklahoma!* but during the rehearsals and afterwards our friendship deepened. By the winter of 1944–1945 I
was going to Oscar not only for professional advice but personal
reaffirmation. Since every man in my life was far away and un-
available for comfort or council, I began to turn to him as big
brother on many nontheatric occasions. The relationship grew
to be one of the joys of my life. He had talked for over a year
about his plans for *Liliom* and I looked forward to the opportunity of working on a second R. and H. production as the happy
reward for being a good girl.

Plans ripened that spring. While the snow fell softly outside
his Pennsylvania farmhouse, Oscar talked as only he can, trans-
forming the material of our common craft into hopeful and lyric
enchantment.

There have been few lasting collaborations in the history of the theater even though the theater is in essence collaboration. The difficulties involved in sharing responsibility and effort, the trial of work conditions, the apportioning of recognition and rewards have proved more than most friendships could encompass. Preservation of equilibrium implies a restraint rather more subtle than that required, for instance, in marriage. Such a relationship obviously presupposes mutual respect and absolute loyalty, consideration, and steadiness of nerve. Rodgers and Hammerstein have worked together in a team that has lasted longer in friendship (if not yet in business association) than Gilbert and Sullivan. They have been able to do this because they recognize their need of one another and because they practice discipline. I had a ringside seat at their first joint effort and witnessed their great, their unprecedented triumph. I saw them at work in three productions; I was privileged to work beside them.

In a union like theirs, bound tight by creative collaboration, business involvements, administration and public exposure, they are locked closer than most families. Their interdependence suggests royal dynasty. And although the two households live apart with summer homes in different states, they present a common front to the public. R. and H. appear publicly together, they refer to one another in all interviews, they make decisions jointly, their joint word is pledged on all deals, they receive joint and equal honors. One might think that a double opinion on all questions would cause delay; it does not. They act with dispatch.

They always hold their first conferences privately, and come to staff meetings united and in perfect agreement. They decide quickly and they stand by their decisions. In the field of art this is not easy, the artist's birthright being to reconsider and alter. But in the theater hesitation is not always practical, especially in matters of casting and staff. And therefore R. and H. examine all newcomers personally, even the totally unknown. They can see, no one better, talent or lack of it in a face, they can hear it in a voice. Whatever I had that was good, either professional or personal, held their instant attention and no intermediary was needed to tip them off. For years anyone could appear for an audition and be heard and everyone, even the well known, had to — a precaution, although seemingly arrogant, designed to guarantee high caliber of production. They were like doctors who refused to diagnose until they had personally taken the pulse. From the time of *Oklahoma!*'s opening, every Thursday has been audition day. They saw and heard literally thousands, took note, and when the opportunity came in their great international enterprises, sent for the applicants and placed them.

This attention to detail has always governed their activity. Every audition, every rehearsal was watched by one or the other. They had final word on every set, prop, hat, light, inflection or musical key. Absolutely nothing was overlooked, not even after the openings, when Dick policed his theaters with a zest and concern extraordinary for someone who had seen so very many shows through long runs. During rehearsals, Oscar usually stayed with the actors, absenting himself only for rewrites, while Dick guarded the dancing and singing. Even with a management as experienced as the Theatre Guild and with directors as distinguished as Reuben Mamoulian, Joshua Logan, John van Druten, Harold Clurman, and Fred Zinnemann, they never slacked their vigilance from the first day of rehearsal. What has made them uniquely effective (beside their talent) is their professional watchfulness. They check every aspect of their productions like mechanics going over an engine prior to transoceanic flight.

The impression on first meeting them was that here at last were the aristocrats of the business. They spoke softly, intelligently and politely. They knew about theater prior to 1919 and outside of

Broadway and Hollywood. They were courteous and charming. Their interests were manifold.

In appearance they are dissimilar. Dick is moderately short and squarish, with a strong compact torso, the developed hands and forearms of a pianist, a strong short neck on which sets and turns a head almost archaic in its concentrated power. When considering, he becomes fixed and monolithic like a primitive. His piercing black eyes grow as opaque as an Aztec's, his face expressionless. The rest of us wait and hold heartbeat because the decision will be Star Chamber and final. "Well," he will say, throwing down his cigarette and smiling so suddenly and graciously that every subsequent remark becomes illuminated by the unexpected release, "I'll tell you what we'll do," and then he outlines a practical course of action, which may not be what you had in mind at all, but while he talks you will be convinced, or at least you will wish very much to be.

"I want you at the end of the dance," he will say, "to get a big hand — not a cheap hand. I want you in your way, in your own style, to stop the show — without, of course, sacrificing any of the delicacy or tenderness you value. I know you can do this without compromise; you have that kind of technique." The challenge has been thrown by Rodgers, S.J. And under the spell of his hypnotic persuasion you rush to meet it.

He kids and jokes companionably at all rehearsals, but he is a figure of some terror, through sheer nervous tension, high voltage, and the unforgettable overtones of his world power. His diction and tonality are straight New York, a flat, crisp, didactic voice, something like an instructor. He is the reverse of talky. He does not converse; he pronounces with judgment frequently unexpected and sharp, like summer lightning. Most of his comments are *coups de grâce*.

But at moments of direct personal approach he can be gentle.

I suspect he feels in some ways cut off, even yearning; the banter
is too constant, the quips too quick and sharp to betoken anything but vulnerability. He moves behind verbal machine guns.
But just as the greatest quality in his music is a lilting delicious
scherzo with overtones of hovering sweetness, so in his manner and
in his eyes (when he is off guard) there is a brooding quiet, a
kind of unappeased hunger, a woe.

Oscar seems solider, more the country gentleman, the pater-
familias, the benevolent, genial, eighteenth-century man of letters.
He looks too neighborly, too understanding, too philosophic for
our gypsy and disreputable trade. Oscar is somewhat older, but his
respect for Dick's judgment amounts to veneration. He is a tall,
broad, heavy and gentle-faced man with a soft voice, a Yankee
twang when excited, and a chuckle that is one of the most aus-
picious sounds our theater ever housed. He has, for all his size,
the quietness and discipline of an athlete. He smokes little, drinks
almost nothing at all, and practices daily exercise and massage.
Like Dick, he is always immaculately dressed. He wears beautiful
custom-made shoes of glove leather that fit over his insteps without laces. He walks quietly; he waits quietly, he watches with
attention genial and silent and can enter and leave a rehearsal
without being observed or interrupting work in progress; but he will
have learned a great deal.

Dick is considerate and quiet too, but always noticed. He takes
a chair by the director, or by the piano, or he sits chatting in the
auditorium with a member of the cast, or he dictates his entire
morning mail. But he misses nothing, not an inflection, not a turn
of the wrist or a grace note. And none of us ever misses the fact
that he is there watching. In music rehearsals he is, of course, an
active participant; he plays well and frequently takes the piano
to give pace and dynamics.

When I started rehearsals for *Oklahoma!* I asked for an inter-

view with him about the ballet music and handed him a detailed
scenario broken down into seconds as I had done for Aaron Cop-
land. He nodded and stuffed it into his pocket, then proceeded
without slackening step into his song rehearsal. "Aren't you going
to read this?" I asked. "You have all the songs, haven't you?" he
answered. And, smiling, he hurried on.

No further word coming from him, the dance pianist and I
began piecing his song tunes together in a kind of sequence —
purely as a makeshift — and without warning, suddenly Dick ma-
terialized like a chef standing over the piano with pepper and salt,
accenting, changing keys, shaping phrases, organizing both pace
and music. But when at last we came to the final death struggle
at the end of the ballet, we found that the score contained no
melody suitable for breaking a man's back. I sent bulletin after
bulletin upstairs to Rodgers, but he was coaching songs and too
busy to come down. Finally in desperation we set the fight in
silence to counts, and showed it this way at the first run-through.
At conclusion Dick came tearing up the aisle and grabbed my
hands. "It's wonderful and I like the silence. We'll put some
tympany underneath to cue in the dancers." And that is how it
remained. I was startled by this seeming casualness, but Dick knew
it would be all right. He added a coda and the whole piece worked
out well. If he had found the effect weak, he would have given
prompt orders.

The most noticeable differences between the men are in their
habits and methods of work. All matters except the writing and
reading of lines are dominated somewhat, I should say, by Dick,
but it is Hammerstein who composes first. His incomparable ear
and flair for metrical form establish rhythms that are later trans-
lated into melody. Oscar works at his farm in Pennsylvania or in
his superb Georgian study in New York, slowly and painstakingly,
beginning at dawn every morning, writing at his stand-up eight-

eenth-century desk and pacing the floor, muttering. Dick works anywhere — his home, backstage, the orchestra pit, frequently in a cubicle in Carnegie Hall — rapidly and easily. (The eight-minute aria of Billy Bigelow in *Carousel,* which had taken Oscar many weeks to conceive and complete, was set by Dick in two hours, as fast, in fact, as he could indicate melody and key changes on paper.) Dick seldom revises or alters. His work is virtually complete when we go into rehearsal. Oscar, on the other hand, does considerable editing; the job for the rest of us just begins. So Dick sits watching. Oscar is more relaxed perhaps, because busier, and not so constantly present. Both are available with ideas and time when needed.

Oscar, who has the reputation of being folksy, down-to-earth and more or less cracker-barrel in his style, is actually prone to considerable daring in his search for new forms. He has attempted startling and lovely experiments. His first version of God in *Carousel* as a New England minister and his wife was extraordinarily imagined but shocked Calvinistic New Haven and was immediately and entirely deleted, the two characters becoming one, the star-tender, the keeper of the heavenly back doors, "The Mother-of-Pearly Gates," but the first version had a dry toughness that the second lacked and a quality that Oscar has frequently had to yield before audience hesitation or surprise. This occurred in one third of the scenes in *Allegro.*

Dick is more conventional, classic, if you will. He is not so interested in experimenting as in reaching the audience emotionally and he prefers the direct and proven methods for doing this. He thinks the words of a song should be heard and understood, and the best place for the singer is, therefore, standing on the footlights and facing front, all but motionless, surrounded and framed by perfect quiet. To this end, the lights are as a rule lowered and the singer picked out by a special spot. This treat-

ment rather handicaps the director and gives small scope to movement invention. It can become monotonous. But monotony to
Rodgers is of no concern beside clarity. If the song is good enough
there will be no talk about monotony. And under his care the
song is generally good enough.

Neither man has an eye for color. And this is strange considering Dick's great love for modern painting. On the other hand,
he can grasp the form and idiom of dance movement with the
skill of a choreographer and has always been creatively helpful
in placing and cutting dances. Oscar has no true visual appreciation; he admits he does not know how to look at painting. Pure
gesture communicates nothing to him. But if he recognizes only
dramatic content, how sensitive he is with this! My feeling for
character, for intimate comedy, for the pattern dictated by situation and mood, even my willingness to forgo the effects that would
ensure a final hand were treated by him with gentle and appreciative intelligence.

In setting stage business for their songs I strove, without con-
tradiction of text or character, to broaden the author's original
intent by adding my own comment. Sometimes quite sly and ex-
pressive jokes could be contrived by playing off one medium
against another. But they always were keyed to scene and mood.
In this way the dances are rooted into the score and dialogue and
have become part of the flesh; that is why they are always reproduced no matter who stages the revivals.

The authors were appreciative. Dick's enthusiasm for any subtle
rhythmic device or a gay "button" at the end of a piece (the trick
that drives the point home sharp and clear), Oscar's joyous and
tender excitement when I did something revealing of character,
when I added speech to the dances in *Carousel,* for instance
(Oscar is in love with language and likes to see it get on), were
the rewards of working with them. They were equally vocal

when dissatisfied, insisting on eighteen tries and my heart's blood, insisting and persisting until the curtain was up. Then time stopped and they cut. I have seen Dick yank out ten minutes of his own music without an attempt to save it. He has also yanked ten minutes of my dancing, but he put the scalpel into my hand.

In spite of their great skill, the tryout periods for their shows have always been quite as hard as any others; but there were little diversions and encouragements peculiar to association with them. There were the quatrains and parodies Oscar improvised under his breath apropos of rehearsal occurrences. Many a lunch ended with a completed song quite as brilliant as any published. There were Oscar's outrageous and superb puns murmured half apologetically as though not expecting the corroboration of a giggle or even the turning of a head, like his designation of a delicate caress on a cancan girl's bustle as a "gosling," or his wordless comment as when at a particularly stringent moment, having ordered a cut against my bitter opposition, "and don't come out of rehearsal hall until it's done," he sent a tray of twenty cartons of coffee where I sat alone brooding (this was, of course, after coffee rationing had ended), or when he had discussed for days the cutting of another number, the *Carousel* clambake dance, he said, sitting down quietly, "Convince me," and sometime later, "You argue well, but I don't agree."

"I don't agree too," I replied patly.

"That makes us even. But I have the choice."

I answered, "That's candid. I can accept that."

"My dear," he chuckled, "you'd better. You have to."

Or again, when hearing me express extreme dissatisfaction with my own work, he put his arms around me and murmured, "You be careful what you say about de Mille; you're talking about the woman I love."

Both men, wise in this difficult business, are generous with

advice. Oscar takes time off to read and consider lengthy manu-
scripts and gives council and help. But one can talk to Oscar
about anything at all. For Oscar one clips items from newspapers
and magazines, marks passages in books, reports conversations overheard, remembers specially, finds drolleries, thinks more lucidly
and perceptively. Oscar is never under any circumstances bored;
everything is new and provocative, even the conversation of adoles-
cents. I have seen him set aside work and spend half an afternoon
teaching chess to an eight-year-old. Oscar has given away a dozen
young professionals in marriage and stood godfather at a score
of christenings. Dick fascinates and amuses, but it is Oscar whose
hand they ask to take at solemn moments.

And at moments of need. I went to him once on behalf of
Ballet Theatre. It was the first time I had ever approached anyone
in his position for money. I had not warned him about what I
came for. I sat down in great disquiet in the beautiful Georgian
chair, surrounded by the fabulous porcelain and books, and faced
him over the mahogany desk with the silver accouterments. He
smiled and waited. I squirmed and moistened my lips. He didn't
speak.

"It's just this —" I stuttered.

"All right, yes," he cut me short.

"Yes what?"

"Yes a thousand dollars. Never mind the pitch. Do you want
Scotch or bourbon?"

Oscar and Dick take on together not only the regulation char-
ities expected of men in their position, but their own foundation
and causes, political issues and social reforms. They work hard at
them, writing pamphlets and sketches and songs. Oscar devotes
a real measure of his time and resources to this.

Both are businessmen in the historic American tradition and
combine the drive and power of nineteenth-century empire build-

ers with eighteenth-century politesse and philosophy, living in ducal splendor and maintaining a suite of offices outside of the law firm they all but endow. Seldom in the history of the theater has anyone approached their business success. Their four great plays have been running very nearly continuously in at least three countries for from ten to fifteen years. They each separately have a dozen or so permanent successes that bring in constant royalties. In addition, they have functioned as producers for others' work with enormous return (*Annie Get Your Gun, Happy Birthday*). They publish their own music and print their own books. They are now currently producing their own movies.

Far from exhausting them, these manifold interests and diversions are like catnip; they revel in the multifarious responsibilities and incomes. In this huge zest for affairs and returns they share equally.

Whenever we boarded a train together, Oscar would stop me and, placing a hand on my shoulder, say in his gentle, even voice, "Now, Agnes, what have you forgot this time?" (This was not a frivolous question. I had been known to forget or leave behind suitcases, brief cases, reading glasses, single shoes, music and, once, myself, when the Oklahoma City fire department was dispatched to find me and fetch me to the train.)

What have I forgot? Oh, so much. It is hard in a few pages to sketch these complex, contradictory, fascinating, passionate and gifted men who played such an overwhelming role in my life and of whom I grew so fond, so grateful to for so much, with whom, in fact, I fell in love, yet who, for all the rich and fruitful hours spent together, the miles traveled, the honors and horrors shared, were bent on preserving what in the end could not be shared. For over the years they became more and more concerned with what tragically and inevitably must raise barriers between their ambition and all collaborators.

Carousel was a tough show for the choreographer because it was based on a strong and well-written play and there seemed small need for dances. The ballet in Act II, therefore, represented probably the hardest challenge I'd ever met. It entailed a real job of dramatic invention, close to playwrighting. I struggled and strained, but at last the bosses avowed themselves pleased.

The opening night in New Haven was a real surprise. This was, as Jo Mielziner remarked, the best musical-comedy script he'd ever read and it had been beautifully directed, but almost none of it came off as we had expected. The staff repaired to a hotel room where sacrifice and a cold supper awaited. There followed the kind of conference that professionals seldom see: in two hours we made a plan, throwing out or drastically altering the better part of Act II, half my ballet, five complete scenes (and with one the services and hopes of an elderly actress who had come out of retirement for the first real chance of her life), a couple of good songs and several verses in the remaining ones.

At the end of two hours we were all well exercised.

Although neither of the authors could have foreseen the audience reaction that night, they must have been to some degree prepared, because they set to rewriting with an alacrity and organization that bespoke foresight.

One of the assistants said as we left the room after that dreadful first *Carousel* conference, "Now I see why these people have hits. I never witnessed anything so brisk and brave in my life." And indeed, not three minutes had been wasted pleading for something cherished. Nor was there any idle joking as at the *Venus* conferences. We cut and cut and cut and then we went to bed.

Oscar went earliest, as soon as he could get away, because he would be up at six, working. And he had a list of required lyrics, scenes and liaison bits that would have daunted any lesser theater craftsman. For the next two weeks he was due to put in five or six hours of creative writing every day from dawn on.

Oscar would be alone and quiet in his room with his wits about him. But I was scheduled to begin in public. And into the room with me would drag the slightly soiled and shopworn brutes known as my dance company. They had to pull it out of their backs. I thought I had better be ready to help. Therefore I was also due up at six.

One might with time, one would think, build up a toleration for the tryout period, but working with Rodgers and Hammerstein always seemed more significant than working with others. Their united force was greater, their passions channeled deeper, their intent more noticeably implemented. One could no more think of their failing than of the war effort failing. One always felt that Posterity sat in on all staff meetings and had a good deal to say. Also our old colleague, Box Office, but this time dressed in a silk hat and carrying a gold-headed cane, and this time with voice mellifluous and venerable. There were elements of Patriotism and Mother Love and Honor in what they expected, and what you were privileged to give. Dick had never had a failure, he kept saying. And were you going to be the one to help him to this unprecedented, humbling experience? Oscar had had several, long before, and at the height of his great fame took a full page in *Variety* and advertised his worst notices with the endearing caption, "It happened before; it can happen again." This public penance, this propitiation to Fortune made him the more worthy of serving. It was only human for others to watch with jealous eyes for the misstep in the splendid parade. But we who marched alongside were very proud and minded the music and the step carefully.

All night I minded and counted and planned. All day I rehearsed. Between times I walked the streets alone in the twilight and thought of how someday I would not have to work like this. I would sleep and waste time and think of frivolities. Someday I would look forward to the evenings.

In Boston the spring freshened and flickered, the young green leaves dancing in the air like insects, and everywhere women lifted their heads and wondered how their men would find them. For the waiting had dimmed and blurred all of us. This had been a time of wrestling to hold vigorously to hope. And like any strong experience it had shadowed our faces. But we believed still that childhood would one day come back to the earth, and not a hat was bought that Easter without a personal prayer behind the act, not a daisy, not a yard of ribbon. In every house throughout the land cupboards were being opened and dresses shaken out and somehow the feminine rustling and stirring was a surer omen than the changing map. It was time for the war to be over. It was the earth season for a new way.

Meantime I was living in a hotel room. And he was in a place designated by a number. And I walked alone, back and forth across the common and up and down streets where families were sitting down to dinner, and men entered doorways and were greeted.

If there is a limit set to dreadful times they become bearable, but if none is known they are unbearable. And yet, they are to be lived through, and whether the end will come today or to-morrow, six years, never . . . they are to be lived through. My friend Arthur Davison Ficke, the poet, dying, said to me at this point, "The European war will be over in five years, but the war in Asia — this is a secret, don't breathe it — the war in Asia will be a thousand-year war." Ideas like this had to be listened to and endured. One leaned into anguish as a dancer leans against space, and the living balance within sustained. And one day passed and one day and one day and that year was done.

We were now getting into the second spring of separation.

Nothing seemed to change. Europe was being recovered mile by mile, but the Pacific and its hundreds of islands stretched across our lives. One could not think beyond this geography. One dared not look at maps or reports. If one read a book, it might possibly be something like *Shore Leave,* that dandy sabotaging of women's morale which, in an agony, I discussed with Walter, suggesting that if all husbands and lovers were unfaithful all the time, it were just as well not to advertise the fact to their women. He reassured me after his own fashion: that he was terribly surprised at my concern about anything so badly written.

Walter's news was broken and sparse. He didn't like the English weather. He had arrived in November at Liverpool, had not been piped off the boat as I had hoped, but had disembarked in a grim clanking, marched down streets without a light in black pouring rain, and had been shut immediately into a transport train for Stone, Staffordshire, where it was still raining. "Out of the frying pan into the mire." In August he had written, "Yesterday, a Monday, we had summer." Elizabeth Bowen had been extremely kind. Lise Harland had invited him to dinner. She had lost the child she was carrying in a recent bombing. He had given her nylons. He had visited a neighbor, the Countess of ———, and here, there was a hole in the paper. But she wrote to me herself directly, so I found out who *she* was. He was camped, I learned much too late, in the paddock adjacent to Rebecca West's farm at High Wycombe, but because I couldn't notify her, she never leaned over the garden wall and asked him in. It was raining a good bit. I was not to buy any more furniture. Couldn't I arrange to rest a little? He saw no end to the war. London was infrequent, but quite fun. He visited a friend of mine, a quartermaster in Westminster, who had a flat. There was, however, fog in London. And rain.

In all this boredom and complaining, I was now and then

drawn up sharp to the realization that he was in the middle of it, in daily mortal peril. There was the simple reference to a toy factory that had got a direct hit in the town nearby; most of the casualties were old women and very young girls. His battalion had devoted New Year's Eve to cleaning it up. There was the casual remark about a job of detonating leftover land mines along the beaches — routine work, he said — they all had to do it. The point was to try to guess correctly in which direction the chain reaction of the explosives would proceed. Sometimes they guessed wrong; they found this wry. I stared at that letter a long time as it sat on my breakfast tray. But he never spoke of active combat or any of the plasterings on his air base — never a word.

We had stopped making plans in our letters. We talked vaguely of Afterward. But Afterward seemed hardly possible and in the meantime we were spending all our time among people neither of us knew. Every episode that had occurred between us in our brief communion had been worn bare with the retelling. I searched the headlines and maps for some name on which to fasten an intimate fragment of gossip or a personal reminiscence, but history was between us, and whisperings and turnings of the head and liftings of the hand were blotted out by world events which everyone shared. There was nothing for us alone. We kept trying to imagine how the circumstances seemed under the other set of conditions; but of course we could not. About this time I realized I had forgotten how his voice sounded.

But once in a while the public sharing was so awful as to destroy space. There was the night in the Ritz elevator I saw the tragic terminal headline "ROOSEVELT DEAD!" In the great gold cloakroom of the Colonial Theatre, to which I had, as a matter of duty, to go, with the paper spread on the marble-topped gilt table, I read the details. The coat woman complacently knitted. Tears of horror and grief fell through my fingers as I read and I was oppressed with terror for the reconstruction without the man whom so many and so disparate people had come to trust.

"Well, it was about time for a change," said the cloakroom woman, "and thank God we are spared That Man." That Man, in this case, was Wallace. "And soon I hope we can have someone sensible and have a change from all this idiotic spending." I continued to weep without answering. On the other side of the wall, June Busted Out again. It was 9:04. I went back in the auditorium and saw Pearl Lang get her hand and retire to the wings, where the cast stood appalled, round-eyed, not speaking.

The same night, in Germany, Walter was smoking at mess with the French officers when, hearing a commotion in the road outside, they all ran out to find the sentries with some Russian D.P.'s. The Russians were distraught and making a terrible noise, begging, apparently, to see the commander. It was hard to understand them, but one name came through, and their persuasive and apparent grief. The D.P.'s had a radio, and they knew the American officers had none, and so they had come hurrying up the road to bring the news. And there, under the moon and the blossoming branches of a Bavarian spring, these two groups of men confronted each other and several wept.

I knew of this only much later. We were in Boston with a show to ready and our minds were fly-specked with our tiny troubles and hurts. Finally one day Dick watched with grim lips the revised ballet and that night the new ending was tried out. "Well," he said in relief as it finished, "I wouldn't have given you a nickel for it this afternoon."

"I know," I said.

He hugged me. "It's all right now, kid. The changes work. You've got a hit."

Opening night in New York my protégée, Bambi Linn, stopped the show cold. This is a phrase often used, but seldom actually witnessed. The first time I ever saw it was when a debutante named Ethel Merman sang "I Got Rhythm" in a Gershwin musical, *Girl Crazy*. At the conclusion of the *Carousel* ballet, the actors four times tried to resume dialogue before they were permitted to be heard, and when minutes later Bambi, having changed costume, made her next appearance, she was greeted with such a roar that she had to step forward and bow. Her face burned with excitement and two little girls in the wings burst into tears. The audience continued to yell. This happens frequently in opera houses but almost never in the commercial theater. The sound in the opera houses is lyric and ecstatic. The sound on Broadway is sharp, instantaneous and important. Behind this clapping is the noise of thousands and thousands and thousands of dollars, of telegraph wires humming, radio stations broadcasting, recording machines turning over, agents telephoning, reporters typing. The roar from a Broadway audience opens every door in the theater world. Immediately. That night.

Bambi woke up to find herself famous.

CHAPTER XV *The Cost*

SO now that financially and popularly speaking I was at the crest, I had first refusal of every script on Broadway, and although I had never been to Hollywood, the offers reached unprecedented heights. Dick (God Love You) LaMarr and I turned quite giddy over the proffered contracts, which bettered automatically as my refusals persisted, refusals due to script deficiencies or time stipulations or my own insistence that I keep free from long-term commitments until Walter's return from war. I had one windfall that netted me in 1945 ten thousand dollars when the management failed to take up an option on a picture I was praying I would not have to do. Walter sent his astonished congratulations from southern Germany, where he was wintering in mud and snow with the First French Army. It had not made me wonder; it was exactly as I had thought. I had learned the lesson hard in reverse. Three years before, my choreography of *Rodeo* grossed me five hundred dollars for five months' work. It seemed as though I were personally safe in this perilous profession. But I knew better; I saw what was happening to colleagues.

We needed a union. Everybody else had one — and choreographers had special difficulties and vulnerabilities. Not only was there no minimum wage or condition beneath which they could not be pushed, down to working without any recompense whatever, but of all the creative workers in the theater they were the only ones with no copyrights, no property rights in ideas or accomplishments, and no means of punishing plagiarism. They could have, therefore, no continuing income from their established works. The general public is not aware of this situation; the managers are, and exploit it.

Copyright in dance pattern exists in no country. It is possible to copyright an idea or a story — but not choreographic design. For this, property rights are guaranteed and enforced by law only through individual contract or private suit. Choreography, therefore, even the best and most famous, can be pilfered and reproduced and nothing but practical difficulties and moral scruple stops the practice, forces which should not be trusted to police the commercial theater. All the great nineteenth-century ballets have been considered public domain since their conception and only the extreme difficulty of reproduction limits the stealing, for if there is no script to protect the author, there is none to help the plagiarist. But most of Fokine's ballets were pirated from the year of their first performance by anyone who could remember the steps, and were played without fee, royalty, or credit given. So great and universal became the swindle that finally in 1935 a group of impresarios, headed by Dame Ninette de Valois and including de Basil, Massine and Marie Rambert, voluntarily set a price for performing *Les Sylphides, Carnival, Prince Igor, Scheherazade* and *Petrouchka* and offered this pittance to the choreographer, Fokine, as tribute and comfort in his none-too-affluent old age. He had no legal rights in the matter and could not have collected a cent by his own efforts.

Choreographers have always made individual terms with ballet companies, specifying certain controls as to casting and programing and small, pathetically small, royalties. As long as the companies have use for the choreographer's services and choose to function with responsibility, they will honor contracts. Chances for breach are manifold; royalties on foreign performances are hard to collect, and even the best terms are shabby — between seven dollars and twenty-five dollars a performance, usually late in payment. Ballet managements argue that there is no money — and after the electricians, grips, costume and scenery executants have taken their cut, there, indeed, is very little. They further argue that it is to the choreographer's advantage to display serious long works and that if the troupes were to go out of business, the choreographers would be done for, artistically speaking. As matters stand, this is unanswerable.*

The situation in the commercial theater, in films and TV has been, and is, much worse. At least in the ballet world the companies exist by virtue of the choreographers' cooperation and must therefore respect their wishes and rights to some extent. Prior to 1943 the Broadway field was monopolized by five or six dance directors who were by virtue of this fact alone able to negotiate passable fees, but newcomers fared badly.

When I signed my contract for *Oklahoma!* I was unknown on Broadway. I had neither union nor precedent to help me. I made what terms I could. They were not good. I cite them because they represent the common lot of any beginner in this business, then and now. I signed for $1500 cash and no royalties. I was to get an extra $500 when costs were paid off. My contract stipulated no royalties at all, but after the out-of-town triumph, the Guild granted me $50 a week. I went to Lawrence Langner later about the matter. If he could make it $75, I explained, I could start paying off debts. But he was concerned with his responsibility to backers and could not see any way clear to raising my share to $75 a week. Langner's concern for the backers bore fruit. By April 1953

---

* At the current writing, April 1958, A.G.M.A. is endeavoring to correct the most grievous wrongs by introducing a minimum-term contract for choreographers of ballet and opera and will force the companies to accept this when they negotiate the annual basic contracts for the dancers.

each investor with a $1500 one-per-cent share had already earned
a profit of $50,000.* One shareholder on whom a $5000 invest-
ment had been all but forced by the Guild Board realized a million
and a half.

The play ran for five years and nine weeks in New York City,
and there was a traveling American road company which played
for nine and a half years. For a great part of this period there were
concurrently two road companies. There have been three New
York revivals of several months' duration. It opened in London
April 1947 and ran three and one half years. It is still playing the
English provinces. In England alone it grossed more than one
million pounds. It played for one million people in London, for
one and a half million troops overseas during the war. It played
for years in South Africa, in Australia, and in New Zealand.
There were productions in Sweden and Denmark. The last
United States road company closed in December 1954. It is estimated that over the world more than fifty-five million persons had
bought tickets. Decca, which made the recording with the original
cast, then an innovation although now standard practice, reports
that by the time *Oklahoma!* closed on Broadway its album had
sold eight hundred thousand copies. It is still selling, both the
original version and subsequent recordings with other casts. In
1955 the seven-million-dollar moving picture was released and a
newly assembled all-star live company sent to Paris and Rome by
the State Department as representative of our culture. One can only
guess what the sheet-music sales have amounted to. Rodgers and
Hammerstein get a small royalty every time a tune is played on
radio, TV, jukebox or band. The Theatre Guild estimated forty-five
million dollars as its gross in ten years. They sold out their rights to
R. and H. for one million dollars. Current published figures, un-

* Robert Sylvester in the *New York Daily News*, quoted in the *Rodgers and
Hammerstein Fact Book*.

official but unchallenged (official figures are impossible to obtain), give the total world earnings over fifteen years as sixty million dollars.

My arrangement with the Guild remained unchanged for four and a half years, the biggest earning period of the show (I was granted, after lengthy negotiation, the $75 a week I asked for the road company only). In 1947, at a grand conference where my total Guild earnings were cited — but not theirs — I was at last accorded one half of one per cent.

When the play was produced in South Africa, Australia and New Zealand with my dances and my name, I had to sign away all claims in perpetuity in order to get any royalties whatever, and when the picture was made I had to accept whatever terms were offered for restaging purposes because the dances themselves were not my legal property and could be turned over to anyone for reproduction, as was in fact done without recompense to me of any kind when *Carousel* was filmed. In this instance I was forced to threaten suit to get credit for my work.

There were no rights and no royalties for any of the stock-company or summer-opera performances of either play. But my dances, or a version of them, are nearly always reproduced.

Hanya Holm with *Kiss Me Kate* and Jerome Robbins in *The King and I* have had the same experience. Both were artists of considerable achievement and great reputation at the time they signed contracts. Robbins had a strong deal with ownership clauses and royalty stipulations for *High Button Shoes,* for which he did his historic Mack Sennet ballet. But in order to benefit by his contractual rights he was obliged to rely on legal action.

Composers and playwrights are in a better position altogether. The copyrights on music and drama are strongly enforced both by law and by societies maintained for the purpose. An institution such as ASCAP monitors all musical performances on and off the air and demands toll with scrupulous exactness. But these organizations were a hundred years building and are the direct result of pirating endured by all the great of the last century, by Beethoven, Balzac, Chopin and Dickens, who reaped only a fraction of their earnings. So gross did the plagiarism of Gilbert and Sullivan operettas become at one point that they were forced to launch companies of their own to put a stop to imitation. Now, entrenched in the rights won for them little by little after decades of struggle, the contemporary composers and managers in their turn seek to exploit creators in other fields (scene and costume designers, music arrangers, but chiefly directors and choreographers) and go to legal and managerial lengths to avoid the paying of royalties, the giving of credit or other proprietary recognition.

Many authors and composers consider the plays the uncomplicated creation of their own imaginations and they buy the services of choreographers, designers, orchestrators outright, sometimes with authorship credit as well, as though these were services like plumbing or upholstery.

Lest the reader concur in this view and believe that a choreographer is no more entitled to ownership rights and royalties than orchestrator or designer, it must be understood that what the dance director furnishes is stage time, in the case of *Oklahoma!* twenty-six minutes' worth, dramatic and lyric invention not specified or even suggested in the original script. He starts with blank pages, an empty stage, and no music except thirty-two bars of melody and proceeds from there on his own responsibility. What he contributes may not be as important as the songs or dialogue, but the creative effort is like in kind and should be so recognized. In practice it is not.

As a result, each choreographer must make his terms individually in an open market crowded by worthy and starving competitors. There are only three veterans to whom secondary rights or percentages are conceded, that is, rights in moving-picture or television sales or foreign productions or stock or summer-opera companies, and yet, if the dances are good, they are reproduced faithfully lest the quality of the show, and therefore the profits, be diminished.

How can this be done with no dance script? Why, very simply by hiring dancers who have performed the work under the choreographer's tutelage. During the last fifteen years, many managers — in point of truth, too many and in all countries — have hit on the scheme of engaging dancers to reproduce whatever choreography they have been performing. By this means, all legitimate choreographic royalties are avoided. Mimeographed transcripts of the dances, bar for bar on the music, are often furnished as a further aid. There is sometimes, not always, legal sanction for this. The ethics seem undeviatingly clear. Dancers, who are more frequently loyal than not, loyal to the point of starvation, will not easily lend themselves to the practice. Alas — there are some who will, and the pilfering of whole ballets without change or disguise has become a useful adjunct to certain dancers' income. Foreign managements quite simply steal and invite suit in distant places with unfamiliar laws. Domestic managements change the names of corporations and sell and resell rights so fast to themselves and their cronies that it is extremely difficult to tell what change has transpired, if indeed any at all, but the choreographer is glued immobile as a fly in a web and must watch his own pupils and assistants, suborned to steal his ideas and livelihood. Several dancers have made paying careers out of doing just this.

The book directors find themselves in much the same position, and while devising stage business and analyzing character, however vital to the success of a play, cannot be placed on the same creative plane as composing — either musical or choreographic — their work is considered sufficiently useful to be recorded exactly in complete detail and forwarded to the producer of each subsidiary or stock company, domestic and foreign. For these extensive and detailed blueprints ("on the word 'cup' Donald sits on the left stool, crosses his legs and takes cup in right hand, looking over his shoulder") they receive neither credit nor fee. The directors also are not properly unionized, and for their services must, like the dancers, negotiate as individuals. Mamoulian's direction in *Oklahoma!* and *Carousel*, for instance, is always reproduced, usually without credit or pay, as is Robert Lewis's in *Brigadoon*.

In the ballet world, the public and critics have gradually been educated, and as no young composer today could, with any success, bring out a Chopin Polonaise as his own, so no dance director can claim the great *Sylphides* Nocturne or the *pas de deux* from *Swan Lake*. Dancers who have never choreographed anything in their lives do claim, however, the ballets from *Oklahoma!*, *Carousel*, *Allegro*, *Brigadoon* and *Paint Your Wagon* and they take regular authorship pay and credit for staging them.

The loss of continuing royalties is no trivial privation. A choreographer's life is slow in developing and more expensive than any other creative worker's. (Any composition involves studio space, music and living bodies, generally paid by the hour.) Taxes annually take all but the smallest profit. Money from good years cannot be set aside for study periods or privately financed experimental projects; losses incurred in rehearsals one year may not be applied against gains in the next. Without royalties, therefore, the choreographer is constrained to constant work, much of it hack. He can never, under any circumstances, stop and consider — or free-lance. Unless privately subsidized, he must always sell his time on arbitrary schedules, for purposes and ends not of his choosing, and among the confusion, threats and interferences of other interests.

Choreography has become, in short, a desperate profession. The answer is plainly copyright and unionization.

In order to obtain a copyright, however, a tangible blueprint must be filed in the Library of Congress through which ownership can be established. There are only two ways of blueprinting a dance: by script and by moving picture. Dance script (Labanotation) can be written and read back expertly by only a handful of people in the United States, none of them choreographers. As a group, we are illiterate. Any dispute, therefore, would have to be conducted with choreographer, producer, plagiarist, librarian, lawyers, judge and jury unable to follow the text and at the mercy of the expert witness. The theater unions have made filming dances a practical impossibility by decreeing that all performers must receive either an entire week's or half a week's pay for the exposure of any negative, even 16 mm., at any regular performance. The filming of a three-minute dance, therefore, runs into thousands.

With all this in mind, the choreographers currently in New York assembled that winter of 1945. We canvassed our colleagues throughout the United States, collating all suggestions and ideas. From our investigation there emerged a history of exploitation that was arresting; the scope, viciousness and variety of abuse surprised even us. For five decades, which was as long as anyone had personal memory, there had not been the slightest attempt at recompense or rights equivalent to those enjoyed by the other arts. Armed with this knowledge and a good plan for a minimum contract, we started the reformation, and ran head-on into seemingly insurmountable blocks.

First, the smallness of our group. We defined a choreographer as anyone who had set an original dance for pay or professional public performance (note that the two are by no means synonymous). At that time we numbered only eighty-one. Since then, I imagine, the figure has tripled.

Second, our poverty. For the very reasons we were organizing we had been unable to make or save much. We were advised that the price of getting a copyright law through Congress would cost at least fifty thousand dollars. No lawyer of repute seemed eager to attempt the work as a public service. We considered joining Equity, but after careful examination on both sides, decided (maybe correctly) that inasmuch as our work was creative, and that of actors interpretative, our interests were not only different but in some ways divergent and hostile. Where we, by nature, belonged was with the playwrights' guild or composers' union, whose key members stood unalteringly and powerfully opposed to our getting representation. For, if ever we were to establish property rights in our own works or ideas, and could implement our claims, the enormous profits of the composers would have to be, to some extent, divided. This was an eventuality they naturally did not favor.

It needed selfless effort to make any headway in this troubled field. Economic reform, of which unionizing is one type, is whole-time work and demands tremendous sacrifice. It means setting aside all career interests for months at a stretch and buckling down to the sweat and turmoil of political organizing. It means refusing jobs and ruining one's personal life. And without pay. The creative artist will not voluntarily stop his artistic activities and give his time for anything on the Lord's earth, including spouse and children. That winter everyone seemed too busy.

At this writing the situation is considerably worse. Producers and managers are aroused by the threat of choreographers' growing demands. Authors go to peculiar pains to write dancing out of the shows or keep it well corralled in unimportant little corners. Rank beginners are brought in at bottom prices. There is a very real rivalry between directors and choreographers for power, prestige and percentages. Jerome Robbins and Michael Kidd have solved matters by organizing, directing, producing and choreographing their own shows. This is a heroic answer and one that is not possible for many. There could be another: simple justice.

CHAPTER XVI *London Town*

ON May 8, 1945, the German Army capitulated. For a time now a good many men would not be killed. At least, not right away. Everyone took a notch in his belt and looked to the east.

Shortly thereafter Ruggles wired that he had obtained all the necessary permits and currency releases and that I was to come to England with all possible haste. He would immediately arrange transportation.

Walter had been moved in midwinter to the Continent and was presumably wandering about Bavaria as liaison officer with a segment of the French Army. There was scant chance of his being relocated in England, but London was closer than New York to Bavaria and I could not believe we would not somehow effect a *rapprochement*. I cabled rejoicings.

The next day I went with my lawyer to the Subtreasury Building on Wall Street and asked for an exit visa.

"Married?"

"As you see."

"Husband's present whereabouts?"

"U. S. Army overseas."

The clerk snapped my passport to and handed it back to me. "Go home, madam. We make no exceptions. You will not get permission to leave the United States."

"But the war is over."

"Only in Europe, and the government is not granting exit permissions. Don't even bother to try. You will only disappoint yourself."

I walked silently out. The lawyer patted me on the shoulder. "I'm sure there is something we can do. It may take a little time."

"We've had lots of that, haven't we? In the meanwhile, at any moment he may be moved to the Pacific. And the job won't wait."

So I had a good strong pot of tea and began to pack. A trunk stood in one corner of the room in case I went by boat. Two bags were readied in another in case I went by plane. And night and day I and my sister and mother pulled every possible wire, including calls to Mrs. Eisenhower and the British ambassador, several colonels and a senator. Somehow it was accomplished. After two and a half weeks, a kind of promise drifted through. My lawyer phoned one noon. "Exit visa granted. You leave Baltimore tomorrow at four o'clock by air."

I turned my shows over to the dance captains, my business affairs to my agent, my domestic affairs to my secretary, my studio to a WAVE, Lieutenant Loia Cheaney from San Francisco, made a will and departed.

The week before I left, my sister's husband returned after two years of overseas service and they went off together on a vacation. This seemed like a happy augury and I took heart from it.

As Mother embraced me at the station, she put into my hand a letter just arrived. It was from Walter and it advised that if I had not already started, I had better drop all plans for proceeding as he was probably being shipped home shortly. I really did not know what to do. Nothing was certain, and I was now under contract. I faced Mother in bleak dismay. Mother, as always, took the cheery view. "Well, at least it will be a change for you — and you can see all the old friends. I've put a package of tea in your bag for Lady Wedgwood and another big one for the Taxation of Land

Values staff. And, of course, you'll see Walter. You can't tell me they'll be able to keep him from you once you're on his side. It would be inhuman!" Mother erased with finality the recent four years with an emphatic clenching of her tiny fist. "Inhuman! Now don't forget Lady Wedgwood. You have to go to her, you know. You can't phone. She's stone deaf. And hug Arthur Madsen for me. And give my greetings to Richard Stokes. Tell him if he wants any more copies of the *New York Times* — Oh! I forgot to give you the Mothersill for the plane! If you get hungry eat vitamins." Her voice trailed after me as the train started to move. "Of course — you'll see him. If he's sent home, just get out of your contract. Explain to them." Her face was a blur. She still waved.

I was making a flight at a time when people still signed dollar bills — short snorters — as a token of the trip — and she was petrified of even the briefest plane trip. She had not once mentioned her reluctance to see me chance this one.

This was June 14, my second wedding anniversary.

We flew high above the clouds and the heavens were clear and splendid with stars and a hard moon. At dawn there was nothing but mountains of changing mist and fume — and then sickeningly we plunged straight down through opaque white and there rose up to meet us, as sudden as a great animal from the fog, but brilliantly green and wooded, the mountains of south Wales. And we were looking at England again, we who had wondered for so long and with such love if ever we would.

I had left London seven years before, November 1938, debt-ridden, hopeless, heartbroken, all my plans, professional and personal, shattered, with not a friend to see me off at the station except two refugee Germans. Now, as I drove into Mayfair well escorted and in Ruggles's limousine, I couldn't help marveling at the contrast. Great bunches of welcoming flowers graced the expensive if sad and unpainted hotel rooms. On the table by my bed lay the bound scripts. There was a list of invitations and appointments for press interviews. Nothing that could be done to make me welcome had been neglected.

I went out to see Berkeley Square. Opposite my hotel window was the home of a friend, a blackened shell now with window shades blowing hideously from one gaping orifice. The three-hundred-year-old trees in the square still stood even though damaged, but the iron fences had long since been removed for scrap metal and the lawns were worn to brown earth. There were no flowers — absolutely none. All the lovely London squares had become throughways, trodden bare. A film lay over the city; everything was covered with dust. No doors had been painted, no brass polished, nothing shone, twinkled, or reflected. The whole town was grayed down, as in a dream. And with the disappearance of color, sound and speed seemed to become muted also. Everyone moved just a little more slowly, a little more quietly, and when a bird's note was heard, as it sometimes was wonderfully in those metropolitan streets, the sound was futile and without resonance, there being no answering vibration in visual tonality. Only the weather was the same — sunlight and drizzle, sunlight and drizzle in dimpled nervous inconstancy.

With dreadful repetition appeared the holes in the earth, the empty spaces where buildings had stood, frequently walled off to make reservoirs for fire fighting. These were brutal accents in the gray shabbiness and these one expected to see. But now and then a sight so overwhelmingly emotional stopped all thought — the columns of a Georgian church cut off idiotically four feet from the ground as though by children's scissors, fireweed growing rank and delicate on the marble floor while a black cat nosed her way through to the chancel. But it was not these extraordinary reminders of brimstone and horror that clutched the heart. It was the gray patience of the city, the lack of dynamics, variance, or zest.

The women wore no stockings, no hats, little make-up and five-year-old dresses. No one looked young except the children, unusually red-cheeked and robust for English children. The faces of the older people were stilled. In their own parlance — they'd had it.

Outside of some French visitors, I believe I was the only woman in London wearing a hat, and I had a selection of gay and charming ones made for me by Gustavo Franklin, my dancer Lidija's husband, especially designed to ravish Walter. Passers-by stared at me and grinned. After all, I was a portent, like the first crocus or a February swallow.

I went back to my hotel, where a reporter awaited me. He resented my coming to England to make a musical; they could, he felt, make their own musicals. He resented my coming to stage dances; they already had good choreographers. He resented my being well fed. He resented my hat and my nylon stockings. He resented my new suit and my lipstick. He resented my accent. He'd met some American soldiers, I gathered, he didn't care too much about. He resented Wesley Ruggles. Ruggles had been giving out some wonderfully ill-advised pronouncements about how he was going to show England the way to make a supercolossal musical, Hollywood style. He indicated that no one in America believed England had any pretty girls but that he would find them somehow and make proper stars of them.

All this the reporter brought home to me sharply, but in the middle of our taut interchange there appeared running through the lobby Thérèse Horner and Peggy van Praagh, who had been members of my London company in the prewar days, and with them was the lovely Lise Harland, who had been my business manager. They were young and beautiful women when I left. But now lines of care and deprivation and terror had been worked into their faces. Thérèse was ill with tuberculosis. And the years for their careers had come and gone. They had simply missed out on the big chance. We clung together and gasped out questions. The reporter tried to interrupt, but feebly now. Lise turned on him.

"But, my good man, you don't understand. She's one of us."

"We worked for years and years together," I explained, "and went hungry, job-hungry, and buttoned up each other's costumes. I didn't come over to teach them anything. I learned most of what I know right here ten years ago."

"Speaking of costumes," said Peggy, "does Hugh still rip off all his clothes whenever he gets mad? I'll never forget the time in Norwich when the bishop's wife —"

The reporter grinned and slipped away.

Oh, if I'd only brought over more lipsticks and nylons and nightgowns!

I read the script in the room among Mr. Ruggles's flowers. The script was far, far worse than anything I feared. I went to bed with a headache. This did not help — the script remained unchanged.

On Monday Ruggles gave me a reading with music in his office. He was trying, with touching sincerity, to imbue me with his enthusiasm, and the audition he put on for me was like a real show. The whole staff attended. He read the script and played records of the songs. There were costume and scene plates for each number and even samples of material. Many of the costumes had been designed in Hollywood and would have done for a night club on Sunset Strip but for nothing I cared to deal with. The music — never mind the music! Or the lyrics! Ruggles had everything ready — in fact, there was almost nothing left for me to do. He had blocked out the dances to the last detail of each camera angle and length of exposure. All he expected from me was which foot, how high, and with what arms.

No amount of courtesy and diligence could mask facts. The songs were terrible and so were the dance ideas. There was to be one number on a grand piano forty feet by eighty, made of white satin, and while twenty girls in evening dress played it, a group of witches were to dance around a caldron on top.

The plot had to do with so-called backstage life. It is as hard to recall now as it was while we were working on it.

"One thing — if I might suggest," he said diffidently. "In matching dancers, try to put the tall girls with the tall boys and the short girls with the short boys — and Kay Kendall is your leading dancer."

"Has she ever danced before?"

"No — she hasn't acted yet either. But if you want to, and I want you to, you can make her dance just as well as anyone in the Sadler's Wells. I'll take time off and help."

Kay Kendall was a ravishing young model with a long slender body, wonderfully long legs and arms, and the face and creamy complexion of a great Edwardian beauty. She had sensitive and gentle lips on which both invitation and appraisal seemed to tremble simultaneously, and eyes which, for the depth and softness of their deep violet gaze, rivaled any I have ever seen. She made one realize why people stood on chairs to watch the fashionable belles drive through Hyde Park. But she was very young at this point, and very shy and intimidated and, although smart, not skilled in the tricks and techniques of the formidable professionals who surrounded her, and who regarded the sudden pushing ahead of this novice into star position with something less than Boy Scout courtesy. It is a very rare thing when a great beauty is guileless. But Kay was that — patient, obedient and guileless. Her next months were not easy; indeed, her next years, due to the false precocity of the start, were to be very hard. She is now an established international star. No less lovely, she has grown deliciously comic. And who would ever have foreseen this as the timid pretty girl glanced uneasily to the right at Sid Fields, the darling of the music halls and the American G.I.'s, and to the left at Tessie O'Shea, the Bomb of Blackpool? They gave short shrift, I can tell you, to her or each other. Kay somehow survived and there is not a wrinkle to tell that she frequently sat in the corners crying with fright. She has since learned to kick and prance around delightfully — but to equal the best in Sadler's Wells, that she has not yet learned.

"If you want my help in showing her how to dance," said Ruggles, "you'll have it."

I was trapped, and dismay made me cruel.

"Mr. Ruggles," I began —

"Call me Wesley," he pleaded with a melting smile.

"Wesley, have you seen any of my work for Broadway?"

"All of it."

"Evidently you haven't liked it."

"I liked it. Why do you think I brought you over?" His eyes became steely — I daresay mine were pretty bright.

"Wesley, I have to work my way and only on what I believe."

"Of course," he said. "That's what I want."

"And with trained dancers —"

But he would not listen or learn. In me he'd bought what he considered the most currently successful Broadway girl, but the last thing in the world he intended was to pay attention to the ideas that had made this success. He knew what a musical movie should be. He knew and that was that. It was going to include the white satin piano.

Nevertheless, he noticed my personal loneliness. And he was more than kind. He tried, while not giving way an inch on any point in the picture, to help me reach Walter. Now that I was on the near side of the Atlantic, all communication ceased. I attempted cabling. Ruggles even tried an Army telephone to the Continent. Nothing resulted but unbroken silence. For all I knew, Walter had in fact been shipped back home or out to the Pacific.

Weeks passed this way — no news and the daily discovery of disheartening details about the picture.

My friend, the American quartermaster who had been so hospitable to Walter all through the last two years, was due to move on to the Pacific and bequeathed me his pretty flat in Dolphin Square. This was the flat that had housed Walter during his London furloughs. He had sent snapshots of his two birthday parties on Christmas Eve, with a tiny cake at each and a ring of strange heads bent over the minute glow, the officers' buttons shining in the light and all the windows muffled in black. The flat held not only memories, which I could not share, but the quartermaster's personal stores of toilet paper, soap, grapefruit juice, orange juice, chocolate bars, nuts, which I could. I became a short-lived but welcome dispensary for everyone I knew.

The quartermaster also bequeathed me his housekeeper, Lily Cantello. She took charge of my ration books, which were altogether beyond my understanding. She took charge of me. So I moved in and was extremely comfortable and altogether unhappy.

Every time I read the scenario I was appalled. Every time I played the music I was appalled. Never before in my life had I done anything I altogether despised. This was a new and unpalatable experience. Walter was evidently on his way home and I was, I informed myself hourly, stuck here by contract for six months.

I remember one particularly dispiriting Saturday afternoon. I finally sent the company away and sat cross and wretched on the studio floor. I said to the pianist, "Play some Mozart. Maybe with another sound I can move in a less disgusting manner." So she played Mozart and I put my head in my hands and cried.

I looked up to see a young man watching. "I don't care to be watched just now," I said angrily, wiping my eyes with a grimy hand. "Go away."

"I would like to talk business," he said very politely.

"You might ask beforehand," I snapped. "I can't talk now. Go away."

He turned slowly but hesitated and then said very softly over his shoulder, "I was sent on behalf of the French Embassy to offer you the Opéra. We want you to take charge of our Opéra for a year and put it on its feet."

Dirty, tear-stained and astonished, I gaped at him.

"Our director is unable to continue."

"Your director has been indicted for collaboration."

"Exactly. So, mademoiselle, if you will consider —"

"I am honored," I said, climbing up and slapping the dust from my legs. "But this is of all times the job for a Frenchman. I am not enough of a classicist to be suitable for the position. And now is the time to turn to great use the talents of your own people."

"Mademoiselle, please think this over."

"I am deeply moved — but you think over what I have said."

(Subsequently they thought it over and, ignoring Roland Petit, Jean Babilée and Janine Charrat, took Lifar out of limbo and reestablished him.)

This extraordinary conversation had occurred at 3 P.M. I had, on the exhilaration of the talk, decided to indulge myself and went out window shopping.

When I returned home there was a letter at last. At last a letter. How I tore it open and stood holding it in shaking hands before I dared read the beloved writing! And what I read was this: that he did not know when he could get to London — possibly not for the next six months. His C.O., a twenty-five-year-old colonel, did not hold with husbands and wives meeting in wartime, and although he, the colonel, made regular trips to England to keep some pretty fancy dates, he forbade Walter to accompany him. Better go home, said Walter's letter, get out of the damn job, go home and wait.

I cried this time as though my heart were dying. I cried from my stomach, from my bowels. But there was no one around and the phone never rang, so after a while I stopped through exhaustion and bathed my swollen, blotched face in cold water and put on my prettiest dressing gown and played Schubert. I might as well spend the evening doing something constructive. I might try to work up zest for one number somehow with Schubert to help. The long July evening stretched ahead. Behind my tousled hair I could see in the mirror as I moved the high northern sky with golden clouds and all the Wren spires that were left straight and perky in the pale happy light. Nothing good occurred in my room, however, nothing good, but I persisted.

The doorbell suddenly rang. I expected no one. I knew no one likely to call. I walked dully to the door. I opened.

Outside stood a soldier. He handed me a newspaper.

"Your evening paper, madam," he said.

It was my husband.

I didn't do much work in the next twelve days. But Ruggles was generous and understood. In any case, we were not to go before the cameras for two and a half months, so there was no need for his fretting. Twelve days later our time was up and Walter was forced to go back, but we were quite cheery. After all, the shooting war was over and he was stationed less then a thousand miles away, a near neighbor, and he promised to return in a short three months.

Later that day I was called to the phone to speak to him.

"Impossible," I snapped.

But is was he. His colonel had been too hung over to fly the plane. So we had one more night together. Unfortunately, the colonel had sufficiently recovered by the following morning.

I went on with my weary exercises. None of the replenishing of the past week had changed the script. The following Saturday we knocked off at noon in our usual week-end disgust, and clad in an old raincoat to disguise my American accent, I went the round of the fabulous antique shops in Church Street, Kensington. How often in my student days had I pressed my face to the glass of these shops! Treasures could be had for nothing then, but in those impoverished times 7/6 had been too much for my budget. Now I had money aplenty but the stock was depleted and the prices up. However, I found a couple of things and brought them home unwrapped in my pocket. (Paper and string were still practically unobtainable.) As I put my latchkey into the door, I noticed that the lock clicked oddly. The flats had suffered several robberies lately and my heart skipped a beat. The mink coat! My only lovely mink! Bought with so many years of work. The mink Walter wouldn't let me wear because he had not given it to me himself!

Obviously the door had been unlocked. The knob turned in my hand. Lieutenant Prude rose cheerfully to greet me.

"Damn you, darling!" I said. "Can't you ever give me warning?"

"I stepped into the plane on eight minutes' notice. I haven't even a toothbrush."

"Why were you permitted to come back so soon?"

"Well, I suppose you might as well know now as later. I'm being shipped East in three weeks. Ordinance work all through the Islands."

I knew what that meant. He was to help clear the litter off the landing fields, the litter being unexploded bombs, wrecked planes, ammunition reserves — anything that could blow up.

I sat down quietly and took his hand. Like the ringing of bells, everything clarified. A knife wound could do this, I thought, or a death notice, or the birth of a child. The world, for a wonder, turned as a unit and direct purpose took over.

At breakfast on the last day, we were sitting in the sunny parlor by our balcony spreading the marmalade which miraculously and inexplicably appeared each morning. Walter looked up from *The Times*.

"They have dropped an atomic bomb on Hiroshima."

"What's that mean? Will it make the war shorter?"

"Honey, you don't understand. This is going to make the human race shorter."

"So long as the war gets shorter."

"Take care of my wife," he said to Lily as he left.

"Very good, sir." I think he did not realize then what a promise from a Cockney meant. But I came to know.

Three days later when he was on a boat in Marseilles heading for the East, the second bomb was dropped and the war was over. His transport was rerouted to New York. But I was enmeshed in four remaining months of contract. I couldn't budge.

With the final peace, everyone's nerve let go. My friends simply disappeared. It was August and holiday time and all who could, went away for six weeks and, in decorous English privacy, collapsed. They had waited so long for sleep and leisure and complaining and losing their tempers and getting angry, or just for weeping. But they had the grace to do none of these things in public. Those who had to stay didn't care to talk. Everybody in town kept to his own room and sat listening to the sound of no bombs. At this point it became a great effort to pick a piece of paper off the floor. One could see the citizens going down the nearly silent streets, hatless, stockingless, very slowly, without talking.

I saw no one except my wretched colleagues, no one at all after rehearsal hours. A terrible listlessness dragged on me.

Mother and Walter were now together in New York, and although his letters were irregular, due to his rushing about on military duties, hers came three times a week and told me how he looked and when he came to dinner and whom he met and what he said. And now I could dream about him, in known surroundings, and the people in each episode had faces. He did not move into the studio. Our friend, Lieutenant Loia from San Francisco, was still there and he was as reluctant to dislodge her as he was to take possession alone. So it was she and not I who stood at the top of the stairs and threw open the door to him. I cabled her to have the fire lit and flowers around and to be sure the place was shiny clean when first he saw it. In the corner was my gift to him — a 1604 Swiss cabinet of beautiful design — and over the mantel hung my anniversary gift — the portrait of me by Elizabeth Montgomery (Motley) in my bridal whites, holding a sprig of Texan bluebonnets, the hands unfinished because I had left precipitously without notice for England. And standing about the wide rooms were the chairs he had forbidden me to buy. He was seeing them all without me. Would he forgive me the chairs? Would he accept them without me there to tease him into loving them? Mother had him almost every night for dinner. He bunked with a friend and a large dog. He did well enough, but it certainly wasn't what we'd had in mind.

He was trying frantically to get a job in case he were demobilized and not sent to the Far East on occupation duty — but he warned me that we could not count on this. I determined that he should not be sent overseas again for another two-year stint before I got back. I determined this, sitting with clenched fists and set teeth in my London flat.

And in the meantime, one by one, he was going to all my shows. Every time I had watched them from the rear of the audience I had thought, Will he like this phrase? Will he turn to me here and nod and press my hand? I never watched a performance but I thought how it would be with him seeing it for the first time beside me. All I could do was to wire the casts. But I was so afraid he might be disappointed. The press wasn't and the public wasn't, but he was my husband. He was the most important and the hardest.

The last time he had visited me in London we had gone as the guests of David Webster to the Sadler's Wells and there Walter saw his first ballet. It was not a felicitous introduction — a light, inconsequential piece full of all the cliché stylizations that balletomanes take such a time learning to savor and which drive the ordinary citizen roaring for fresh air.

"Is that," said Walter to me as we struggled through the crush bar, "what you do?"

"No," I answered. "No, it isn't."

"But," said a well-known enthusiast and critic, standing by, whom my mother always referred to as "the housebroken mouse," "it's not a bad little work. It has an atmosphere, a sort of — how shall I say? — a certain quality, a good deal of that — and then her *batterie!* Poignant! Absolutely poignant! Don't you find it so?" He chewed over each half-formed opinion as though he were nibbling at something that was very dear to him, which, as a matter of fact, it was, being the result of his own processes. One could no more disagree with his opinions than his face. "We need ballets like this," he added.

"Why?" asked Walter.

"Didn't you like it?" happily prompted the little man.

"I thought it was pure rot!"

The critic was so surprised and disappointed in the bluntness and unfriendliness of the response and the disrespect to a native English work that he drew back with widened eyes.

"I can't be unique in this," said Walter. "I'll get another opinion," and stopped a bristling and empurpled British colonel studded with pips and ribbons. "I beg your pardon, sir, what was your opinion of the last piece?"

"Balderdash!" shouted the colonel with such gusto that he nearly spilled the two pink gins he was carrying. "Uncompromising balderdash!"

Now as I sat waiting for his opinions about my work, the echo of that terrible word knocked at my heart. Was Walter watching my pieces with tight lips and disappointed eyes, shutting his teeth on sick realization?

"Balderdash," I said to myself and wired my dance captains to rehearse the troupes again.

I used to go where I knew he'd been, and look at what he must have looked at, and try to imagine how it was for him when he had been there without me, so that I could salvage some of the experiences we had not shared, so that I would not be left too far behind.

I walked a great deal alone through London, and one night, just at dusk about nine-thirty, I crossed Piccadilly Circus, and standing at Amen Corner was a group of American soldiers. They did not move and they barely spoke. They waited, watching. They waited with gathering energy, baffled but in power, and they knew they were a force to reckon with. The citizens gave them wide berth, except for the hatless, stockingless young women who darted among them like little fish, committing small incomprehensible signals of notification. But the main group of men never stirred. They were savoring what they might do if once they got good and ready to.

The dark blotted out their faces. But they were still there, a lot of them, watching. Their cigarettes glowed unmoving. They seemed to breathe together, and the only variation was the young girls hurrying between.

I used to stare through the long evenings at the sights he had seen so often without me, through the windows that could then only be opened in daylight.

I put my head on the sofa and stared at the spires brilliant against the softly darkening sky. I left my supper untouched. I just sat. I didn't care to read and naturally I couldn't talk since there was no one there to talk to. These rooms had been electric with fear and fun and sharing during the war. They had been gay and full of comfort during our weeks together. Now there were no voices, no laughter, no creaking of chairs or scraping of boots, no tinkling of glass, nothing except slow footsteps outside down the street and a woman calling to her child across the areaway. And at long intervals, Big Ben, right over my head, throwing out a pall of sound that signaled my progress toward November.

When it was dark I went to bed.

At six-thirty the next morning, Lily would wake me for the rehearsals that would surely lose me my professional reputation.

Lily did her best to cheer me. "Never mind," she said every morning. "You'll be going home soon," and there was marmalade on the tray and an egg.

"How does all this marmalade happen?" I asked.

"I promised the lieutenant I'd look out for you."

"Your rations?"

"It's a pleasure, madam."

"And your husband's?"

"It won't be for long."

"And the egg each day?"

"Don't ask, madam. It's our hen. But the government takes all the eggs — all except one."

"When did you last have an egg?"

"You're not used to this, madam."

On coming home from work I used to find notes all over the house. *There's a bit of fish on the stove. Light the gas and when it is warm try to eat it.* Or with a threepenny bunch of violets: *Dear Madam, I thought you might be lonely.*

Besides the disgusting scenario and shoddy dances and the yearning to share the homecoming experiences with my bridegroom, there was a possible better reason for my listlessness. I badgered the doctor. Surely? Surely? Not yet, not yet, she said, no one could be sure so soon. But I knew. The first rabbit was negative. "This is an outrage," I cried. "Science has failed — or the animal kingdom."

"Probably both," she answered. "They often do."

Two weeks later, coming home from a dinner with my Hollywood agent, who had flown the Atlantic to straighten out certain matters — among others, my predicament — I entered my empty flat to find a note from the laboratory. This one was to be definitive — so I opened it with considerable tension. I was alone as I read.

Shaking, clutching the paper to my breast, I walked up and down. The note stated simply: "The test for pregnancy is positive."

I rushed onto the balcony and looked at the few lights going out, and the churches and the frosty towers of Parliament cold and quiet, and the rows of chimney pots turning their heads about like cats. Whom could I tell right then, right that moment? Whom could I shout to and embrace? Whom could I share this with? "Hear what's happened: I too!"

Thérèse, Peggy and Lise were all across the city and sound asleep.

I picked up the telephone and called the one person on earth to be sorry for the tidings. I called my agent. He was a gentleman. He rallied.

"Congratulations. Splendid. Dorothy Lamour is, too." And through his kindness I could hear the deductions he was making from his yearly budget.

"Will you inform Ruggles?"

"Yes, I'd better be the one."

"I'd be grateful to be spared that."

Ruggles felt, not without justification, that he'd been used. He was offered back every penny he'd put up. But he declined to release me and threatened suit. Since my health was splendid, no medical discharge was possible. "We kept our girls in the factories well into the fifth month," said my doctor heartily. "There is a well-established precedent here —"

September 18 is my birthday, and on September 27 the birthday call Walter had attempted all week was finally accomplished. I heard the phone ringing at four-thirty in the morning and knew instantly what it must be. There were several official voices announcing a transoceanic enterprise, and as I waited, I saw the dawn glowing behind the houses of Parliament. Then, finally, we were established and he was able to say:

"Happy birthday, darling."

"I've news for you!"

"You're coming home! Thank God, you're coming home!"

Static intervened and a British "Please excuse this."

"No, quite different. We're going to have a baby."

"What?"

The static was fearful. Several British disclaimers. I had fairly to scream.

"We're having a baby!"

"Good God! Are you sure?"

The line broke. A clear British voice spoke this time: "I'm really very sorry, madam. It won't be long re-establishing you. Hold steady."

It was twenty-five minutes.

"Walter, are you all right? You're not alone?"

"I'm being supported on either side!"

"Have you something to drink?"

"A bottle of Scotch. I'm well along in it." There was a transatlantic gurgle.

"Aren't you glad?"

"Are you all right? Who's looking after you? Oh, take care. Oh, Lord, if I could get to —"

"I'm all right," I shouted. "Do you like the way I fixed up our flat?"

"That is all, madam. The time is up. You were completed, weren't you?"

Lily's marmalade and eggs continued. "This is my baby too, madam," she said. Lily's son had been killed by a direct hit on a tank. She had found the official telegram in her box on Christmas morning: HIS MAJESTY'S GOVERNMENT REGRETS TO INFORM YOU — She served the Christmas dinner before she told the family.

The minute she learned my news she arranged a quart of milk a day. It seemed cheating to come to her country, an alien, and take advantage of the milk supply, but everyone appeared heartily in accord with showing hospitality to the unborn citizen, alien or no. I was given vitamins and extra butter.

Friends rallied. Honoria Plesch, our costume executant and designer, bicycled across the city many evenings in her ill-fitting W.V.S. uniform with a cabbage or a fresh head of lettuce and even an occasional egg. Simone, who lived below and who knew the Free French Air Force, was sometimes the recipient of good French beef or a bottle of real olive oil straight from the Mediterranean, and she rushed to knock on my door. She was the daughter of a Cordon Bleu chef and she cooked without disguises. One could recognize meat from vegetables at a glance. She worked in the largest beauty establishment in London, and tired as she was from standing all day in an atmosphere of wet soap and hair, she washed and dried mine late at night as her gift to the situation.

The men at the studio shortly became aware and as the autumn damp intensified, trained their lights on me for warmth where I sat in the yellow fog in my mink, no longer an unpardonable luxury, but the means of life. There was absolutely no heat anywhere, dressing room or stage, and we endured the unchecked river mists from eight in the morning until seven at night. One man gave me an orange. It was the first any of them had seen since before the war. I could not force myself to eat it in their faces, so I sat like Henry the Eighth for two days with it in my hand, and then devoured it publicly, slowly and ceremoniously. Plesch owned a jar of peanut butter stolen from somewhere and cached in her paint cabinet and when she saw me going lavender about the mouth, slipped me a well-spread cracker.

We all, high and low, ate in the commissary and the food was dreadful. My colleagues had developed mouths of sawdust and ate doggedly. But the smell of old fried fats, of old margarine, the flannellike bread, the little dried pieces of meat, the watery sprouts, the greens always bearing a thumb mark made my bowels turn to water. Everyone dreamed of clean food. The war was over and so deprivations became insupportably irksome.

The studio was up the Thames and right on the river margin. It had been used during the war as an airplane factory and often bombed. What Ruggles took over was the shell of a plant and some acreage and he attempted to build the physical workshops and stages while setting up a functioning organization and simultaneously filming and recording. His company had not been in existence as a unit before, and while they stood shifting their feet in the damp and making lists of what they needed, carpenters were laying the planks for them to shift on. Most of what they needed, like six miles of electric cables, was unobtainable. But they persisted with the ingenuity which had built chicken coops in every British back yard and raised beets and sprouts in every city square. Naturally it was slow. And Ruggles fumed because among all else he was responsible for the budget. He had several tense dinners at Claridge's explaining to J. Arthur Rank just where the money was going.

Ruggles had set himself an impossible time schedule, one that refused to acknowledge the late war, and what's more, he nearly kept to it. The stages and laboratories were constructed first and then a block of dressing rooms in raw cement which sweated without covering or rug. The wood was new and green, the wet ground covered by plank walks, and the stages remained for some while large undifferentiated hangars, there being material for sets but not for screening. When the air inside became too close the great doors were rolled back. Immediately the atmosphere of the Thames Valley took over.

It found you with its fingers in all your joints and in your throat and guts. It wrapped its dirty veils about your eyes. And all you could do was watch the crew hazily through the fog trying slowly, because of their terrible fatigue, to make do with inadequate, unfinished equipment, as they'd made do for so many years with guns or bullets or shovels.

Ruggles established his own quarters on the premises in what had been a great Edwardian house. The library was particularly comfortable with a roaring fire and rugs and books and real furniture. I was allotted neither office nor dressing room since the actors obviously had to be accommodated first. Plesch put a cot in her office and there, wrapped in Douglass Montgomery's fur-lined military sleeping bag, I managed to keep warm.

Ruggles sat in his director's chair scowling, always on set, always in the middle of the work, always silent and unhappy, trying by sheer force of will to make them hurry, to shock them out of exhaustion. He made no impression. They were underfed. They were used up. Furthermore, they did not see any particular reason for hurrying. So they downed tools regularly and had their tea and Ruggles sat grinding his teeth and studying his wrist watch as they laughed over the great steaming mugs. "They're lazy. They're lazy," he said to me. "They never learned to work." The men heard him and seemed to pay no mind. But I think they did not care for his point of view.

One day, as we were working around a garden pool, a light fuse went out with a bang. Two electricians threw themselves face down into the water and were dragged out shaking and cursing. "Another delay!" muttered Ruggles. Bunty Kelley, my youngest dancer, who had been dug out of the rubble of her house three times, didn't bat an eyelash — nor did anyone else. The men were taken to the tea wagon and given towels without comment. But, of course, there was, as Ruggles said, a ten-minute delay.

The inevitable errors and petty accidents took on, under these conditions, unwieldy proportions. One finished set of costumes was rejected, a natural occurrence in any production, but here it proved near disaster. There was no more cloth. The coupons for cloth and materials were kept in a safe. Any mistake in design or calculation entailed the bleaching out of dye with acid and the ripping of every seam before altering. It was done — but it took time.

It was under such conditions that the British produced the best contemporary opera of the period, laid down the foundation for their great ballet repertory, filmed Olivier's *Henry V*, introduced the Christopher Fry plays, and continued the Old Vic and Stratford traditions with productions as fine and opulent as any in the world, all this while cleaning up rubble, rebuilding cities and establishing without bloodshed social and economic changes more profound than any set by the French Revolution. Ruggles should not have fretted. He should have read history and learned.

He continued, however, in his own style with foreseeable results.

From time to time, like a dreadful warning, he would bring up the subject of the white satin piano. I had nothing to do with the white satin piano, although the scene was made later, I'm told, by someone else. But I did have a daffodil vale — a real Wordsworthian spring. There was a hill of wire frame, felt mats and paper grass, and ten thousand yellow paper daffodils, fluttering and dancing in the air currents of electric fans. On these we romped barefooted and goose-fleshed while patient Englishmen straightened out the wire stems after each passing. I remember running up and down the slopes in my rubber-soled shoes, my mink flying around me as I showed the girls where to jump and roll, the paper flowers scrunching underfoot and the worried grips pulling me back and making me sit still. "If you should slip," they said. But I knew I wouldn't. And I didn't — except aesthetically.

This idyll completed, my relationships with the director rapidly went to pot. I was forbidden to talk to my girls on set and finally constrained to work through a system of signals with Peggy and Thérèse, until they also, in their turn, were banished. I was forbidden to see a foot of printed film. I never at any point was permitted to meet my boss, J. Arthur Rank. I was forbidden to absent myself from the studio or the set for even half a day. I was on set from eight in the morning until six at night, six days a week. The drive to the studio took one hour each way through fog. I rose at six-thirty. I might have staged a revolt, but somehow I hadn't the energy.

These circumstances maintained for four months. I nibbled at my peanut butter, I snuggled into my sleeping bag, and I counted the days, I counted the hours, I counted the quarter hours.

If my condition became known, and surely it would be obvious in another month's time, no airplane would take me aboard, nor would any boat. The risk would be too great on the North Atlantic in midwinter and I would find myself stranded in England until after the baby's birth. Walter's leave might by then be up and he dispatched to the Far East on occupation duties.

I wrote impatiently back. Pop, who had a tendency to accept matters as they came, who had spoken very sharply when I apologized for my work in *Oklahoma!* — "These dances may not be the best you feel capable of, but get on your knees in gratitude for the success. And shut up" — now wrote with the same vigor. "Never mind the picture. First things first. Take care of the child." The family sent all kinds of food packages. Trude sent food and classic salutations: "Courage, dear Sister." Mag sent nylons and lipsticks. And thrice weekly came the letters from Mother: how he looked, what he ate, the friends he brought to the house, the new dresses and hats Mag and Judy had acquired, the sending of my studio curtains to the cleaners, the purchase of twin beds, everything, anything, throwing her gossamer web into the air so that I was caught on the weather, the sounds, the smells, voices, dinner-table sentences, the continuing presence on the other side of the world, of days coexistent with mine, so that at any hour as I looked through the damp at my watch in Dolphin Square I knew to the minute what was happening on Ninth Street. It was a kind of spiritual osmosis. I passed over and back. I lived in two places. And Walter wrote, but now briefly, with terseness, "It doesn't matter what I do or whom I see. Come back. Come back. In God's name, finish and come home."

Come home. And what would that be like? After, I mean, I had found his arms and had realized once more what a conversation was like where I did not have to invent both sides of the dialogue. Would the baby distract me from him? Could I still dance? I had always lived with none to please but myself, coming late to meals if I were in rehearsal, bedding down at dusk to wake at midnight and work until dawn, shutting myself away for days, concerned with little beside my professional bothers, expecting my clothes to be cared for, my studio cleaned, my meals readied, expecting to be nursed, cherished and comforted for the betterment of all that mattered to me, MY WORK. I never had attempted to live with anyone while working.

Of course, for a time I would not be working. But someday later I knew I would again want to.

How would the child fit into the Carnegie sweathouse? Could I take it along and hang it papoose-style on the wall? And how could I serve child and husband with a rehearsal schedule that hitherto had never provided sufficient leisure for hair washing? What would I talk to him about during out-of-town dinners? Whether to move Susie to the other end of the line or take her out of the dance altogether? Would he become interested in these goings-on? Enough to forgive poor housekeeping and late meals? Would he include me in his work? During the five months of physical inactivity ahead, I could teach, I could make notes and scenarios of ballets (the one about Lizzie Borden, for instance, the one that Edward Sheldon had always wanted me to start). I could make notes for a book and — oh, yes — I could learn to cook. I could fix up the flat better and fuss with clothes, mine and the baby's, and every night, every night he would come home to dinner. I would not have to eat alone. The fire would be lit and I would be waiting and he would come home. All other problems and questions disappeared before this certainty. First let me put my head on his shoulder and life would work out the rest.

THE week before I left, a wire came from Walter saying he'd been formally demobilized and had accepted a job as assistant to Sol Hurok, the impresario. And from my other world there also came a wire and a letter from Dick and Oscar outlining a new show they were working on, *Allegro*, an original story to be told largely through stylized movement and dancing, and they asked me to direct the entire production as well as choreograph. This was a tremendous honor and it sent shivers of anticipation, pride and uneasiness through my marrow. As far as I knew, it was the first time a woman had been put in charge of a big Broadway musical. It was the first time, certainly, I had been offered a major show to direct. But all the years of organizing, composing and producing dance companies would now surely pay off and I felt that if trusted, I could meet the challenge. The show would not be ready before I was; I could have my baby in peace with the anticipation of this wonderful job awaiting me.

The picture was nowhere near done when I walked out of the studio on a November Saturday after shaking hands all around and with secret embraces in the dancers' dressing room.

Kay Kendall, beautiful and sweet, now browbeaten, was wandering through the vagaries and the angers of these months like a punished child. This was her first job; it was like to be her last.

I said good-by to her against instructions in the upstairs hall out-side Plesch's office.

"You're lovely," I said. "I wanted to help you."

"I was forbidden to talk to you, or listen to anything you said."

"That's a pity," I answered. "Perhaps someday."

I never saw the film, but knowing what I did about it, I paid four thousand dollars to get my name off the picture. I might have saved the cash, because after one preview showing in America, the stunned exhibitors refused to release it. It had cost one million pounds sterling in a country that had no butter for its toast nor paint for its houses.

I packed up quickly, Thérèse and Lily helping, and on a gray Tuesday at five in the morning, we had early tea and I drove to Euston Station.

"Do you want to follow me to America and look after the baby?" I called as Lily kissed me good-by.

"Oh, yes, madam!"

And so they waved pocket handkerchiefs that fluttered like moths in the darkening tunnel behind me.

The ship I was assigned to was the motor vessel *Empire Ettric,* a captured German freighter built for duty in the Mediterranean and fitted to carry twelve passengers. Thirty of us climbed aboard. It had never tried big waters before. However, it seemed sea-worthy to the Cunard officials and there didn't appear to be any reason why, given time, it could not complete the crossing. I in-quired at the shipping office in Liverpool the possible date of ar-rival and was answered by a hearty laugh in which all the clerks joined. When they stopped exchanging glances and jocosely slapping papers around I pleaded for an approximation. The clerk was instantly and quietly polite. "Well, say, as a guess, sixteen days — but don't promise."

This message was accordingly relayed West.

We embarked, a mixed group, half military, half members of diplomatic corps, returning nurses and special-service officials, a few civilian invalids going to America for complicated operations, and one kilted and bonneted Scotsman just out of Japanese prison camp whose wife, last seen in Singapore, awaited him in New York. As his foot hit the extraordinarily narrow deck, he bowed to all of us and said, "Good day, ladies and gentlemen. Now, thank God, I can start malingering." He took to his bed and we didn't see him again. But then he hadn't had a bed in six years.

The quarters were mean, cramped and uncomfortable, the saloons bare and small, supplied only with tables and chairs. The bare dark patches on the wall testified to the portraits recently torn down. George VI had not yet replaced Hitler, but we trusted he would on the next trip, provided there was a next trip.

We started off jocular and chatty, but after two days of weather and diet those that could move about turned up jaundiced and lethargic and sat in the swinging and creaking cabin sighing intermittently and turning the pages of whatever book failed to take their mind off conditions, the while their yellowing eyeballs moved hopelessly toward the portholes, where nothing was seen but flying spume and oily smoke.

The ocean that winter made nautical history. Old captains who had followed the seas thirty years and more limped into harbor swearing they had never known the like. Hatches were stove in, rigging torn off, cargoes saturated and destroyed, plates ripped loose, ships driven from course. November 1945 is memorable in every shipping office. The losses were enormous.

And through the boiling wilderness of opposing seas, our little toy beat its way against mountains of green water, lifting and plunging, careening from side to side until the white froth laved the deck like soap suds, and its ridiculous plume of black oily smoke blew impertinently before the glazed windows or streamed behind in the unending downpour. And when we mounted up on the endless terrifying power we saw suddenly the columns of spume marching on the white-laced waters like trees bent in hurricane and the scudding skies driving around us. And then we fell and looked through sheer water into death. But it was not death. The little heart beneath our feet kept beating. The boat moved slowly forward and took the blows.

The weather on deck was foul, wetting with sleet, and evil with the diesel oil blown straight into one's eyes and mouth. It was not pure air, but it was salty and cold and better than the fetid bins in which we were locked.

It was on a slanting deck, hanging to a hawser, my feet planted in wet, hair blown wild among banners and flags of mist, halfway between the worlds on the watery crust of oblivion, that I looked into the fretful sky and laughed. I had experienced the sublime impertinence: the child kicked.

One of our fifteen-year-old stewards bent double to the weather and, reaching with a raw hand for whatever support he could grasp, yelled through the crashing and swishing:

"Did you speak?"

"I laughed. I'm having a good time."

"Thank you, madam," said he, taking it as a tribute to England.

The ship tried again and that day we made, I think, half a knot.

I had always been seasick every time I crossed green water, the Catalina Channel, the English Channel, the Gulf of St. Lawrence, the North Sea, the North Atlantic, the Hudson River, any safe harbor with a ground swell, any coast line. I had always been sick. This trip I was neither sick nor cold. Perhaps because, for the first time, I was living up to my nautical inheritance — my grandfather, Henry George, as a teen-age cabin boy, had sailed before the mast twice around the world — perhaps because the son I was carrying was going to love boats and the sea most wonderfully. All the other passengers were very sick.

Every night I asked the captain how much progress we had made, and since some days I am convinced we lost ground and just chugged up patches of spumy water without moving and some days I believe we actually drifted backwards, he grew cross with me. "Madam, there's nothing you can do about it. The boat and I are hurrying all we can."

It was maddening, though. So close, and so endlessly long — thirteen days and the same awful dinner, fourteen days. I asked the boy steward, "Could you give me some dry biscuits to keep in my pocket? I'm going to have a baby."

"Why didn't you tell me?" said the youth. "My sister's going to have a baby. I could get you extra things."

"Another blanket perhaps?"

I was impatient but I was not bored. I was driven by a tremendous excitement.

I used to lie awake and realize that I need make no effort, need not think or analyze or plan, that God would do the baby for me. It would take not the slightest effort on my part. There it would be, eyelashes and teeth and leg muscles, all differentiated without my counting a single bar of music or quarreling with a single producer. It was the easiest venture I'd ever engaged in, and I was precious, for once, not by anything I was doing, just by being.

I planned. I planned with such immediacy that my mind dazzled. It was over, the waiting. As I lay in the swinging bunk I remembered our bridal days set apart and framed in glory. I remembered the unknown flowers glimmering in the road ruts at Hobbs as we ran to meet each other across windy acres under a whanging great canopy of airplanes. I remembered that the young men about us were hopeful and full of high excitement and that we had been hopeful and had respected ourselves and our companions. And in the long months and years that followed, how day by day and month by month we had grown to trust, searching our hearts in the lonely hours for the very best to tell one another, the best, the most amusing, the most zestful to keep for one another.

And now it was done, the waiting.

Fifteen days. There were rumors of land and sunshine. We all went topside and cheered up.

Sixteen days. We were packing with feverish excitement. We forgave the food. Most people were bilious and jaundiced with body toxins, but they began to exchange jokes.

Seventeen days. Ambrose light. Land at dusk. We put on powder and lipstick and our city suits and stood at the railing. Home by midnight. A passenger came up with horror and urgency on his face. "I heard the stewards ordering early tea and breakfast."

Impossible! We were to sit out the night in the Narrows, watching the cars drive along Fort Hamilton within shouting distance, but unable to wire or phone or send messages. For all the tangible good, we might still be separated by a wartime sea.

We barely undressed. We were up in the dawn and felt the motors working again. And this time the gray shore slid by and the towers of Manhattan, rain-drenched and faded with mist, stood to meet us. We were bumped and pulled into berth and rushed to watch the quayside. And then we were herded back down again. We had not passed quarantine yet. The Cunard office with bigger ships on their mind had somehow neglected to note the hour of arrival or the position of this very small one and the quarantine officers were even now steaming down the harbor to where we had been but were not while we were safely and impotently drawn up at Pier 57. We were to be confined to the saloon for two hours until the doctors could be returned.

And there on the shore, yards away, there on the shore were the others, running up and down, and beating their fists against barriers and officers.

I saw him in uniform — and I saw my mother behind him, trying to keep up, gray with cold and stamping her little feet and taking her hands from her muff to wave, her eyes straining to the ship.

And I simply walked past protest and restraint, the kilted Scotsman right behind me. Walter stepped over whatever intervened, some of it human, and reaching between shore and ship, we found each other's hands. The Scotsman embraced his wife last seen on the dock at Singapore six years earlier.

An embarrassed Cunard official danced between. "This is quite out of order, you know. I do understand, but you must stop. You're not supposed to meet or touch until the regulations have been complied with."

"Mon," said the Scotsman, lifting his bonneted head and fixing the official with a northern stare frosted over with triumph, "don't be absurrrd!"

Index

DATE DUE			